The Year of Indecision, 1946

Also by Kenneth Weisbrode

Churchill and the King

Old Diplomacy Revisited

A Brief History of Americanism

On Ambivalence

The Atlantic Century

The Year of Indecision, 1946

*A Tour Through
the Crucible of
Harry Truman's
America*

Kenneth Weisbrode

VIKING

VIKING

An imprint of Penguin Random House LLC

375 Hudson Street

New York, New York 10014

penguin.com

ISBN 978-0-670-01684-6

Printed in the United States of America

1 3 5 7 9 10 8 6 4 2

Set in Albertina MT Pro

Designed by Francesca Belanger

For Akira Iriye and Bruce Mazlish

Contents

Preface

Nineteen-forty-six was a cold year. It ended with the coldest winter anybody could remember in Europe, when much of the Continent, as well as Britain, starved or nearly did. It began with one almost as bad in the United States. The new president, Harry Truman, had been in office only a few months, since the previous April. Apart from 1949–50—when the Communists seized power in China, the Soviet Union detonated a nuclear weapon, and the Korean War began—this year, 1946, was the nadir of his troubled presidency. Postwar arrangements broke down with the Soviet Union, and just about did with Britain. The United States suffered inflation, shortages, and strikes. In November, Truman's party, the Democrats, lost both houses of Congress.

It was a bitter, dark moment in our history. It was also wondrous. In literature, music, film, and the visual arts there began a renaissance. The year was baseball's "victory season." Americans could, and did, rejoice.

This book interprets the history of this important and overlooked moment, just after the biggest war in modern history, and right before another of a kind nobody had fought before. The moment was strange and scary, but not hopeless. This book therefore is about fear. It is also about optimism.

It takes a look back at 1946 in order to explain and understand this contrast, not just for its own sake—to fill in a gap—but also to consider its legacy for today. For we still are living with stark contrasts in America. They are not the same as the ones faced by some of us in 1946, or by our progenitors. But they rhyme in numerous ways.

Speaking of legacies, the British diplomat and writer Harold Nicolson once said that he kept his diary for his great-grandson. This person could best appreciate the mind and method contained there, with the right mix of familiarity and distance from the historical moment, and could learn from it without being trapped by it. I have written this book with a similar bias. It is not for my own imaginary great-grandchildren but, rather, written in the mind, as I have imagined it, of my great-grandparents and their children, my grandparents, who lived it. Their generation needn't be qualified as the "greatest" or as anything else. Their lives and histories are facts. For all the millions of words written about them (even in praise), they deserve to be understood better on their own terms.

Books with years in their title, annohistories, have become common. This, alas, is not a book about a single year. It presents the year 1946 in synecdoche, as a thematic portrait and progression of people, events, and concepts of the era just before our own that is also still our own. It begins with Harry Truman and his entourage, tells what they did at home and abroad, describes some aspects of American life, then cycles back with a meditation on our country's place in history. Everything significant for the era didn't happen in its twelve months, but 1946 acted also as a fulcrum. America moved then to accept the burdens of being a world power. It began to exploit the benefits and endure the costs—to its prestige, its compass, its way of life. It tried to master fear (and it succeeded, albeit only partially)—fear it both hated and needed. Or so said its leaders, teachers, parents, and citizens.

It is still too early to tell whether or not they were right. Fear has yet to be mastered fully in America. So we go back to 1946 and revisit one of the most confusing and frightening times in our history and ask how our predecessors did it. We learn, among other things, that they met it less by firm, clear decisions than by the opposite. Hence the book's title.

In the following pages we will see several manifestations of indecision. We begin with the disorientation of the Americans returning from the war and of the civilians who welcomed them, or did not, and of the big question many of them asked: *What now?* We proceed with a description of the country, its president, and its other leaders now faced—more suddenly than many of them had anticipated—with assuming many burdens of international leadership and, for the first time, a strange new "nuclear" world. Related to such burdens were a number of questions about the aims, intentions, and capabilities of the Soviet Union. Back home, there were decisions to make about reconverting a wartime to a peacetime economy, and how best to promote prosperity—or more likely, *whose* prosperity. Its leaders having failed to resolve that question to everyone's satisfaction, much of the country took refuge in the (apparent) certainty of the bigger pie—that is, when in doubt, don't do nothing, grow. The mood and spirit of the country—in art, science, and culture—reflected the promise of plenty, which was an old American idea, recycled now with a habit of preponderance. Postwar America was preponderant by scope, degree, variety, and frequency rather than by sheer force and presence, as traditional empires were. Yet its preponderance, both at home and abroad, was manifest piecemeal, temporally, like moving islands on a map. This was as much the result of Americans' own difficulty with understanding or even choosing their country's postwar role as it was of the variable nature of preponderance itself in the mid-twentieth century.

Americans usually like convention delivered in bold, "transformational" packages, not the other way around. Some, perhaps many, of them felt the future was still too much to take on, and looked back to an idealized past; others went a step further, resorting to a familiar trope—Know-Nothingism—although here too it came in a somewhat different package, no longer directed against real or imagined sophisticates per se but rather against a foreign ideology, namely, Communism. The Know-Nothingism of 1946, soon to be renamed McCarthyism, was preponderant as well in some places, but it did not last very long. Today it is remembered more for its style than for its substance, which recalls one further trope of American history:

simplification. So complex and diverse a society has always needed simple, clear ideas, slogans, messages, images, and beliefs to hold it together, or to divide it, as the case may be. America in 1946 was at one of its most confusing moments, and so forced its way not only through a series of tough choices but also to embrace the concept of decision in as simple a way as possible. Whether the image and the reality of decision were consistent in every manifestation mentioned in the following pages is open to question. However, many Americans, starting with Harry Truman, sure liked to think so.

In the simplified history of the United States the nineteenth century was one of conquest and narrative while the twentieth was one of expansion, consolidation, adjustment, and interpretation. The model for this book is another, related account of a moment that took place a century before the one I describe. Bernard DeVoto's *The Year of Decision: 1846* appeared in 1943. It told the story of the wars against Mexico and nature through the eyes of the country's leaders, its soldiers, and its settlers, westward pilgrims determined to color the map American all the way to the Pacific Ocean. It made for a brave, gallant, dramatic, and troubling tale of the interaction of individuals with historical forces, centrifugal and centripetal "energies" compelling, inviting, or deterring them hither and yon.

I try in a modest way to honor DeVoto, one of America's finest historians and writers. Each chapter that follows here features a short epigraph from his monthly column in *Harper's* magazine titled "The Easy Chair." As it happens, he spent much of 1946 wandering westward across the country in a Buick that gave him more than a bit of road trouble. Then, as did the subjects of his own book, he stared toward that particular occidental sunset.

Here we reverse the orientation. In the middle of the twentieth century, America looked back east, to Europe, all the way back again to Asia, and to itself, intermittently. There was no single decision to do this. There was no president this time swearing he would conquer territories and change the country's boundaries—well, not quite in the same way, at least—even though there were still plenty of adventurers and pathfinders, and one or two dreamers.

My title notwithstanding, 1946 was full of decisions, at least on the surface. Truman and some other characters in this story put the word in the title of their memoirs. To do so was not meant to deceive. Rather, decision and decisiveness are aspirations, as is the freedom of choice, enshrined in the country's creed. Indecision, however, is the leitmotif of American history. Do we revolt against the British Empire? Do we defend the Union or stand up for states' rights? Should we go off to fight in Europe? In Asia? Which do we do first? Should we stay or come home?

The remarkable thing is that the country so far has held together, and indeed much more, amid so much indecision. It found a way around resolving itself, oftentimes by the paradoxical satisfaction of adversity. That sentence would have made DeVoto cringe, for he liked strong subjects and verbs. He taught a generation of Harvard students to use them, before Harvard, in its wisdom, let him go. But, we must ask, how can indecision be strong? DeVoto has equated decision with optimism, but what if we find deciding too difficult? May we still be optimists? Can we?

Harry Truman made one big decision in 1946: he decided not to decide. He did not impose what he thought was right with his country upon what he and others said was wrong with it. He decided from then on to play it by ear. That was not easy. Some people wanted him to be firm, so he acted that way. Some people wanted to feel that no decisions had to be made at all. So he would make a few. He hardened a foundation. He committed his country to defend and enrich parts of Europe and Asia, to support a new nation called Israel, to go to war in Korea, and to use and augment an atomic arsenal and military-industrial complex. These all involved tough choices but not necessarily careful, deliberate decisions. He opted for the reactive position. He let events dictate most of the choices, and when they did not to his satisfaction, he passed the big decisions on to his successors. It would take another decade, at least, to strike something of a balance between America's role in the world and its preferred way of life at home; yet even now that balance eludes us.

This is not meant to be a denunciation. It was Truman's contemporary, the French politician Henri Queuille, who supposedly said that "no problem is too intractable to resist an absence of decision." We students of history are left with the question: So what? What if Truman did not really have an option? What if he was incapable of making such grand decisions? Wasn't he right to wait? To think them through just a while longer? To do less harm by buying a bit more time? Survival had to come first. Or what if, by playing the hard decider so often, he had lost the consensual capital he needed to lead the country along a particular direction? How many other Americans had done—and still do—just that?

We too may be undecided, or at least as much as our predecessors were in 1946. History continues and we may change our minds, but it is not too late to reconsider these questions. It matters that we try.

Chronology

1945

January

Franklin D. Roosevelt inaugurated for the fourth time.

February

Yalta Conference.

Battle of Iwo Jima (ends in March).

March

U.S. troops cross the Rhine.

April

Battle of the Ruhr continues.

Gallup poll shows 81 percent of Americans "in favor of a world organization with police power."

Roosevelt dies.

Soviet troops reach Berlin.

Truman insults Molotov.

San Francisco Conference begins (lasts until end of June).

U.S. and Soviet troops shake hands across the Elbe.

Mussolini executed.

Hitler commits suicide.

May

Victory in Europe.

Demobilization begins.

Harry Hopkins meets Stalin in Moscow.

June

United Nations Charter signed.

Office of Price Administration life extended by one year.

July

First test of the atomic bomb at Los Alamos, New Mexico.

Potsdam Conference (ends in August).

August
Atomic bomb dropped on Hiroshima.
Atomic bomb dropped on Nagasaki.
Japan accepts terms of surrender.
Victory in Japan (officially September 2).
Rationing of gasoline and fuel oil ends.
Lend-Lease canceled.

September
Strikes force Ford to close plants for three weeks.
Coal strike (into October).

October
War Production Board replaced by Civilian Production Administration.
Truman calls for peacetime military training.

November
Truman-Attlee-King statement on atomic energy.
Nuremberg trials begin.
General Motors strike (lasts until March).

December
British loan agreed.
Marshall mission to China begins.
Moscow Conference.

1946

January
First session of UN.
General Motors, General Electric, and Westinghouse strikes; also
   meatpackers and steelworkers; largest strikes since 1919.
Iran submits Azerbaijan issue to UN.

February
Joseph Stalin's speech.
Canadian spy case revealed.
George Kennan sends his Long Telegram.

March
Winston Churchill's Iron Curtain speech.

April

Soviets begin withdrawal from Iranian Azerbaijan.

New strikes in coal and railroads (through May).

June

Bernard Baruch delivers his atomic plan to UN.

July

Bikini Atoll bomb test.

The Philippines gains independence.

Paris Peace Conference (lasts until October).

September

James Byrnes's Stuttgart speech.

Henry Wallace's speech at Madison Square Garden.

October

Meat price controls end.

November

Republicans sweep both houses of Congress.

Truman removes most other price controls.

New coal strike.

December

Bizonia agreed.

Official end of hostilities of World War II declared.

1947

January

George Marshall gives up mission in China, becomes secretary of state.

February

British notify State Department about aid suspension to Greece and Turkey.

Teachers' strike in Buffalo, New York (ends in March).

March

Truman Doctrine announced.

Truman orders loyalty oath for government employees.

June

Marshall's speech at Harvard.

Sugar rationing ends.

Taft-Hartley Act passed over Truman's veto.

Coal mines restored to private ownership.

July

Kennan's "X" article appears in *Foreign Affairs*.

National Security Act signed.

October

House Un-American Affairs Committee launches Hollywood hearings.

November

"Hollywood Ten" voted in contempt of Congress.

December

A *Streetcar Named Desire* opens on Broadway.

Wallace announces third-party candidacy for president.

The Year of Indecision, 1946

Chapter 1

The Uprooted

The trains were full of soldiers, sailors, and marines coming home. . . .
Jason and Ulysses, d'Artagnan and Johnny Inkslinger are coming home
to Muddy Creek.

—"The Easy Chair," January 1946

Millions of Americans had left their homes and families to fight in the war and now millions of them returned. By June 1946 more than twelve million were back. Munitions contracts worth billions of dollars were terminated. The armed forces at the end of 1947 would shrink to just one and a half million. The pace and magnitude of the demobilization were such that Harry Truman called it a disintegration. For many, though, it couldn't happen fast enough; demonstrations took place on military bases and installations across the world. Many more millions would relocate from their war postings in the United States back home, or to some new place altogether.

They were not alone. A greater movement of people had not been seen on earth, it was said, since the Middle Ages. Many tens of millions of refugees, of displaced human beings, moved around the world. Hundreds of destroyed villages, towns, and cities, some like junkyards, and cultures, societies, and lives—and ways of life—would never be seen again. People made do like insects—in Berlin, they made Truman think of "termites"—in the ruins.

Americans could count themselves lucky. If luck can be counted, let us recall that other nations lost millions of their citizens in the war as combatants and victims of extermination. Many more were left homeless, destitute, and subject to forced labor, including those who were abandoned in one place or another and would not in some cases be repatriated for several more years. The dead were just gone. The Soviet Union lost, for example, twenty-seven million. The total number of Americans lost was just over four hundred thousand.

It was still time to cheer a victory, albeit in stages. First, in France, was the Liberation in 1944. It would happen later in Italy and other parts of Europe, but not for a while in Asia. Anyway, what was liberation to countries that had been, and would remain, colonies? Meanwhile, to Parisians, V-E Day on May 8, 1945, was akin to a burial. To American observers in China, it came "with bland urbanity." However, in America, victory in the Pacific followed in August and Americans were gleeful; women were seen carousing naked in city streets and in fountains; couples embraced, and did more, in public. A uniform was seen as a ticket for almost anything a young man could want.

The euphoria did not last long. Now it was America's turn to be disoriented, dizzy. Maybe because Americans also had become accustomed to stages, to gradualism. After all, the war had begun this way, through fits and starts, until the United States joined it following the attack on Pearl Harbor. It finally entered the war united on the surface but badly divided beneath, for a large number of Americans had opposed entering it right up to the last month of 1941. The country then unified against infamy, but there was not, many later "good war" commemorations notwithstanding, an eloquent definition of what the country was fighting for. This also took some time.

Following the war, there was some residual victor's guilt, for a few Americans must have realized that millions of Germans and Japanese warriors also were returning home to a strange adjustment, yet they were denied the benefit of victory. Americans, no matter what they had done in the war, had the fact of a victory on their side. But like the chronology of the war, it wasn't clear-cut. This was the first war anyone could remember, or that most people knew of, that had been anticipated so long in advance. So too with its aftermath. The atomic bombs ended the war before many people thought it would finally be over, yet the remains of those killed in action didn't begin to come back in large numbers from their temporary burial places until the latter part of 1946. Families were given a choice to repatriate them or leave them where they were. Veterans had been coming home for some time already. Government officials had long been planning for the postwar period, some (the State Department, for example) since before the war even began. By 1943 Franklin Roosevelt had ordered Bernard Baruch to oversee a postwar adjustment program and to plan accordingly; both houses of Congress had set up special postwar committees. Secretary of Commerce Henry Wallace, who had received warnings for at least two years about the adjustment, noted in October 1945 that the nation's GNP could probably contract by about $40 billion, with a loss of wages of around half that amount, which meant between seven and eight million unemployed by the middle of 1946.

How well did they do?

From the perspective of the twenty-first century, they did all right. There was no economic or social collapse in America after the war. Considering the millions of people on the move—and the altered country they found—it was remarkable that there was not a bigger disruption. Americans, however, were used to that. The World War II generation was only one removed from one of the largest generations of immigrants; nearly thirty million came between 1880 and 1920. This does not include another big move, so big we now call it the Great Migration: that of African Americans from the rural South—where most of them lived—to the northern cities, where by 1930 their population is said to have grown by some 300 percent. This accelerated, from around three million in the North and ten million in the South in 1940 to more than five million in the North and ten million in the South in 1950, many of whom had already migrated to southern towns and cities. In other words, almost 75 percent of African Americans were found in the rural South in 1900; in 1950 this figure had fallen to less than 20 percent. How much of this change was anticipated or planned, and how much happened arbitrarily, cannot be known. All we know is that it happened, and had been happening for some time. The war generation was used to disruption.

We begin with the soldiers. They were not the first to be sent to fight in a European or Asian war. They were not pioneers. Yet how strange it was to leave the world you had known, be sent to a boot camp in some part of the country you had never been to or had thought you would see, head shaved, clothes replaced by uniform issue, bedroom with barracks, dining room and parlor with mess, saddled into a platoon with boys more or less your age but with strange accents you'd heard only in movies, if at all, then sent to the other end of the earth in order to kill people you had never known much about either. Boys from places we've never heard of, dying in places we've never heard of: that is said during every American war. It is true for every war. Today's stereotype—Americans being a warlike people—is a Vietnam-era conceit. Some Americans are bellicose and violent, and Americans have fought many wars, most of which they, like the British before them, preferred to call something else. The British use the term "emergency," as in the Kenyan or Malayan emergency, or the "troubles." Americans like the term "conflict." But who can say for certain whether Americans are any more bellicose or dangerous than any other people? We can only be reasonably certain that it was not the universal perception in 1946.

Some found families waiting for them more or less as they had expected. Some did not. Some had wives, girlfriends; others no longer did; many did not talk about what had happened during the interval on the home front either—at least not then. More immediate problems needed taking care of. Where would they live? Where would they work? The government came up with one of its better ideas back in 1944, called the GI Bill. You could use it to buy a house, start a business, or go to college. Veterans flooded university campuses. It was one of the most disorienting but also one of the most creative periods in American higher education, courses teeming with worldly-wise veterans, many who would never otherwise have considered going to college, and many who were the first in their families to do so, and were therefore determined to make the most of their "unintended juggernaut." This campaign for human capital coincided with the growth of Big Science and then the Cold War, and the major universities now became professional, segmented, and competitive places with their entrepreneurial fiefdoms. Later they would grow more selective. For now, everybody was in it and you had to push.

What did veterans want? What did they expect?

Security. That's the obvious, appealing answer. It's also obviously simplistic. This generation knew too well how easy it was to squander capital. It could buy security but didn't guarantee it. What they really wanted were strong, permanent roots. Yet for many returning veterans, roots were harder to come by than they had imagined, so some pretended not to want them, while others pretended that the roots remained there, firmly in the soil, against all evidence to the contrary.

We shall return again to this paradox of 1946, which was a paradox of adolescence, of the roots and the wings. Good parents are meant to provide both to their children. They are meant to keep them safe and feeling safe, and also to allow them to feel free. But the parents of this generation were also torn, most by now convinced that the nation had lost its way when they were young; that intervention in the First World War had been a terrible mistake; that it had brought little glory and instead the Spanish flu, the Great Depression, and an even bigger war. The wings would have to be clipped. But the parents, especially the millions of first-generation Americans, had also been told, and tutored since Pearl Harbor, that "isolationism" was a bad word, an "ism" to be repudiated. Was it possible to take solace in preparedness? To make it a source of, or anchor to, the proverbial lost or misplaced innocence?

For many of their children who went overseas to fight in the war, their actual return was not much easier. Being uprooted had an exponential effect. Like their immigrant parents or grandparents, many had left behind all they had known and crossed the sea, only in reverse. Even among those of older American stock there was still a notion that they had "returned" to the Old World whence their ancestors had fled so that they, those ancestors, could plant new roots. Now they, their descendants, re-returned to the New World—uprooted, then, in theory, rerooted like a multigenerational boomerang. For those who went from one theater of war to another, from Europe to the Pacific or vice versa, the effect may have been even stranger. But now at least they were home.

How much of America's later postwar success can be attributed to the drive and enthusiasm of its returning GIs is open to question. There are many later obituaries with the familiar formula: war vet; first in his family to attend college; prominent citizen; corporate executive; father of four children, nine grandchildren, two great-grandchildren; et cetera. The greatest generation became conscious of its greatness, as most generations do, but in retrospect. Enduring the worst of the Great Depression as children did not necessarily convey a notion of greatness, nor did surviving the worst of the war. Riding the postwar boom as specimens of human capital may well have done. There was no better time, in the twentieth century at least, to have "made it" in America. And there was every sense that making it meant you had earned it, that you deserved it, that you had not won a lottery but had instead paid your dues and had proven yourself by the American creed. It meant that you had planted stronger roots. But only a few people questioned this pattern with clarity.

Gertrude Stein, for example. The journalist Cy Sulzberger paid

her a visit at the end of August 1945. They talked about a book she
was writing about the soldiers, *Brewsie and Willie*, "about GIs and
how they worry and how she worries about them and how they
worry together about their worrying":

> Are we isolationists or are we isolated is what I want to know. . . .
> I am worried. And the GI is terribly worried. He is quite as wor-
> ried as I am. We are quite worried together. I am worried as they
> are worried and they are worried as I am worried. . . . Their
> minds are being deadened. They lack spiritual courage. They
> lack interest in home politics except locally. They don't believe
> anything is true. It is kind of a dark picture. Compared to Euro-
> peans they don't take any active interest in things. They have a
> leadership complex. I say to them: "Can any of you lead your-
> selves? Do you all have to be told?"
>
> They are beginning to feel this thing in themselves but they
> haven't any religion any more. You don't see any Bibles around
> like you did after the last war. They worship efficiency and
> only efficiency and maybe subconsciously they're puzzled
> because Germany, which was the most efficient country in
> Europe, has "gone West" [been destroyed]. . . . They feel these
> things subconsciously and it makes them sad. The French ask
> me: "Why are they so sad?" I say they've been away so long and
> they're homesick and they're young. And the French say: "But
> they don't look young."
>
> At the same time, when all Europe is going left our boys are
> terribly conservative. They're more conservative than anyone
> on earth. That's one thing that makes them nervous. They
> dimly realize the Germans were all these things.

The extrapolations tempt us. We must be prepared to assume
that many Americans knew that there was no more of life antebel-
lum, that there was no going back, but also that new beginnings,
new eras, new histories are torn between the wish for something

better and the knowledge that hope may also be false, or the things hoped for delayed, given all that they had just seen.

They had been young and green. They had been excited. They had been scared and "scared of being scared." Now they had mixed feelings. Many of them didn't like to speak of the fighting. They alluded to it but usually didn't dwell on it. For some reason veterans of the Second World War, the good and noble war, the war that is still the most commemorated of America's wars, have been the most reticent about its details. "In 1946," Ben Bradlee, the journalist and editor, asked, "who cared what you did in the war?" For him the war meant a great deal. Yet he "thought that people who sat around and talked about their war were terrible bores." Maybe now they aimed to forget. Or maybe, at this early stage in their new lives, there was just doubt. Stuart Chase, a sympathetic man, was commissioned by the Twentieth Century Fund to write four volumes about wartime and postwar planning. The final volume appeared in 1946, titled *For This We Fought*. It is about the soldiers.

Jeff is a combat veteran. He was brought up by middle-class parents in a small town near a big city. He was a blue-eyed, open-hearted boy, chiefly interested in football and gliders. The Army caught up with him just after he finished high school, and made a navigator out of him. He was overseas for almost three years. . . . Jeff is just old enough to vote. The rest of his life is before him. Yet how can it be anything but an anticlimax? . . . Just now the only job available is shipping clerk in a nearby mill. His father thinks he should take it before some other hero gets it. . . . He has lost his open smile, and his eyes are darker, his face lined. Sometimes he looks sullen and trapped. Is this what he fought for, just to come back and pack metal parts in a shipping room? . . . Even if he is not a casualty, his nervous system is conditioned to active response for any unexpected happening.... Civvy Street calls for different responses. It expects people to be patient when thwarted.... They won the war, and that was all the goal they had. The tie with their parents has been greatly loosened. The tie with wife and children may have been changed.... The feeling of comradeship, of risks and dangers shared with one's buddies, is mostly lost in peacetime.

Now, surely not all has been lost. Chase has segregated the feeling, in a manner that is becoming familiar to us, by stages: "When they first get home they want to forget the war, to rest, to sleep late, relax.... In due time, they wake up, often quite suddenly, and ask, Where am I personally? What am I going to do? ... The final stage is when they begin thinking about matters *beyond* their immediate personal interests.... How about the atomic bomb? How about Russia ...? How about the full employment bill, UNO, China, wages, inflation, strikes?" He has elaborated with a survey from June 1945 of soldiers awaiting their return, conducted by the Kiplinger Washington Service:

We want to go home
  We don't think much of foreign parts.
  Most of us want jobs, and are afraid we won't get them.
  We don't want the old job back very much.
  Strikes and strikers are so and so's—a rich vein of four-letter words was opened here.
  We are worried about getting a house to live in....
  We are pretty sore at racketeers in Miami and elsewhere who rob soldiers, at John L. Lewis and Caesar Petrillo, at civilians who grouse about gas rationing, at black marketeers, at advertisements in four colors puffing products for "doing their bit," at Hollywood war heroes, at commanding officers, at rules and regulations generally.

We want to do quite a lot of studying when we come home, and our favorite course is engineering.
We want a hard peace for Germany and Japan.
We are worried about the future peace of the world....
We think of ourselves as civilians temporarily fighting for our community.

This is joined by conversations overheard among veterans in New York and Bridgeport:

Listen, mister, I don't want sympathy. I just want a place to live....
Are there any good jobs around Hartford now?
How can I learn to be a union carpenter?
Can I finish my last grade of high school at night school somewhere? Can this come under the GI bill?
Where can I get some legal advice about a divorce? ...
Is there anything new to read about raising chickens?
Will they take my mother's house away from us?
How can I get a land grant in Alaska?
What do I need to get a job as a mail clerk?
What is the best engineering school? You see I learned a lot about radar.

Stages move back and forth from past to present and future, and also from the particular to the general, or, as Chase described it, between the individual and the community. Where the former had been prepared to sacrifice all for the latter, it was now the latter's turn to rehabilitate and reintegrate the former: "The town cannot lie low waiting for the veteran 'to get over it,' or else he may never get over it. The town must meet him half way." That is to say, families and friends of returning GIs had to help replant roots; they were not themselves the roots.

The town may not have understood. The lives of many Americans, at least as they saw it, had not been affected directly by the war. The soldiers knew this. Some were distant, even antipathetic, toward civilians. In surveys a majority of veterans said they should be given special preference for jobs over civilians. Competition, including among veterans, whose job prospects improved by how quickly they were discharged, was fierce. Even major-league baseball players who had gone to war—Ted Williams, Stan Musial, Joe and Dom DiMaggio, Bob Feller, Enos Slaughter, Pete Reiser—were noted for their feistiness, as were their fans. Some veterans moved into politics, declaring themselves reformers, superior to the old gang. In one small Tennessee town, for example, a bunch of veterans under the command of the local schoolteacher pursued the town's mayor, sheriff, and other officials to the jail and then deposed them after a siege lasting some six hours.

Yet for many the homecoming, such that it was, was empty, uncomfortable, even dark. There were assaults of civilians upon returning soldiers, especially those of a different race, with traditional enmity reinforced in some cases by the unfamiliarity of return, and by intervening trauma. For some it took the form of withdrawn hatred. For others it became a resigned, almost silent, loneliness. They had been small-town nobodies. Then they were somebodies, with great responsibilities, seeing, feeling horror. Then all of a sudden they were nobodies again. Their nostalgia for civilian life, if they had had it, was burst. They may not have been so willing to go in the first place. But they did, reluctantly in many cases, and now returned to a country that, like many of them, wanted to bury all that had happened.

"Skinner, what the hell do you want? It's not 1937, and you can't go to Spain. This is our war, for better or worse."

This is Skinner Galt, the protagonist of Vance Bourjaily's novel *The End of My Life* (1947):

"I want a nice, small war, Jeff, with clearcut issues. There should be more than just a villain you can hate. There should be a side you can love, too."

"I don't think so," said Jeff. "I think it's enough just to love the guys you're fighting beside...."

"So what do you want?"

"I want to do something decisive. It's too damn hot for indecision."

This was true before, when their parents were their age. Then again, it wasn't, not really. The First World War had been for the United States a war of choice, but many young Americans went off to it as to a great adventure. Rhetoric aside, they had, at least at the outset, less to lose. It was something altogether new, unfamiliar, and even in some cases romantic. The effects were dire, to be sure, and many doughboys, as they were then called, returned chastened, damaged, even bitter, but there was less of an engagement at the center, a less responsible, more detached notion of the war for a few as something to be observed and then regretted. For this reason we call them the Lost Generation. They had lost their innocence and their separation from the old world through combat and death. They now had to live with that. They were also uprooted and few could deny it.

Not so with their children in the Second World War, whose displacement was less stark. They had seen war before, secondhand, at least. And they had seen much, much more now. They had less innocence to start with and even less after. They, or some of them, had experience and were more familiar with the wider world than their parents had been, but inside there remained a hole that was run through with a skein of relativism. It was said they lived in a gray world where glib metaphors took the place of symbols, and where nearly everything looked different from different angles. They returned to a country that was, by outward appearances, determined to get on with business as usual. Still indifferent, gadget-loving, self-absorbed, and increasingly coarse. Still insisting that wars could be won rather than settled, security could be found rather than earned, fears could be conquered rather than managed. When none of that happened, there was an easy response: there were traitors, villains, and incompetents among us.

Uprooted from without—and now from within. Some gave in to despair: An "anti-suicide police" was formed in mid-1946 to keep people from jumping from the Empire State Building. Others felt frustration, confusion, and occasional rage, joining outbursts that had taken place in their absence. The latter included the "zoot suit" riots in Los Angeles and other cities in California in 1943, when thousands of rioters set upon mainly Mexican-American victims. These riots were followed by others in Detroit; Beaumont, Texas; and Harlem. The Detroit riots were the worst the city had seen in twenty-five years, resulting in three dozen deaths, hundreds of injured, and thousands of dollars of damage.

Some things back home ought to change or were about to. There is the now familiar statement of the black soldier coming back from Okinawa: "Our fight for freedom begins when we get to San Francisco." The fight had been under way for some time, but, as with many other things, the war gave it a push. More than a million more African Americans were employed in civilian jobs during the war than before it; more than half a million had joined unions; the number of members of the National Association for the Advancement of Colored People had grown fivefold; illiteracy among African Americans was down fourfold; life expectancy was up by over twenty-five years; and, thankfully, there were fewer lynchings.

Life was different also for women, black and white. In one survey, eight out of ten women said that they meant to continue working after the war. This was a long time coming. The number of women in the workplace had more than doubled between 1880 and 1920, and did so again by 1940. The effects, on both women and men, were not altogether welcome. Some women had left domesticity behind. Many would return to it, but domesticity had become laced with suspicion. Certainly many men had strayed during the war; so had many women. The guilt could not be purged in America, as it had been, for example, in France with the brutal shaving of heads of female "collaborators" and their being paraded naked in the streets. Instead Americans stifled doubt or channeled it into novels and films with female characters, at once alluring and threatening, and into the classic formula of social panic. Newspapers featured headlines like "Veteran Beheads Wife with Jungle Machete," "Ex-Marine Held in Rape Murder," and "Sailor Son Shoots Father."

Then came the Kinsey Report. Something like this could only have come after the war. Not that the 1920s and 1930s weren't years of liberation in mores and practices; they certainly were. So were, for that matter, the 1940s. But the Second World War introduced a different culture of quantification, of scientific certainty, and it was this aspect of the Kinsey Report—which measured human beings and their sexuality by percentages, experimentally and purportedly objectively, that is to say, empirically—that many people found so jarring. Again, some people asked: Is this what we fought for?

People adapted to peacetime in a predictable way: this was the marriage and baby boom. Divorces climbed too. There were twice as many in 1945 and 1946 as there were in 1939, and many lawyers switched their practices to divorces.

A major source of marital tension was the housing problem. A majority—perhaps as many as two-thirds—of married veterans were living in the houses of relatives or friends. Housing was not just scarce; it was naturally much more expensive than before or during the war. It was not unheard of for apartment ads to receive thousands of responses. The homeless in America's largest cities numbered in the tens of thousands. President Truman appointed a "housing expediter," the mayor of Louisville, Kentucky, Wilson Wyatt. He promised more than two and a half million new dwellings before 1948. Because these were meant mostly for veterans, and were public, Wyatt was tarred with being a Communist. A housing boom would come soon enough, thanks to private initiatives, led by William Levitt, having started the previous year.

Many veterans bought their new houses with money provided to them by the government in the above-mentioned GI Bill. It is now regarded as one of the more popular and successful pieces of social legislation in American history. The bill had been passed in 1944 and had already been declared insufficient by war's end. It was extended to all honorably discharged veterans. Many of them used the money for education. It was in great demand. For now at least there was enough supply, although housing all the new students was a problem. The result was by 1970 a doubling of the college-educated proportion of the labor force. Any veteran could obtain, at government expense, a university education for the amount of time served, so long as it was more than ninety days and not interrupted by attending a university. There were additional provisions for veterans (graduate students, for example) whose education was interrupted by the war. It also allowed veterans to borrow funds to start a business or buy or mortgage a house. Nearly everyone—future Supreme Court justices and presidents among them—who wanted it benefited by it. This included many who would go on to become purveyors of cultural capital as well: Robert Rauschenberg, Norman Mailer, Gene Hackman, Joseph Heller, Harry Belafonte, Arthur Penn, Paul Newman. Such status continued even for those professional officers who remained in the service. Peter Drucker, who had escaped Austria in the 1930s for a renowned academic and literary career in America, remembered middle-aged officers in the 1950s and 1960s coming to him because they thought earning a doctorate was the best thing they could do in retirement, which had, incidentally, been forced upon them because of their age and failure to be promoted.

So some Americans moved upward. Some just moved. Seventy million of them in 1947 lived in a different place from where they had lived in 1940. About one-fifth of the total population had moved to a different county or state. They were migrants, wanderers, searchers, some satisfied, others not. The American dream—the prosperous, comfortable, safe world—still existed in the minds of many people, even the families of returning soldiers. It had been not so much a fantasy as a postponement, one that many people somehow wished to earn but did not expect. It is difficult to parse the distinction. Herbert Hoover, in noting that "'the victors suffer almost equally with the vanquished' in economic misery and 'spiritual degradation,'" addressed himself to our basic question:

> When these men, whom we fondly call boys, come back from the wars, what sort of country will they find? What sort of a country do they want to live in? ... They will, under the experience in this war, have increased individual initiative, dignity and skills. They are the self-reliant. They want the security and self-respect of a job, not a dole. They want to be free to choose their own jobs and to prove their own worth. They want the rewards of their own efforts. They want to be free to plan their own lives.... They want a government that will keep the channels of opportunity open and equal.... In war, the altruistic impulses rise above all others and they mainly drive the economic machine. But regrettable as it may be, the self-interest group are the dominant drive force in peace.... It is this impulse that makes the difference in war. In war our people are willingly the servants of the State, but in peace they want the government to be the servant of the people.... Men cannot be free in mind and spirit if government is either to operate or dictate their economic life.

Also in 1944, Hoover's nemesis, Franklin Roosevelt, promoted an economic bill of rights that defined rights as rights, not simply as aspirations. The bill included rights to employment, medical care, housing, education, clothing, food, and recreation. "All these rights," Roosevelt concluded, "spell security." But they did not amount to a social revolution; some Americans may have wanted or expected it, but they did not seek or feel entitled to, as the British and others did, a wholly new system, a full-gone welfare state in name and in deed. This was not why they had fought the war.

Yet there was a challenge: how to square freedom with security; how to strengthen roots as well as wings. The postwar challenge of rebuilding sounded straightforward, so why did it prove so difficult? Why had it still not been achieved? One reason is that it was conflated with ideology, and in Hoover's and perhaps Roosevelt's case, with patriotism. The preferences of one or the other were easily tagged with the un-American label. However, both men presumably believed in democracy. Democracy justified the war. Democracy also must define the peace. But the country was divided over the history of the concept. Democracy to some was the prewar norm, and the value of any war president was measured by the extent to which he could return the country to the life it had known before the war demanded so much sacrifice, before it took so much away. To others, the war presented a call to master the future. To restore the past—especially in name—was in a way admitting a defeat. Yet in America as well as in Europe, continuities persisted from the prewar (or interwar) period to the postwar. One historian of Europe has gone so far as to declare the entire period from the mid- or late 1940s to the 1960s a "twenty-year truce" in the great political and ideological conflicts of the twentieth century.

Our indecision over what to call this period in the United States and how to characterize it—as a dawn or as a departure—is as illustrative of our own perpetual yearning for security as was that of 1946. So, yes, Americans planted roots. Women returned home from their factory jobs; the "housewife" became the middle-class staple, along with the "nuclear family," hence the baby boom. Americans were used to booms, of course; they usually followed, and were succeeded by, busts. But this one kept on booming for another twenty years at least. For the sacred middle class, the nuclear family represented not only confidence but also security at its most basic and visceral. A good job, your own house, a family: the American dream was really a postwar dream. A generation earlier it was called a promise. It could be kept or broken. Sometime later it was a way of life, defined mainly by standards of prosperity. But now it was a dream, it was meant to be fulfilled, "manifest" in the nineteenth-century sense, a blessing and a birthright.

This was what the country took from the war. Never again would it allow itself to feel so insecure, so exposed, so vulnerable. Never again would it allow a foreign power or alliance of powers to catch it unawares. Never again would it let someone, somewhere, deter it from a special destiny that would not, could not, be denied by anyone but Americans themselves. The war rewrote the American creed along familiar lines. But those lines had been overstepped by many Americans during the strange interval after the last war. Things would be different this time. The roots now were stronger.

But not in 1946, not yet. People may have returned from the war hopeful. They may have found jobs, bought houses, started families in an optimistic way. But it was a chary optimism. The war had exposed them to so much that was evil and ugly, much, again, that they preferred to deny to themselves, however much they fought the right of others to deny them anything at all. They did not yet fear another war, or another depression, but they did not yet know how not to fear. They had not yet found safety in a sense of superiority. They had gained in confidence, but not trust. They had become more determined, but not self-possessed. Part of them was like the man who knocked on wood, feeling lucky to be alive; another part was looking over their shoulder, wondering, just sometimes, whether it was safe yet to feel this lucky; and still another part held that thought in check, the part that knew that there was more to it than luck, and that this generation of Americans was meant somehow to carry on and do well at it. Some parents and children were just better at advancing, others at staying put, few at both.

This is one way of understanding the collective state of mind just after the war. Where Roosevelt's Four Freedoms—of speech and worship, from want and fear—then resided on a stage of fulfillment, they conflated the two things that most people wanted, indeed needed: wings and roots. The war generation decided that the latter took precedence over the former. This was the conclusion they reached during the confusion of the immediate postwar period, when everything the country had just gained in the way of security was about to be lost. The country had barely celebrated a victory when new fears—of poverty, nuclear destruction, Communism—overtook whatever serenity people had felt. The appearance—the threat, rather—of a Pyrrhic victory would persist for another decade at least, but it was no worse than at the very outset. The remarkable thing about the mood of 1946 was that it combined wariness so well with the logic of purpose. What was freedom from fear, after all, if you couldn't face fear directly? Yet facing fear is not the same as conquering it, especially if fear results from having partial or bad information. This was what the disruption of the war, and the further disruption of the peace, taught. Fear could not be conquered anymore, at least not permanently. Nor were these Americans conquerors, at least not the same type of conquerors. Earlier Americans had cut forests, dug holes, planted farms, raised animals, tilled fields, built villages, towns, and cities. But they had kept moving. Once they settled one place, they moved on to settle another. Conquest was expansive, dynamic, constant.

It was not this way anymore, simply because Americans no longer enjoyed the "free security" that existed during the latter part of the nineteenth century, or so many believed. It had never actually been free: it was a fact of geography but was underwritten by the British navy, which reminds us that oceans connect as much as they divide or insulate. In any case, this was no longer so relevant by the middle of the twentieth century. There were no more continents to conquer but there were still conquests to come: the space race, eradicating polio, and so on. Military conquest had been delegitimized by the war. American troops would return to, and stay in, Europe and Asia, but they were neither conquerors nor liberators. They were, to put it baldly, insurance agents against aggression, as it was said, or simply against fear.

A similar principle held at home: job, house, family—an armature. Americans were still mobile, but the old pattern was gone. You moved because your employer relocated you, or to be closer to a job, or to find a better one, or a better school for your children, or more space in which to raise them. You did not move for the sake of moving. That nineteenth-century practice has been ascribed, since the time of Tocqueville, to the condition of plentitude, beginning with the land. Americans then, it was said, could afford to waste it. They just moved on. To the mid-twentieth-century American who had endured the Depression and the war, moving was cumulative or destructive. You moved up, or sometimes down, but not simply on.

Yet Americans were still the world's people of plenty. This much we know in retrospect. How many felt it in 1946 is difficult to say. Some planners at Bretton Woods two years earlier certainly did, and so did some of the same people negotiating the British loan, as we'll read in chapter 10. But the average man or woman who laid down roots right after the war was more likely to have dreamt it. Or better yet, they may have just felt it somewhere, somewhere inside where they knew that the strongest roots were not the ones that extended outward in every direction but those that entwined themselves inward, buried deep inside the person.

There was something about this generation that has made it easy to call them the greatest, although the specific reason escapes us if we think hard about it. The appellation is not entirely fictional; it is just impossible to compare. How can anyone judge these people against those who lived through the Civil War and then rebuilt the nation, or against any number of others? Greatness is a strange concept. Usually it says more about the beholder (and his life and times) than the beheld. Still, there was something about the members of this particular generation that counts for more, at least by their descendants, who cannot help compare them to the baby boomers who followed. They were *stronger*. Their hands and arms were thicker, larger; their voices deeper, more powerful. Their gaze was more direct; even their syntax was clearer.

This is an image, a bias, a prejudice, perhaps true of most people looking back (or up) to their forebears. But few generations had been on the winning side of a war so vast. Few had then lived through the most glorious period of national prosperity—at least for the middle class. Few had seen their country become the most powerful nation in modern history, all in the span of a few decades, indeed, of their own lives. And so the texture of the roots—the source of great confidence—came to matter a good deal. What remains of this uprooted generation, then, is that texture, at once strong and sensitive. It once lived as though nothing at all could be taken for granted or assumed; it was an existential generation in this respect, which found its worth through the mere act of living, and occasionally loving, as if that were enough for the moment. That sentiment was more often than not reflective. As the years went on, the uprooted came to feel a satisfaction and even a nostalgia for having done as well as they had. Somehow they came to overlook the tenuousness they had once known. They did not like to admit or even think it, but they had come to relish having once been in the war, if only because they had that confidence, and therefore the security, of having done so.

Back then, as we have seen and shall see, it was anything but. There was more to the sensation, for it was not mere confidence but, in the words of the writer and early student of existentialism William Barrett, an "exuberant confidence." He remembered later asking the artist Saul Steinberg if he didn't share the feeling, and if so, where it came from.

Steinberg's "memory focused," wrote Barrett, "he gave me that sharp and reflective look of his, like a jeweler squinting sidewise at a questionable gem. 'No,' he said, 'there was something else there too. Something simpler beneath all our big ideas. It was the simple feeling that we had survived.'"

Chapter 2

"Harry Who?"

For the process of revisionism has developed a habit of understating certain things and passing quickly over others.

—"The Easy Chair," February 1946

A popular historical falsehood is that Americans don't do irony. We rather like such myths. This is one of the biggest, for American history is full of ironies, which in good old American, that is to say adversarial, fashion usually come in the form of a paradox.

Harry Truman was a paradox straight out of central casting. Who better could follow the most beloved president in anyone's lifetime, yet who had also been one of the most despised? Nobody could fill Franklin Roosevelt's shoes, it was said, except the sort of man whom nobody ever would expect to do so. "I just can't call that man President," Grace Tully, Roosevelt's secretary, repeated over and over. It was not that she disliked Truman; she just barely knew him. Nobody stood when he entered the room; they did only when they saw Eleanor Roosevelt arrive. He asked the senators and pages and even the reporters he saw to pray for him. Not many outside the Senate or his state had an opinion of him when he stepped forth to take the oath of office on April 12, 1945. Probably Roosevelt hadn't much of an opinion either. To those who did, Truman was the caricaturist's dream of an American everyman, precisely the type of man Roosevelt had been championing all this time, and precisely the type of man FDR was not.

Truman was an exaggerated everyman from Missouri. Now he was the president.

He had one problem. Everymen weren't meant to be president. Americans had nothing against them; there is a long tradition of anti-elitism, or, as we prefer to call it, populism, in American politics. However exceptional or aristocratic they may be, presidents were supposed to play to the people. Roosevelt understood this better than most. Truman probably did too, but the problem is, he really *was* of the people, warts and all, which is not necessarily what most people want their presidents to be.

To recall the reality and the myth: Truman was a small-town haberdasher who went to the Senate and then to the White House. Don't shrug or smirk, the old Washingtonian says to the grandchild, passing along Pennsylvania Avenue, you too may end up there someday; it's always the ones who least expect it who do. Humility and chance feed with the ambition of the mystic who accepts what comes but prepares for something greater, and accepts that too. Truman, however, was no mystic, nor did he fit the log-cabin archetype. The only president who did in the middle twentieth century was the last of that genre, Lyndon Johnson. Truman was provincial but not rustic. He was prim. This was the image conveyed by those round spectacles, the hair combed neatly, the pursed lips. The image went back to his earliest years. If we did not know any better, we would say he modeled himself upon Twain's model of the Missouri mama's boy.

It sounds like an oxymoron. Missouri had long had the reputation of a rough borderland. Its people resembled its famous mules: hard, sturdy, difficult, with a "kick" to them. Missourians also take pride in being both a juxtaposition and a microcosm. They see their state as comprising America, with all its problems, "in peppery miniature."

They are also known for their pride. The writer John Gunther found that out directly: "One thing I know about Mr. Truman is that he loves Missouri. . . . 'They're ornery, mean folk!' he chuckled. 'They're against everybody but themselves!' I asked Mr. Truman what they were for. 'Missouri!'"

It was true. Truman often heard the "Missouri Waltz" played when he reviewed troops. He liked to be introduced to the Missourians among them. He was sentimental about his state in just the right way.

These are qualities Americans are supposed to relish. Truman's first approval ratings, bolstered no doubt by national grief, were well over 80 percent. So it may be ironic—or just predictable—that he left the presidency shunned, indeed with an approval rating as low or even lower than that of Nixon, Carter, or the two Bushes, and has since only grown in the public estimation, today being regarded as a near-great president. The shift had been under way for some time, but much of the credit for it now goes to the popular rehabilitationist David McCullough, whose 1992 book *Truman* outsold many other biographies. McCullough has found a nice formula for rescuing such people from the condescension of posterity. He did it for Washington Roebling, who built the Brooklyn Bridge; for George Goethals, who built the Panama Canal; for the young Theodore Roosevelt; and for John Adams, another president who may have deserved better, although hardly an everyman. His heroes are complicated, even troubled, men who rise above tough circumstances and enemies, and their own flaws and neuroses, to greatness. But to McCullough and to his readers at the turn of the twenty-first century—including the president in 2001, George W. Bush, who probably resembled Truman more than any other of his predecessors, as we are about to see—Truman may have had the furthest to go.

To honor or to disparage Harry Truman is symptomatic of the times, perhaps more so than for most leaders, because he did not seize or rise to the office of president, or at least that was never obvious. It fell into his lap, or as he put it, on his head, like the moon, the stars, and all the planets, and a load of hay. It is tempting to depict him as uprooted too; in fact it was the presidency that had been uprooted beside him.

Yet he was said to worship the office. He treated the moves of adversaries as challenges not only to himself but to the office that he held. At the same time he regarded himself as a student of leaders and leadership. The story has often been told of his having read all the books, some three thousand, plus encyclopedias, in his local library as a boy. This was an achievement, for Truman was a very slow reader. His eyesight was dreadful, which was why he wore such thick glasses, which in turn was why he spent so much time reading, because, by his account, rough games were out of the question. The other children poked fun at him. This gave him, he said, a passion to better himself—to learn—and "to fight for everything you do." Fighting meant conquering: he was taught to avoid actual fights and tried hard to be liked. He also probably wanted to be admired. He prided himself especially on a vast historical knowledge gleaned from this early immersion in books, but nearly every time he mentioned it, he cited great men—emperors, conquerors, statesmen. The young, tormented boy who found solace in the great deeds of great men always remained a part of him. He would rattle off their names as if playing back a magnetic tape:

I wish I was seventeen instead of sixty-seven, with the same urge I had at seventeen to learn and to know world history. I spent a lot of time reading about the World's Great. Moses, Joshua, David, Solomon, Darius I and Cyrus the Great his uncle. Alexander, Hannibal, Caesar, Antoninus Pius, Hadrian, Titus, Marcus Aurelius Antoninus, Rameses III, Cleopatra, Mark Antony, Augustus Caesar, Thothmes III, Plato, Socrates, Pericles, Demosthenes, Cicero, Catos, both of them, then Charlemagne, his father Charles Martel, Roland, John Hunyadi at Belgrade, Saladin, Suleiman the Magnificent, Jenghis Khan, Kubla Khan, Tamerlane, John Sobieski, Richelieu, Gustavus Adolphus of Sweden and Charles XII of Sweden, Alfred the Great, William of Normandy. The greatest of French Kings, Henry IV of France and King of Navarre, Francis I of France and Charles V of Spain. Elizabeth of England and Mary of Scotland. Sir Francis Drake and Captain Kidd, Martin Luther, Frederick the Great and Maria Theresa of Austria. Wellington and Lord Russell, Disraeli, Gladstone, Washington, Jefferson, Jackson, Lincoln, Grover Cleveland, Wilson, Franklin Roosevelt and the end!

Truman's historical knowledge was not perfect or rote. It was what we call applied knowledge. He was fond of analogies, and of declaring that this or that problem was "just like" another he recalled learning about in the local library so long ago. In recalling the negotiations at San Francisco for the founding of the United Nations, he

> had hoped that someday we could build an international organization that would eventually work on the same basis as the union of the United States. I had made a study of the "Grand Design" of King Henry IV of France. This plan called for a kind of federation of sovereign states in Europe to act in concert to prevent wars. This, as far as I know, was the first practicable international organization ever suggested. Woodrow Wilson must have thought of it when he planned the League of Nations.

In explaining the nature of his office and his approach to governing, he noted that

> the Presiden[t] . . . has more duties and powers than a Roman Emperor, a Gen., a Hitler or a Mussolini; but he never uses those powers or prerogatives, because he is a democrat (with a little d) and because he believes in the Magna Carta and the Bill of Rights. But first he believes in the XXth Chapter of Exodus, the Vth Chapter of Deuteronomy, and the V, VI, & VIIth chapters of the Gospel according to St. Matthew. . . . He should be a Cincinnatus, Marcus Aurelius Antoninus, a Cato, Washington, Jefferson and Jackson all in one. I fear that there is no such man. But if we have one who tries to do what is right because it is right, the greatest Republic in the history of the world will survive.

Since Truman's time a large body of scholarship has formed on the subject of presidential power and leadership. One man who gets much of the credit for starting it was a young assistant in the Bureau of the Budget and then in the White House during the Truman administration named Richard Neustadt. After observing Truman and his circle up close, Neustadt went on to earn a PhD and to launch his career, as he put it, as a professional "president watcher." Neustadt's simple idea, which he told in his text *Presidential Power*, was that the American executive was little more than an agent among catalysts. His power was the power to persuade. For there was very little you could do in the American system (or in most other nominally democratic systems) if you could not persuade a good portion, probably a majority, of others to support what you sought to achieve.

Persuasion was one of Truman's deficiencies. He was an above-average go-along-to-get-along type, so long as the matter in question was largely decided beforehand. Had he stayed in the Senate, he could well have become one of its stalwarts, not by any shred of legislative brilliance but by reliability and, probably, fair-mindedness. When it was up to him to choose and implement something, however, he suddenly became, to himself, a stubborn, solitary man. When faced with opposition or abuse, he dug in. Then he would be stiff and awkward, looking as he thought a strong leader ought to look, after giving it a few minutes' thought. Yet to others he just looked like a failed haberdasher with the perfectly folded handkerchief sticking out from his suit pocket.

There were opponents, enemies, traitors . . . undercutting, cheating, thwarting him when all he was trying to do was the right thing for the American people. He had little tolerance for complexity, for "gray areas." The image set in of a man frustrated. As time went on it got worse. "Give 'em hell Harry" became an epithet, for good and for ill. It could signify strength of character, or it could mean a tough façade meant to disguise something far less: "erratic, petty, and a cut or two below his responsibilities." It could even mean hypocrisy, for some people said that Truman only told the world he'd given you hell after he had agreed with you, whether or not he understood what you were saying.

The worst costume of stubbornness is self-righteousness. It was demeaning to the office to take everything so personally. That may have worked for an Andrew Jackson or a Richard Nixon because both men, and the style they had, corresponded to a resentment that was widespread among the American people. In Neustadt's terms, it was a means of persuasion, for it bolstered their popularity.

With Truman it was the opposite. Americans had become used to a style of presidential rule that was avuncular and cheerful even in the face of duplicity. And FDR was hardly uniformly admired or even liked. Roosevelt smiled through the years of invective from the ranks of his many haters. He learned from his onetime ally Al Smith the pros and cons of being the happy warrior. He knew how much more enjoyable the political game could be if enemies were hoisted with their own petard, how easy it was to drive them to distraction by coupling, indirectly, their opposition with your success, and how much more freedom to maneuver you had if you could rely on their emotions to do your bidding. Roosevelt was blessed by his temperament and by the quality of his enemies. They rarely went for the kill. On the other hand, he retained his outward dignity and popularity while cutting their throats as well as any tough politician, such as the time when he worked to destroy the career of William Bullitt—whom we'll meet in chapter 5—even to the point of ordering party officials in Philadelphia to move heaven and earth to prevent Bullitt from being elected mayor, the man's final grasp at public office. For FDR this was an indication of toughness and political talent; if Truman had done it, it would simply have been regarded as spiteful.

Truman could not feel one way and appear the other: genial and stubborn. He didn't discount political hardball, and he moved with some very tough and devious politicos. But to deceive was not his personal style. He could be shrewd instead. A good example was the way he handled his nomination to the vice presidency in 1944. He had probably known that he would be asked to accept it, but said that he didn't really want it, right up to the last minute. Listeners to that line had a predictable reply: you must do it, Harry, for compromise and for the country, because otherwise Henry Wallace will stay on the ticket, and by now we all know him to be a dangerous prospect. Roosevelt as usual played all sides, needing and wanting to appease his party bosses (most of whom no longer would back Wallace) but also the liberal wing of the party. Roosevelt, however, was tired, weak, and ill. He delegated the choosing to one of the most stalwart bosses, Bob Hannegan, who happened to be from Missouri, and so Truman's name was proposed even though he had already agreed to support another candidate, James Byrnes. When Truman moved to the head of the line there was little he could do but accept graciously, for the honor of his party, his state, and his country. As always, he attracted support by leaving himself open to it, and by not offending too many people. But once he was in power, the stakes and the style were different.

Most often, then, he chose the frontal assault or the bulwark defense. Either way, when he seethed, it showed. This was his "mulish streak": he'd glare straight ahead, harden his expression, and become immobile. He had made his choice.

The usual diagnosis for Truman's most visible traits—his briskness, bumptiousness, precision, stubbornness—was that they were the result of a deep insecurity. There is some truth to that. He knew and admitted it in reference to his boyhood. But there is less evidence that he understood the distinction between being firm and being quick to decide. The latter in Truman's case was as much instinctive as retrospective: he later described his decision to intervene in Korea as taking just seconds to make. His basic instinct, however, was not to act or fight, in fact, but to flee—if only temporarily—to relieve the pressure, the fatigue, and, as would later become evident, an intense anger. In pre-presidential days he took to hiding in a hotel, where he kept a secret diary; as president Key West became his sanctuary. Unlike the young Eisenhower, for example, who was said to relish the scrape and the brawl, young Truman was ordered sternly, mainly by his mother, to avoid them. As time went on, he made more of an effort to gauge the views of his advisers and to master the brief when necessary. When it came to making the choices for which he is best known—recognition of Israel and the firing of General Douglas MacArthur, for example—he could take his time. Generally, though, he held out for his luck to turn; failing that, he placed himself in the roles of judge and enforcer, and sometimes confused the two. His burden, as he described it, was to have to make so many "immediate decisions." He portrayed this as a source of pressure, a duty and a requirement. "I am here to make decisions," he said, "and whether they prove right or wrong I am going to make them." The one concession in the form of a qualification was having claimed, following the Lend-Lease fiasco mentioned below in chapter 10, that he needed to make the time to read the documents he signed. Maybe he also took digesting them, understanding them, for granted; or maybe too many other people did.

Truman's method of consultation has been described as a wheel with spokes. The spokes all met more or less at his central point, where the old buck was supposed to stop. Actually, it did no such thing. He took decisions but then delegated the execution of them to the cabinet departments, which under Roosevelt had been less accustomed to being granted clear duties. At least that was Truman's version of his leadership style. In truth his administration could be as arbitrary, confused, duplicative, and inefficient as Roosevelt's but without his predecessor's famous talent for juggling people and interests, that is to say, for masterful dissembling. Soon people began to notice. The Washington press corps, which had initially found Truman's Missouri gang a refreshing bunch of good old

boys, turned hostile as soon as Truman showed his other, cantankerous side and shut them out. Staffers complained of feeling unsat-
isfied and low after meetings; even when they lost arguments in the
Roosevelt White House, they would still leave with a spark and an
ounce of passion. As for Truman, he stuck to his own trusted circle.
Others he confronted.

There is a notable caveat, perhaps contradiction, to this familiar
portrait of the man. Truman possessed an odd fatalism. It often
took the form of self-deprecation or humility, as with his use of the
word "termites" on his visit to the ruins of Berlin. He referred not
directly to Berliners but to all humanity, small occupiers on or
beneath the earth's surface, subject to forces far vaster than themselves. Over the door to his office he kept a large horseshoe. One of
the words he used most frequently was "hope." On his desk he kept
in a leather portfolio the lines of Lincoln, "I do the very best I know
how—the very best I can; and I mean to keep doing so to the end. If
the end brings me out all right, what is said against me won't amount
to anything. If the end brings me out wrong, ten angels swearing I
was right won't make any difference." Many of his private letters,
especially to his wife, mother, and sister, take a similar tone. He was,
he wrote to Bess, when she accepted his proposal of marriage, just "a
clodhopper who has ambitions to be Governor of Mont[ana] and
Chief Executive of U.S." Or he would just "keep peggin' away and I
suppose I'll arrive at something. You'll never be sorry if you take me
for better or for worse because I'll always try to make it better." Many
years later, he added:

> Well I'm here in the White House, the great white sepulcher of
> ambitions and reputations. I feel like a last year's bird's nest
> which is on its second year.... This head of mine should have
> been bigger and better proportioned. There ought to have been
> more brain and a larger bump of ego or something to give me
> an idea that there can be a No. 1 man in the world.

His aim was to try his best. If he succeeded, it was because of perseverance and luck. If he failed, he had still tried, and he would keep on trying. That was a curious attitude for a president. The columnist Joe Alsop put it a different way in his memoirs, written several decades later. Truman, he wrote, "is an overrated president, although he had more guts, more sheer, naked guts, than any leader the United States has had during this century, barring, perhaps, Theodore Roosevelt." His problem, Alsop went on to admit, was his judgment. Again, when he was blessed with good advice, his firmness and willfulness came in handy; but this didn't happen all the time. Such an attitude could backfire with a president who sometimes had great difficulty in knowing good people and policies from bad ones.

Truman deferred only to one group consistently: women. He had an old-fashioned reverence for them and is rumored in trivia contests to be the only American president in the twentieth century to have remained faithful to his wife. He adored Bess and never showed more determination than in courting her. Other women—his mother, sister, and daughter, and even his beloved teachers Tillie Brown and Margaret Phelps and Grace White, who taught him to play piano—figure prominently in his diaries, letters, and memoirs. His defense of them was as aggressive as his deference was pure. There is the infamous story of Truman's letter to the columnist who insulted the musical talents of his daughter, Margaret. Truman often wrote angry letters. He rarely sent them. But this one he did, to his and his daughter's embarrassment and much of the country's amusement. There is another story, or explanation, of why he never invited the powerful Luce couple to the White House. It was simple. Clare Boothe Luce had once said an unkind thing about Bess Truman. There was nothing more to it than that, permanently.

Truman reflected the strength of the women around him. When he once groused about the refusal of Congress to allow him to enlarge the West Wing, he said he would hire a bulldozer and do it himself. "Harry," said Bess sternly, "you will do NO SUCH THING!" This was accompanied by a hard punch on the knee that left the president looking momentarily crippled.

Truman's mother had a similar reputation. "Every day is Mother's Day in the White House," it was said, "with a bitter snicker." Back in January 1945, when he became vice president, he went to telephone his mother back in Missouri. "Now you behave yourself up there, Harry. You behave yourself." . . . "I will, Mamma."

These women were on pedestals. They reinforced Truman's odd acceptance at face value of the power of those forces of human nature greater than his own. Feminine power was one of them. He was not known to relax around women. He preferred the company of men for that purpose, and even on occasion could tell ribald jokes about women. There was the story told by Henry Wallace about the time Truman joked that he really never should have become president but would have been content as a mere "piano player in a whorehouse." The secretary of labor and Truman's former Senate ally, Lewis Schwellenbach, retorted, "That would have been too bad because then we never would have known you!"

"Why be so high and mighty," Truman fired back, "as though you had never been in a whorehouse!"

This was Truman's observed dual personality. He was an honest man, a faithful son, husband, and father, a hard worker, a put-your-best-foot-forward sort who always stood up when it counted. Then there was Truman the backroom pol, the bourbon and poker aficionado and man's man, the man who proved, despite great odds in 1948, that he knew how to count a vote, and to twist an arm or two, by almost any means at hand.

Truman the politician emerged from one of the most corrupt urban machines in the country, that of Thomas J. Pendergast and his brothers, sons of immigrants from Tipperary. Pendergast was ruthless, combative, charming, and large in every sense. He had wanted to play baseball but his father forbade it, it was said, because the man couldn't really understand the game. His brother Jim had already built a small patronage empire. So Tom switched to politics with all the passion for winning and for power he could summon. Very little got done in Kansas City without Pendergast's approval, and nothing at all concerning public works.

Truman was a Pendergast man and never disabused himself of that, even after Pendergast went to prison. Truman owed his first important electoral victories to the Pendergasts, starting with brother Mike. Later Tom Pendergast kept bestowing favors, although (or maybe because) he regarded Truman as "the contrariest cuss in Missouri." But Truman himself was honest. He justified the rest by qualification. "I am obliged to the Big Boss, a man of his word," he wrote in his secret diary, referring to Pendergast, "but he gives it very seldom and only on a sure thing. But he's not a trimmer. He, in past times, owned a bawdy house, a saloon and gambling establishment, was raised in that environment but he's all man." Honesty was Truman's strongest asset, certainly once he arrived in the Senate. For if anyone had heard of him when he was the surprise choice of the party operatives to replace Henry Wallace as Roosevelt's running mate in 1944, they knew him as the earnest head of the Senate committee investigating waste in war procurement. Truman's committee was one of the best known in either chamber, and with probably the highest reputation for toughness, integrity, and simple hard work. Truman, somehow, was able to finesse the two worlds.

He invited the contrasts. There is the Pendergast contrast. The Roosevelt contrast. The MacArthur contrast, with the onetime army captain. For once Truman put it best himself: "Mr. Prima Donna, Brass Hat, Five Star MacArthur. He's worse than the Cabots and the Lodges—they at least talked with one another before they told God what to do. Mac tells God right off. . . . Don't see how a country can produce such men as Robert E. Lee, John J. Pershing, Eisenhower & Bradley and at the same time produce Custers, Pattons, and MacArthurs." There was the contrast, described below in chapter 5, of Truman and his counterparts at Potsdam. Truman said he could learn to respect Stalin and even Churchill, "a most charming and a very clever person—meaning clever in the English not the Kentucky sense." He figured they would do all right so long as Churchill "doesn't try to give me too much soft soap." Churchill did, but not Stalin. "You know," Truman added for effect, "soft soap is made of ash hopper lye and it burns to beat hell when it gets into the eyes. It's fine for chigger bites but not so good for rose complexions. But I haven't a rose complexion." Later, in 1948, there was another marked contrast with his Republican opponent, Thomas Dewey, the man nearly every person in the know assumed would defeat him.

Dewey, as it happened, was also a midwesterner—the son of a postmaster and editor from Michigan. A couple of decades younger than Truman, he had an easier upbringing. Somewhere along the way he became ambitious. At the age of thirteen he was boss of a small team of pint-sized employees. The high school yearbook, of which he was the editor, declared him "first in the council hall to steer the state, and ever foremost in a tongue debate."

He headed to New York, where he made a name for himself as a prosecutor, and then a fortune in the law. He became governor and then the standard-bearer of his party after putting his name forward for its nomination in every presidential election since 1940. He found it hard going. He was young—all of thirty-eight when proposed to stand against Roosevelt—and, even worse, short. There were the usual jokes: that he rode his dog to work; that he looked like the little man on the wedding cake; that he was "the chocolate soldier of Albany." Probably more damaging was his lacking a sense of humor and the slightest talent for public endearment.

He compensated by slick preparation and presentation. His 1948 campaign brought out everything that was provincial about Truman, his character, and his times. Dewey's campaign was a professional media extravaganza, now alas the norm. He served up the right words at the right time in the right way to the right audiences, and they repaid him for saying exactly what they wanted to hear. There were professional bands, posters, and entrances. Truman toured the country on the back of his train, taking pride in the "whistle stop," playing it by ear at rallies and speeches, missing many cues and speaking the familiar but fading language of the barnstormer, the small-town crier. The contrast showed even in the drinks and games observed on the two campaign trains. For Dewey they were mostly martinis and Manhattans, with bridge; with Truman they were the Kentucky highball and poker.

Somehow Truman won, despite having said many times that he had secretly hoped to lose, right up to the very end when he insisted, against all expert opinion, that he would surely win. At long last he could stop acting humble.

We know, therefore, that Truman was no simple man. He was a man of contrasts, uncommonly compounded. He had come of age in the rough political back rooms of Kansas City. He was content, indeed happy, to spend hours drinking bourbon at a card table. His prim small-town world was just one generation and a few miles removed from some of the toughest borderlands of the Civil War. Truman himself was a product of that divided, hostile, brutal place. His father, a failed farmer and jack of several other trades whom people called "Peanuts," was a cussed fighter who nevertheless bred in his son a firm sense of right and wrong. His mother, whose people's sympathies were on the southern side of the great divide, could chastise her son, perhaps jokingly, perhaps not, from her bed, where she lay, aged ninety-two, with a broken hip and shoulder, for placing a wreath at the Lincoln Memorial. He was a man who once described himself as descended from "these contrary Kentucky feudists. . . . We don't forget our friends and we remember those who lied about us—and I'm afraid I don't forgive them." He had fought bravely in the First World War; he had seen death in France and had survived. There is an oft-mentioned photograph from that time, his army identification, that shows him without the thick eyeglasses. It is one of the few photographs that do. And there another Truman appears, transparently: hard, direct, obdurate, bloody-minded.

Truman was a man of the borderlands in more than one sense. He was not a Deep Southerner but was the bone tossed to the southern wing of his party. He was not a New Dealer and would be chastised by the true believers as a conservative. For his part, he distinguished between an "advanced 'Liberal'" and a "professional one . . . the latter the lowest form of politician." His career was made on the face of inoffensive honesty: he was the one they chose who tolerated the excesses of others and made the rest of us feel all right, but never crossed the line himself. He spoke the language of the nineteenth century and appealed to the small-town romance of the early twentieth, but ushered the people into a world of superpowers. He was mild, easygoing, friendly, and courteous, and he fought as doggedly as any man could when challenged, especially once he said he had made up his mind.

He also was appealingly self-conscious. When Truman opened the baseball season in 1946 he arrived accompanied by Bess, Admiral William D. Leahy, General Eisenhower, and some three dozen other people. The crowd in the stadium gave him an ovation as he made his way to the box. He was the first president ever to walk thus through the stands. Truman was left-handed but had been taught to use his right. He promised, for the sake of the southpaws, to throw the pitch using his left. But instinct (and maybe nerves) saw it begin from his right. He caught himself, "switched the ball to the publicized duke, limbered it up with two short waves of the soupbone, drew it back behind his ear, and fired an overhand delivery of about

50 feet into the cluster of players of both sides deploying for the throw." In other words, after a moment of indecision, he tossed it as hard as he could.

Truman rose to power on his honesty; he wielded it, and eventually lost it, from stubbornness. Few presidents until George W. Bush were so quick to issue directives. And few were so reluctant to second-guess. Doing so, they said, was a measure of weakness. Both regarded decisions and decisiveness as the chief virtue of leadership. Both defined their job in this way. Bush even called himself "the decider." Yet both men, apart from some notable exceptions, put little work into deciding. Choosing and deciding are not one and the same. We associate the former with courage, the latter with wisdom, but also, and perhaps more important, with diligence. It is curious that both Truman and the younger Bush were succeeded by deliberative, almost painfully deliberative, presidents who liked to be seen as above politics, "weighing options" and issuing verdicts on what they determined was most in the national interest. Bush and, even more so, Truman did not judge so much as they just acted, relying upon their subordinates and successors to handle the consequences.

The main difference was in the quality of the advice they got. Truman, unlike Bush, was fortunate to have good advisers, a number of whom, as the next chapter describes, he inherited from Wall Street by way of wartime service in the Roosevelt administration. Such decider-presidents more often do as they are told than reach independent decisions. The important thing for them was to stand firm. They conflated, usually in retrospect, firmness, decisiveness, and leadership. This was how they judged their worth. To their credit, on most matters they stood about as firm as anyone could have done.

If we ask today who was Harry Truman, our answer would not be too different from what most Americans would have said in

1946. He was a limited man who was thrust into a position for which he was unprepared, apart from the commitment, we have sensed, to do the best he could. Truman's best may have been short of what the country needed or wanted, but the country could be pragmatic. He was who he was, so we had to help him. Eleanor Roosevelt's famous line—asking him what he needed us to do for him when he asked what he could do for her (Truman's reply: "Before I had a chance to answer her question, Secretary of State Stettinius came in. He . . . was in tears")—was about as apt as could be. Truman, for all his small-bore persona, for all the times he put fear into the minds of his advisers like Dean Acheson that, for no good reason in particular, he would "stick peanuts up his nose" and buck, could also listen to and take direction. The longer he was in office, the more direction he sought. He was in this respect the ideal president of a plutocracy. And this is why, as we shall see, some people came to dismiss him. They knew he was in over his head, fearful of his own limitations, and did not have the decency to make way for a more formidable leader, if he had existed. He was determined to stand his ground, to do his duty, no matter how much damage it might do.

Truman's own oft-quoted comparison of the presidency to the act of riding a tiger may suggest more about the tiger than the man. The tiger of people, politics, and events could not be tamed; you just had to stay on. To do that all you had to do was to stay firm and hold tight. And what made you hold tight, Truman said, were your convictions, your belief, self-serving as it may be, that you were doing the right thing for the right reasons and in the right way. If not, then let the tiger win, as it should. A cousin gave him a message from his mother: "Tell Harry to be good, be honest, and behave himself, but I think it is now time for him to get tough with someone." That was a concise formulation of his creed.

Whatever he may be when viewed nostalgically, Harry Truman is today an overrated president—not as overrated as he was underrated during his time in office and right after, but nevertheless a figure of misdrawn historical proportions. In another sense, however, he is the perfectly drawn emblem of the self-conscious and unsure mood of his fellow Americans in 1946. He did his best, just as his country did, eventually, in coping with a dangerous postwar muddle of politics and social change. He did not win the old war, and the actions and processes he set into motion did not win the new one. But they did not lose them either. America persevered, and survived. Given all that we now know about how difficult the Cold War was, and how precarious the condition of the country and the world throughout much of it, survival was no small achievement, especially when so many Americans were not sure they were up for waging any war at all. They could have done much worse.

Chapter 3

Empire Men

History is supposed to learn from the experience it studies and from those movements it calls historical processes. Forty-six years into the twentieth century it is supposed to understand the relationship of events in the nineteenth century. Finally, it is supposed to understand that in the nineteenth century some Americans were mistaken, some ideas fallacious, and some actions in error and certain to fail.

—"The Easy Chair," March 1946

"Empire" is a hoary term, becoming more so with the decades. Some nineteenth-century Americans embraced it—as in Jefferson's "empire for liberty"—and drew a moral distinction between their continental empire and an overseas, colonial one like the British, which their forebears had repudiated. By the end of the century the distinction lost some of its difference, when the United States "acquired" a group of far-flung territories from the defeated Spanish Empire, from the Caribbean to the South China Sea. This was, after all, the age of high imperialism. Why shouldn't America take part? Surely, as the historian Frederick Jackson Turner announced to the country in 1893, the frontier was closed. So the American people and their institutions had matured to the point where overseas expansion and even overseas possessions were no longer synonymous with depravity and corruption. In any event, the closing of the frontier made it so. New frontiers were needed. They could be conquered in the American way.

However, much of the country, and a good number of opinion leaders, did not share this view. The 1898 war and its jingoism left behind a bad taste in the mouths of the more enlightened classes;

another war in 1914, which President Woodrow Wilson pledged
over and again to keep the country out of but in the end failed to
resist entering, left behind an even bitterer taste and one that was
more widespread. Entering it was seen soon after it ended as a giant
and unnecessary mistake. It brought, among other things, the devas-
tating influenza. George Washington had been right in his Farewell
Address. The peace and prosperity of the United States depended
above all upon one principle: stay out of other people's politics, especially their wars. The problem Americans had in 1946 was in knowing whether or not this rule could still apply. If so, what alternative
was there for what was by now the world's biggest industrial economy? If not, how to make empire, or something like it, work?

The generation of Americans born during the final decades of
the nineteenth century and who came of age during the first decades
of the twentieth did not need to be reminded of Washington's principle. They were imbued with it. They also saw a paradox. For while
their teachers reminded them of how correct he had been, they
could also see how big their country had grown, how prosperous it
had become, how fortunate it was in spite of all the errors of policy
from the first Roosevelt to the second. For there was another principle dating back to the country's founding that also still held, evidently: Europe's distresses equaled America's successes. What to do
now with so much success?

To some members of this generation—notably its elite, or
what later came to be called, somewhat inaccurately, its Eastern
Establishment—the new frontiers were different from those their
forefathers and many of their more provincial contemporaries disparaged. They were commercial, financial, cultural, not necessarily
drawn boldly with lines or colors on a map, but rather in the hearts
and minds of would-be allies around the world who looked to
America as the most modern, progressive, and successful country
on earth.

This impulse wasn't so new either. Aspects of it are found in the language of the Young Americans from nearly a century earlier, one of whom, the editor John L. O'Sullivan, made popular the term "manifest destiny." For our subjects' generation, reaching adulthood during the boom of the 1920s, the manifestations of American success and influence had finally become facts of life. American banks and bankers now dominated world finance; New York had begun to occupy the commanding perch long held by London and Paris. American manufactures cornered markets in everything from sewing machines to automobiles. Hollywood films deflected and then defeated whatever competition may have come in the early days from elsewhere, and gradually American universities began to do the same.

The one area where the United States still fell behind—very behind, as it happened—was in its capacity to project military power. Its army in size ranked seventeenth in the world on the eve of World War II. Its navy fared somewhat better but was tiny compared with what it was about to become.

Among other things, the war forced a good number of thoughtful Americans to reconsider their basic understanding of empire. They also must have known, or felt, without really knowing it, that the British Empire as it evolved over the course of the nineteenth century was an institutional and political fact. It could be denounced or shunned as much as they liked, but it could not be denied.

Not for much longer. That empire had begun its long process of liquidation, just when those thoughtful Americans had begun to cast a more favorable eye upon it, and to realize what it did and did not do in and for the world. They did not envy it so much as they wondered, and worried, what would follow it, and how this would affect them.

Those who survived the Second World War, as we have read, have since called it the "good war." It was not that, at least not then. The war generation made it so, first by fighting what was one of the bitterest— perhaps the single bitterest—political fight in the twentieth century:

the one between interventionists and isolationists. The fight ended in a draw, or rather it never really ended; the attack on Pearl Harbor suspended it with an armistice. It would be fought in varying dimensions over and again: in the 1950s over China, in the 1960s over Vietnam, in the 1970s over the Middle East, in the 1980s over Central America, in the 1990s and beyond over more than half the globe.

In December 1941, however, duty called. Isolationists became a different breed of patriot overnight. Until then many of them were Anglophobic. Transatlantic communication and travel may have made them less so. Others had been simple yet sincere idealists. This group included the Anglophile journalist Herbert Agar and Roosevelt's Republican opponent in 1940, Wendell Willkie, whose bestselling book about his circumnavigation, *One World*, was a striking experiment in the reverse logic of the double negative, the repudiation of a repudiation: the world was now America's world, so America could feel at home everywhere, in fact isolated from isolationism, yet at the same time surpassing the need or the will to intervene controversially "overseas" by negating the resistance to separation.

Soon all but the most doctrinaire pacifists saw their sons enlist and gave their support. For most of them the imperial idea was an abstraction, if they thought about it at all; others did elsewhere. Winston Churchill certainly treated Franklin Roosevelt as the rising or presumptive emperor, and there is little Roosevelt did, apparently, to dispel the notion. There is the famous image at Yalta, with the tired, ill Roosevelt, cigarette in hand, nonetheless propped up in the center, with Churchill on his right and Stalin on his left. There is another one shortly after, on the deck of a ship meeting Ibn Saud of Arabia, the latter wrapped in robes, FDR in a large cloak. To FDR, the "[w]hole party was a scream!"—including the sheep, slaves, and astrologer the Saudi had brought along. When Ibn Saud admitted that he too had wounded legs (and was missing an eye), Roosevelt offered him one of his wheelchairs (as well as an airplane). The confident smile on Roosevelt's face said everything: the emperors commune.

Binary opposites, reformulated, tempt the historical imagination. There were still plausibly two groups—interventionists and isolationists, to be rebranded once more as imperialists and anti-imperialists. They were different from their turn-of-the-century forebears; the distinction, as today's popular terminology puts it, was no longer so much one of choice but of necessity, even of predetermination, as Henry Wallace, for example, noted with regard to the above communion: "If the oil resources of Saudi are as great as people say, there is a lot of trouble ahead for these simple-minded Arabians." How should we rate the impression that the would-be emperor Roosevelt looked comfortable with kings and courtiers? That he clearly enjoyed the company of these people, from Ibn Saud to King Farouk of Egypt and the emperor Haile Selassie—whom he visited on the same journey—to the procession of exiled royals in and out of Washington during the war, to the greatest monarchist and imperialist of his generation, Winston Churchill?

Put differently, how to account for the expediency of Roosevelt, a man who at Yalta even saw fit to haggle with a semi-Oriental potentate called Stalin, yet who also touted the doctrinaire line of anti-imperialists? Which were the means? Which were the ends? An all-American world with Roosevelt as emperor would remove the rationale for both camps; Willkie suggested as much. But even for Roosevelt's hero, Woodrow Wilson, that was the means to a greater end: a permanent peace—one so permanent that it would vitiate the need for the United States to intervene anywhere by force. It could at last do what it was meant to do: cultivate its own progressive garden. That summed up the zeitgeist of the short period from the middle of 1945 to the middle of 1946: the time to make amends for the failures of the past with yet another experiment, to translate wartime methods into peacetime ones, and to find the right people to implement them.

John Dos Passos, making his way from the political left to the right, saw the risk in so "unworkable" a "proposition": American virtue. He agreed with an acquaintance who blamed Wilson and his successors, including FDR. The man, a wizened Washington reporter, added, "Roosevelt's ardour for social reform means righteousness multiplied by itself. We get the righteousness and we don't get the reform." Dos Passos and the man were having a meal. In the next booth were two marine sergeants. They invited them to join them at their table for a beer. Suddenly the Greek proprietor of the establishment stopped them: "No more drink."

"No can move," said one of the sergeants. "District regulations . . ."

"That's the sort of thing," said Dos Passos's acquaintance. "The last war gave us prohibition. You just wait and see what this one will give us."

The image may be overdrawn; we cannot know how consciously this proprietor was a man of the times. Still, many Americans then idolized their president as the man who saved democracy (as well as capitalism) during the Great Depression and then again in the war. They did not necessarily view him as monarchical, even regal, and certainly not as imperial. He was the common man's president, the traitor to his class, but he delivered the United States an empire. And this one was not merely representational—a few islands, coaling stations, and sea-lanes—or exclusively informal, but rather an empire in the traditional, full sense, for by now the United States was without a doubt the world's strongest military and economic power. Distinctions between the two forms of power in fact blurred. In one or two decades they would have their own abbreviation: "pol/mil." Proconsuls, viceroys, satraps, and the rest wore different uniforms, most military, some civilian, some none at all, because the mission—empire and, presumably, peace—was the uniform everybody wore. Another word for this is "hegemony." Call it whatever you like. It too was now a fact.

A hegemon needed foot soldiers, soldiers who did not relax;

who did not count their blessings following the defeat of fascism but instead turned their attention to new "challenges"; who wondered always where the next war would happen and how to prepare for that; who lived for action and from crisis to crisis; who spoke in strategic platitudes but acted and planned with tactical and, occasionally, operational creativity, that is to say, like the hard-boiled engineers they had known and whose ranks the midlevel ranks of big business now mirrored with former dollar-a-year men; who clipped the wings of isolationism and made sure they stayed so. They were the soldiers who insisted on rebuilding the military power of the United States, to include a constellation of foreign bases, pacts, and arrangements—insisted, again recalling Wilson, that the only true security was a forward policy, what would later be termed in the soberest of tones "power projection." These were earnest men, the scientific-military-industrial professionals who staffed the upper reaches of the federal agencies. They also were broad-minded and ambitious. Even some former New Deal die-hards had come to welcome the "new regimentation," the *dirigisme* that predominated in Washington and elsewhere to come, as a "glacial conformity, a chrome-plated American version of what George Orwell saw ahead for mankind."

Flanking them in the Truman administration were a number of Main Street Münchhausens, silly sorts who were in it for what they could take from it. That was all right. They helped cloak the powers behind the throne. The latter group had not come from Babbitt-land but instead from Wall Street, in fact, or from the leading law firms nearby. In time they could hold their own with such people; they had become, in contrast to their "quiet-spoken" interwar predecessors "with combed-down hair and . . . rimless spectacles, frock coats, and shirts with detachable collars," different types of men, "smart, buttoned-down, hard-fisted, gum-chewing guys who could speak out of the corners of their mouths when on the telephone while puffing on cigarettes at the same time." The war had done this to them. Their wartime migration to Washington as public servants struck few of them as strange or unnatural. It was their duty, they said. They and their champions had a remarkable capacity to deny whatever signs of private or partisan interest seeped through their formidable shell of altruism. They were regarded, without irony, as practical, objective, patriotic, even special men whose destiny was here, in the official sphere, and for whom no other place, certainly not the "private sector," held equal charm or necessity. Washington called them, and they belonged to it.

They were nearly all men—yes, it was a man's world, an arid, harsh, technical, striving world—but we do not write women out of the story. Many of our new foot soldiers had wives, and the wives set the social tone and managed the social universe that made Washington so fashionably competitive at midcentury. Yet Roosevelt's administration, perhaps taking a cue from him, was eclectic in gender: women were playful pets or objects to be kept at some distance.

This was not true of his successor. As we have noted, Truman's attitude toward women was one of sentimental reverence. There were none in his cabinet or, so far as we know, in his official inner circle. His was a more masculine crowd. The men, described in the pages that follow, were powerful, opinionated types: Byrnes, Acheson, Johnson, Forrestal, Vardaman, Snyder. There was nobody like Sumner Welles, Lauchlin Currie, or even Harry Hopkins, the creative, sometimes slippery, loyal jack-of-all-trades in the next room. The Truman men were different. Clark Clifford, who perhaps came closest in the public eye to the former type, given his looks (and his tendency to be photographed with the president in matching Hawaiian shirts), was no Hopkins. Clifford was a shrewd but simple careerist, nothing more. He was as dependable as they come when not in business for himself. But he was no empire builder.

Hence the paradox of the empire men of '46. They reaped more than they sowed, but were not satisfied, so they sowed some more. They did not seek a world empire and came into office promising to prevent it from being foisted upon them. Their predisposition, if there was such a one held in common, was basically, instinctively nationalist, although they paid due homage to internationalism when called upon to defend it. Yet they displayed none of the comfort that Roosevelt and his men did with tutelage. Their expressions were hard and tight, as Truman's own could be, and they often looked as though they had a loaded gun behind their backs.

The political defenestration of an idealist like Henry Wallace, described below in chapters 5 and 9, would have come as no surprise to most of them, nor would the prosecution, justified as it may have been, of an effete Alger Hiss. These events were merely surprising in taking as long as they did to happen. The species was out of fashion, except in certain New York neighborhoods, college campuses, and a few parts of Washington. It had not lost its ideals, those of its helmsman Roosevelt. It kept to its humanism, its cosmopolitanism, its progressivism. It deplored the blinkered mood now overtaking all it had worked so hard to build. It was far from the likes of Truman; and history, or rather Joseph Stalin, did not make allowances for it to recuperate its strength. The second half of the 1940s, following so brief an interlude, was less idealistic by the year. The idea of empire is one of the most idealistic of all. How then did the empire men come to assume its mantle? How did some— Harriman, Stimson, Marshall—navigate the transition from a presumptive empire that dare not speak its name to some other contrary condition: an assertive, even aggressive, posture that prompted the very charges of imperialism it sought to combat, that is, an imperialism before empire, rather than the reverse? And if we can discover how they did it, can we then figure out why?

Dean Acheson for one left little doubt. The title of his memoir, *Present at the Creation*, justly regarded as the most literate memoir by a secretary of state besides whatever may lie hidden in the vast papers of John Quincy Adams, stated it well, but ironically. For Acheson did not show these men to have been passive bystanders. Yet they did not create an empire; they inherited and ultimately embraced one after having overcome doubts. Just as it is hard to imagine this having worked for Truman without their service, it is also difficult to place any of them in a similar position under his predecessor, a genuine imperialist. We need not ask whether this or that action would have been taken had Roosevelt lived in order to appreciate the distinction. For while Roosevelt's men failed to enshrine the empire that he may have desired, Truman's men acquired one their chief professed not to want or choose.

Men like George Allen, Thomas Finletter, Bob Lovett, Stuart Symington, Ben Cohen, William Batt, Leon Keyserling—many, even most, of their names are forgotten today. A short introduction to a few more-familiar characters, spanning Truman's full presidency, shall serve as emblems in cross section for the remainder of the story.

First there were the holdovers:

Henry Stimson, born 1867 in New York City, was the elder statesman of the Roosevelt administration, having been secretary of war under Taft and secretary of state under Hoover. Roosevelt hired him along with Frank Knox in 1940 to bring some bipartisan credit to his team on the eve of war. Both men were prominent Republicans. Stimson remained in office as secretary of war following Roosevelt's death. He was among the few people to advise Truman on the use of the atomic weapon. He was also one of the few who resisted the hawkish shift over the Soviet Union, urging the president to share as much nuclear weapons technology as he could as part of a Soviet-American modus vivendi before the Soviets developed their own weapons, which he regarded as inevitable. Stimson's influence traveled far and wide. He was the link in the tradition of Republican internationalism from Theodore Roosevelt and Elihu Root all the way to George H. W. Bush, who was said to have volunteered for military service after hearing Stimson speak.

George Marshall, born in 1880 in Pennsylvania, was the army chief of staff. He sat during most of the war in the office just next to Stimson's. Like Stimson, he was revered, probably more in the way that generals are worshipped (unlike civilian cabinet secretaries). Besides a high intelligence, great discipline, a formidable bearing—at once serene and strong—Marshall was best known and most respected for his judgment, which was superior in both military and political matters to that of nearly everyone else in public life, or so they said. He was, in Churchill's famous words, the "architect of victory." He stayed on to serve Truman, first as army chief of staff, then as envoy to China, then as secretary of state, and finally as secretary of defense. Truman relied on him not only for his views and guidance, but also for the perception he gave to the public of a steady and trusted hand to guide the new, inexperienced president. With Roosevelt, Marshall held to formalities, including formal titles, and refused to laugh at the president's jokes, lest he be tempted to lower his professional standards or adjust his advice. His well-known retort was, "I have no feelings except those I reserve for Mrs. Marshall." So far as we know, the same restriction and others applied to Truman. Last names were always used, however close Marshall was to a colleague or subordinate. His few indulgences were snacks of maple sugar, cheap fiction, and ice cream during films. "He was," Dean Acheson put it as well as any could, "in a phrase that has quite gone out of use, in command of himself."

James Byrnes, born in 1882 in South Carolina, was the son of a dressmaker. He quit school at age fourteen. At some point he gained proficiency in shorthand, which led to a job as a stenographer. On the frontispiece of his memoir is a page of shorthand from the Yalta Conference. Inspired by the law, he became a lawyer and, it was said, a lifelong conciliator. Entering politics, he was elected to the House, then to the Senate; later Roosevelt appointed him to the Supreme Court. From there he resigned, following the outbreak of war, to become Roosevelt's so-called assistant president, in charge of preparing and managing the war economy.

A chummy, agile, cunning man, Byrnes was confident in his ability to make a deal with almost anyone. Stalin was said to have called him "the most honest horse thief he had ever met." He placed a priority on the quality of flexibility. But when people showed less of that, he was known to reciprocate in kind. He was otherwise given to platitudes, was not especially thoughtful, and was not much interested in the views of people if they made things complicated. To himself, probably, this was all for the best. To others, especially the diplomats and other officials with whom he had to work, and to the presidents he served, it could amount to an infuriating tendency to play situations by ear, as George Kennan once put it. For Roosevelt this often meant that Byrnes could be relied upon to keep problems from accumulating on the president's desk: "Jimmy will handle it and won't bother me." That may have been all right for an assistant president, but not for a cabinet secretary.

He was not popular, therefore, with Truman. Roosevelt had chosen the latter as his running mate in 1944 when Byrnes, with some justification, expected it to be himself. Even Truman, as noted in the previous chapter, endorsed Byrnes for the job. Roosevelt had also considered Byrnes for secretary of state, but this was probably scuttled by Harry Hopkins. The appointment finally came, under Truman, but it was not a happy arrangement. "Byrnes' attitude," the columnist Joseph Alsop wrote, "was like that of the head boy in a school who found himself, by a bizarre chapter of accidents, under the leadership of the man who had been the smallest and least-regarded boy in his class." It was just a matter of time before the arrangement disintegrated. At the beginning of 1947, Truman fired Byrnes for freelancing.

The old saying held true: a president can be his own secretary of state—and some are—but not the other way around. Especially if the secretary of state wasn't altogether suited to the job. And the timing in this case was terrible: the diplomatic plate was full at the end of the war. Byrnes, in spite of his self-confidence, had precious little experience and judgment in what he was meant to do. The world fiddles, went the quip, while Jimmy Byrnes. His attempts to prevail—especially in courting, then contesting, the Soviets— while keeping Truman in the dark were, not surprisingly, fated to end in disappointment. He was nonetheless pleased to be named *Time* magazine's Man of the Year for 1946.

William Leahy was born in 1875 in Iowa. Franklin Roosevelt had gotten to know him back when Roosevelt was assistant secretary of the navy in the previous war. He later made him a five-star admiral and named him chief of naval operations, governor of Puerto Rico, and ambassador to Vichy. In the meantime Leahy had become his chief of staff. Truman kept him in the post. He was a staff man from central casting—quiet, skeptical, cautious, sometimes taciturn and deferential. Like Wilson's Colonel House or Roosevelt's Hopkins, he kept mainly in the background; unlike them, he not was tempted to leave it.

Once, for example, he was confronted in the Roosevelt house at Hyde Park by a family cousin. She asked him, "Do you live here?"

"No, Mrs. Roosevelt, I am the chief of staff to the President."

Truman gave Leahy more freedom of action than Roosevelt had. Truman called him "Admiral," often adding "five star" after it; FDR preferred "Bill." Truman depended upon him more. There was not much mystery to Leahy. His face and posture betrayed his convictions and attitudes. They were of the period and profession. "Limeys, Frogs,

Wops, Chinks, Japs, Krauts or Huns, and Russkies" were terms he often used. Toward the final category he was as conservative as one might expect from an elderly midwestern navy admiral. As we'll see in chapter 5, Leahy bridged the anti-Soviet axis from the White House to the State Department, deferring again (unlike his old rival Hopkins) to bureaucratic formality, often making a point to ask, "What does State think?" even though on this subject he generally knew what they thought and may have agreed with it.

Next, there were the converts:

Bernard Baruch was born in 1870 in South Carolina. The less said about him the better, only because so much was said—rather, he said so much—during his lifetime. The "Adviser to Presidents," as he fashioned himself, is one of the most overrated men in American history, and one of the neediest in public life. Bruce Catton, in *The War Lords of Washington*, described him thus:

> He had become a great name, a sage, an elder statesman, a Sacred Cow . . . for publishers and for editorial writers, an oracle whose word it was sheer impiety to doubt. He was girt about with a kind of Wall Street homespun; when he visited Washington it was widely reported that despite his years he shunned such luxuries as ordinary office suites and did all of his work on a wooden bench in Lafayette Park, impervious to the suns of summer, the chill winds of winter, or the impudent squirrels on the prowl for peanuts. All in all, he was a reputation that reached from here to there, and he was exactly what the administration needed.

Catton referred to Roosevelt's administration, but the same could be said, with qualification, of Truman's.

Baruch had made a fortune on Wall Street and concocted a reputation from that. Georges Clemenceau called him "*Le Grand Bandit Américain.*" His was a persona of wisdom, reliability, and eminence that was several shades removed from gray. But he had gifts. He was told at a younger age that he belonged not on Wall Street but really in Washington, and he took it to heart. He had mastered wartime supply for Woodrow Wilson. He did the same, indirectly, for Roosevelt through those to whom he gave his patronage—"Baruch men," they were called. Louis Johnson (see below) and, most conspicuously of all, Jimmy Byrnes, whom Baruch had discovered reporting in a South Carolina court, took him under his wing and made him a success. Baruch was second only to Felix Frankfurter in whispering names into a president's ear. Presidents responded predictably. Roosevelt liked to call him "that old Pooh-bah." Truman simply put him down as a "show-off."

Baruch persevered. He had money and a first-rate publicity desk in the person of journalist Herbert Bayard Swope. He would continue advising presidents well into his nineties.

Dean Acheson, born in 1893 in Connecticut, was the son of an Episcopal bishop. From an Anglo-Canadian family, he preferred English tailoring, sported an Edwardian mustache and manners, and had a secretive streak that made him prone to freezing out journalists. He had been a troublemaker as a boy but found his way eventually, and trained as a lawyer. He was a Frankfurter protégé, perhaps the favorite. Frankfurter enticed him to public service, and Acheson joined the New Dealers in the Treasury Department. Laws for him counted more than politics. He was, George Kennan later wrote, "[b]y education, training, and profession ... in every inch a man of the law." Bureaucratic, institutional, and even political loyalty came second. He resigned (or was fired; the accounts differ) over his insistence that Franklin Roosevelt had broken the law in the way he withdrew the United States from the gold standard in 1933.

Frankfurter continued to promote him for secretary of state should Cordell Hull vacate the post. It did not happen in this way. Acheson became an assistant secretary there when the war began, but he was not close to Hull and was not especially trusted by him.

Acheson remained following Hull's replacement by Edward Stettinius, and then by Byrnes, when he was promoted to undersecretary, continuing under Marshall.

Acheson was known principally for his intelligence and then for his cleverness, especially when principles were at stake. As we'll see in chapter 12, when Truman's party was beaten badly in the November 1946 midterm elections, the president's popularity had fallen to its lowest point to date. He was almost an untouchable. And when he returned to Washington, D.C., on a cold night, the only person waiting there for him on the train platform was Mr. Acheson. Truman didn't forget that.

Truman elevated him to the secretaryship following Marshall's retirement in 1949. In time Acheson would also become unpopular. Caught up in McCarthyist hysteria, called, among other names, the "Red Dean" of the "College of Cowardly Communist Containment," Acheson handled the attacks "of the primitives," he called them, with customary aloof and oftentimes vicious condescension—that is to say, badly. They struck him, Kennan noted, as few (apart from McCarthy) had deigned to strike Marshall. It embittered him, hardened him ideologically (on the right), and probably puzzled him, given how much faith he placed in the law and in courts. He left office almost as despised and unhappy as Truman. But some years later he reemerged as the wisest of Cold War wise men. He wrote an excellent memoir, which won a Pulitzer Prize.

James Forrestal was born in 1892 in New York. A son of Irish immigrants, Forrestal, by grit and a knack for selling bonds, became rich on Wall Street. Like Baruch and Louis Johnson, he trained as a boxer. He moved to Washington during the war and became secretary of the navy. Like Stimson, John McCloy, Robert Lovett, Robert Patterson, Ferdinand Eberstadt, and Paul Nitze (whom Forrestal first enticed to government service), he was a typical migrant along the

New York–Washington axis. In a moment of weakness, Truman was said to have blurted out that he regarded Forrestal as nothing more than a "God-damn Wall Street bastard."

There was something not quite buttoned-down about Forrestal, however. He had not done everything according to script. He got into Princeton but dropped out, for example. He married the right sort of woman, but she turned out to be a mentally ill alcoholic whose problems wore on him. He left the Catholic Church. He gave a tormented impression that conveyed less gravitas than misguided intensity and a desperate, divisive vulnerability. "Poor Forrestal," Truman wrote. "He never could make a decision." A contemporary has described the "quiet, animal quality about his apparent physical perfection. He has the carriage which movies gave dramatically to better gangsters, swift, easy, with the suggestion of possible violence and the surface of perfectly contained restraint." That about summed up Forrestal.

He served in the navy during the First World War and later, during the Second, rose to become its secretary. From there, as noted, after many a big fight over resources and independence, he was named the first secretary of defense by Truman in 1947. Clark Clifford said that this happened only after he told Forrestal to stop being so ornery; if he did so, he'd get the job. He did, but it would be his undoing. Unifying the services was a huge, nearly insurmountable headache. That it happened at the moment the Cold War was declared, and then militarized, drove Forrestal over the edge, or so it was said. He lost weight. He said strange things like, there were Russians everywhere out to get him. His characteristic focus and concentration, even his patriotism became a mania. Journalists, led by Drew Pearson, smelled blood. They even challenged his courage.

Forrestal resigned in March 1949. "Did you hear the news?" asked the famous hostess Perle Mesta. "That stinker Forrestal is out. My man Johnson is in." A few days later Forrestal checked in to the

Washington Naval Hospital. During the night of May 21 or in the early hours of May 22, he read a few lines of Sophocles (Chorus from *Ajax*), then threw himself from the window of his room.

W. Averell Harriman was born in 1891 in New York. The son of the railroad magnate E. H. Harriman and therefore one of the richest men in America, Harriman pursued his passions with intensity and, more or less, in succession: polo, the Union Pacific Railroad, diplomacy, and finally politics. (He would later return to diplomacy, serving, for example, as Lyndon Johnson's doomed negotiator at the Paris peace talks to settle the Vietnam War, but preferred being called "Governor.")

During the war Harriman worked hard on two fronts: in Britain, where he carried on an affair with the woman who later became his wife, Pamela Digby, then married to the son of Winston Churchill; and in the Soviet Union, where he went as ambassador in 1943. Harriman had long claimed to have a special insight into the minds of the Soviets. He had negotiated railroad concessions from them before the war. Even as late as the Carter administration, he would insist on being heard at the highest levels on all matters Soviet.

Harriman became hard of hearing as the years went by, and he liked to tinker visibly with his hearing aid to demonstrate how little he thought of what others were saying. His youthful bluff turned into a rehearsed scowl and bark that earned him the epithet "Crocodile." Dealing with so many Soviets probably had something to do with it. Like almost everyone who spent any time with them—including his famous deputy, George Kennan—Harriman came to mistrust and disparage Soviet ways. He became hostile to them and influenced Truman strongly in that direction. Truman conceded to include him in poker games, where Harriman was watchful over every chip. It was a big relief to him to be named ambassador to the Court of St. James's in 1946. Later he was called on to replace Henry Wallace as secretary of commerce. Then he headed the Marshall Plan. He counted himself one of Harry Truman's most loyal servants.

Finally the imports:

Louis Johnson was born in 1891 in Virginia. A lawyer, he had been a boxing and wrestling champion at the University of Virginia. He worked his way through school selling Bibles and on the Norfolk and Western Railway, got a law degree in 1912, set up shop in Clarksburg, West Virginia, and joined Philip Steptoe, who became his mentor. Roosevelt appointed him the number two in the War Department to Stimson's predecessor, Harry Woodring. Johnson and Woodring barely got on. Johnson pushed hard for preparedness, especially in aircraft, and he was often thwarted. He was a difficult personality. Said by some to be mendacious, even amoral, he was a combative, aggressive person, with great ambition that he kept poorly disguised. He was said to expect that Roosevelt would choose him as his running mate in 1940. He then thought he would be named secretary of war. Roosevelt as much as promised it to him, he said. Instead he found himself out of a job when Henry Stimson relieved him. Truman later named Johnson secretary of defense to replace the ailing James Forrestal, presumably because of Johnson's major role in bankrolling Truman's 1948 reelection campaign (after Baruch had declined the role).

Back in government, Johnson got on badly with nearly everyone, and especially with Dean Acheson, who regarded him as being "nuttier than a fruitcake." Johnson insisted, with some justification, that his role for Truman was that of lightning rod and enforcer, Truman's "battering ram," or perhaps a necessary foil. It was his job to keep defense expenditure down, although the opposite had been his mission before the war. Now, as then, he would receive the brunt of institutional and political resistance to the line he thought was right. He claimed to have saved the country nearly two billion dollars.

Johnson's official career ended after he was caught conspiring with Averell Harriman to depose Acheson as secretary of state.

Harriman turned the tables on him, and Truman was forced (or probably by now was relieved) to fire his old friend. Johnson was said to have wept in the meeting; Truman kept the resignation short and simple: "Lou, you've got to sign. . . . Charley, work up a press release."

John Snyder, born in 1895 in Arkansas, had known Truman for a long time. They were buddies in the army during the war, and later as reservists. Moving to Missouri, Snyder worked as a bank cashier and bookkeeper. Truman trusted his financial acumen, his sixth sense, and his loyalty. No matter how many times Snyder said or did the absolute wrong thing, Truman stood by him. They were said to resemble each other. Snyder "looked like . . . a Truman twin—the same gray suit and small stocky figure. He spoke with the same casual Missouri twang . . . dull and humorless. . . . [H]e always appears slightly pained, as if his food did not agree with him."

Snyder moved to Washington in the 1930s and served in a number of posts mostly concerning bank regulation. He had returned to Missouri and was president of a bank when Truman, now president, brought him back to Washington to run the Office of War Mobilization. In 1946 Truman named him secretary of the treasury.

It was not a happy appointment. The Keynesians still held sway and Snyder knew very little of Keynesianism. What he knew he didn't like. Wartime controls had to be lifted and he was happy to do it, no matter who objected. Like Truman, he became taciturn and ornery. The events that will be described below shortly—the deteriorating economy, the labor strikes, the attacks on the administration's economic policies—drove him to distraction, even though he probably did not feel responsible for any or most of them. In one cabinet debate late in 1946, for example, he lost his temper: "These people have enough. They wouldn't even know how to spend the money if they got any more!"

Truman's appetite for the conservative small-town banker lasted a long time. But Snyder took it too far. He developed a bias against Clark Clifford, whom he identified with the liberal camp, and even tried to turn Truman's daughter against the president's new golden boy. Still, he stayed in the job until the end, in 1953.

Which brings us, finally, to Clark Clifford. Born in 1906 in Kansas, Clifford was a successful St. Louis lawyer who joined the navy when the war began and eventually found himself assigned to the White House as a naval aide. Above him was Truman's crony James Vardaman, an unpopular figure who picked fights wherever he could, especially with naval officers, whom he had disliked ever since he himself had joined the navy. He even disparaged the First Lady. Truman got rid of Vardaman in January 1946 by naming him to the Federal Reserve. Clifford got a promotion, and then another, becoming the president's chief of staff.

What did Truman see in this young lawyer? Mostly what everyone else did. He was, the journalist Tris Coffin remembered,

> [t]he glittering young man . . . a handsome, matinee idol type and a St. Louis lawyer. When the heavy fog of gloom covering Washington after the elections lifted, there was Clifford as the beautiful white knight who was going to save Harry Truman from a low Gallup Poll rating. . . . Clifford sang the lead in college musical comedies and looks like one of those exquisite men identified with advertisements featuring stainless steel and chrome. He has light wavy hair, broad shoulders, big brown eyes, just the right mixture of authority and deference in his personality, and faultless manners. He is easily one of the best-groomed men in Washington . . . [whose] sharp, but not profound mind dazzles like a Christmas tree decoration amid the cheerless mediocrity of the White House advisers. . . . From out of the gloom of the White House marched this Sir Galahad.

That's more than enough to take in but probably can't be better put. Clifford glowed, literally. He still did, even many years later when he adopted the identity of an elder statesman (becoming, for instance, Lyndon Johnson's secretary of defense) and his skin had acquired the color and tone of parchment. Truman relied upon him more than anyone besides Bess. Clifford, in turn, relied on anyone his cunning mind realized could be of some use—from Roosevelt's old speechwriter, Sam Rosenman, who taught him the tricks of the business, to Washington's premier hostess of the era, Pauline Davis, an heiress and wife of, among others, a onetime secretary of war and founder of the Davis Cup. The friendship was so close some people "took to calling him 'Pauline Davis's counter jumper,'" a term once used to describe the young men in department stores "assigned to woo the clientele, most of whom were women." Truman was curt when he first met his young savior. He may have believed that Clifford was more jackal than lion.

So were the empire men. None was a revolutionary. None was a prototypical "new elite." The changes they sought, and made, were small and sometimes subtle but in a way foundational. The renewal they furthered was staged and oftentimes compensatory, substituting the appearance of command for intellectual laziness. Unlike more familiar "public entrepreneurs" of the middle century—J. Edgar Hoover, Robert Moses, Hyman Rickover, for example—they accepted and manipulated as many facts as they made. They were not, again, empire builders. They were the empire's inheritors, its servants, its defenders, and its beneficiaries.

Chapter 4

Dynamo

Mortal scientists, Satan explained, had not yet learned the secret of liberating the energy locked in the atom. When they did learn it they would add "a new world to the planet's possessions."

—"The Easy Chair," April 1946

It is tough to exaggerate the impression the nuclear explosions made in August 1945. Nobody had seen a weapon like this. No American, apart from the president, a few advisers, and his scientific team, knew about it. Churchill and Stalin knew about it, but they did not have it. Would they have used it if they had?

General Leslie Groves, who oversaw the Manhattan Project to build these bombs, once described Truman on the subject as "a little boy on a toboggan." Perhaps it was the same for Groves, not a man who lacked ambition. As time went on, he used every chance he could to secure his bureaucratic independence by hoisting the flag of the Russian bear. But what real choice did he have? What choice did Truman have? Technology, especially destructive, diabolical technology, constrains the human will as often as it liberates it. When Truman was told that the American people would execute him if he didn't make use of this tool to end the war, he probably believed that. Still, he tried to fudge. He told Secretary Stimson to make sure the objectives were strictly military, that the main targets would not be "women and children . . . [e]ven if the Japs are savages, ruthless, merciless and fanatic," and to spare both Tokyo and Kyoto.

Truman had the support of the American people. A poll taken a few months later revealed that only about 20 percent of them felt "ashamed" that the bombs had been dropped. Some respondents said there ought to have been more.

The debate over dropping the bomb, in retrospect, is another hoary one, yet also one that brought multiple misgivings and uncertainties. Was it right to kill so many people—mostly civilians—in an instant when war in Europe was over and war in Asia, though far from over, was probably entering its final act? Was it justified by the lives Truman said it saved by ending the war when it did? Was it justified by the message it was meant to send—presumably to Stalin— that America was now also "boss of the Pacific" and more; that the postwar world was to be dominated by the United States, which not only had such weaponry in its arsenal but also had the willingness, the audacity, to use it? As to the actual bomb, it was morally neutral, wasn't it? It did not drop itself—but who had the right to welcome or despise it? There are many permutations of these questions to ask and still no perfect answers. They are valid, important ethical, moral, and even spiritual questions.

They are almost all ahistorical. For there was only the slightest chance that Truman would have done anything other than what he did. He was told that many more millions of Americans and Japanese would die once a land invasion of Japan took place, and that such an invasion was the only way to defeat the empire, short of the nuclear weapon. He was told that the U.S. and Allied armies were not ready to launch the invasion for some months, during which many more would die. He was told that the United States had precious few of these weapons and that they had to be used and seen to have their intended effect. He was told all these things. He may also have been told, but did not need reminding, that in wartime a nation uses the weapons it has. The only goal is victory. What war president knowing that such a weapon could possibly bring an end to so terrible a war would not decide to use it directly on the enemy? What leader would choose instead to firebomb so many millions more of the enemy in conventional raids, and sacrifice so many more of his own side?

Asking whether or not Truman should have dropped the bombs is a strange historical question. We would find it hard to draw an alternative historical account, with a different president, a different body of advisers, a different army, a different enemy, and a different international calculus of power. Truman would be judged by his Creator, and by posterity, on other grounds. Anyone, in theory, can always say no, not this time. But historians waste their time here. He had almost no choice.

Regret would come in due course. The man poised to become the Cold War's stock theologian, Reinhold Niebuhr, declared that dropping the bombs had been morally indefensible. The Federation of American Scientists published in March 1946 a book of essays, *One World or None*. It sold over one hundred thousand copies. In August, John Hersey's "Hiroshima" appeared in the *New Yorker*. It brought the bomb to life:

> A Noiseless Flash. . . . At exactly fifteen minutes past eight in the morning, on August 6, 1945, Japanese time, at the moment when the atomic bomb flashed above Hiroshima, Miss Toshiko Sasaki, a clerk in the personnel department of the East Asia Tin Works, had just sat down at her place in the plant office and was turning her head to speak to the girl at the next desk. . . .
>
> The Reverend Mr. Tanimoto got up at five o'clock that morning. . . . In this disarray, he walked out onto Kyo Bridge, beside which his hospital had stood. The bridge had not collapsed. He could see only fuzzily without his glasses, but he could see enough to be amazed at the number of houses that were down all around. On the bridge, he encountered a friend, a doctor named Machii, and asked in bewilderment, "What do you think it was?"
>
> Dr. Machii said, "It must have been a *Molotoffano hanakago*"—a Molotov flower basket. . . .

About a week after the bomb dropped, a vague, incomprehensible rumor reached Hiroshima—that the city had been destroyed by the energy released when atoms were somehow split in two. The weapon was referred to in this word-of-mouth report as *genshi bakudan*—the root characters of which can be translated as "original child bomb."

There was little chance of discounting Hersey's patriotism. He was the man who wrote the story of PT-109, which transformed the sickly young Jack Kennedy into a war hero and brought Kennedy all the way to Congress in 1946. "Hiroshima" was an altogether different piece of writing. In Hemingwayesque simplicity, it described a daily routine through the eyes of its six urbanites that struck readers as very normal, so much so that the tone of the essay, which mimicked the actual event that made time stand still, seemed not only diabolical but also familiar. That is, these are people we could recognize; this could just as easily "happen to us."

So normal yet unworldly, nightmarish. Reprinted as a book, the essay sold in the millions and inspired something of a national catharsis. Yet it joined a chain of attempts to grapple with the import of the new weapon. Secretary Stimson wrote and published a defense of the decision. Norman Cousins, editor of the *Saturday Review of Literature,* wrote an essay—also reprinted later as a book—of his own, "Modern Man Is Obsolete," granting it world-historical significance, the violent handmaiden of "a blanket of obsolescence not only over the methods and the products of man but over man himself." Bernard Brodie, a navy planner who pioneered a new category of strategist, the so-called defense intellectual, at a soon-to-be-founded organization called the RAND Corporation, rushed to print what was probably the first serious book to gauge the military and political import of nuclear weaponry, *The Absolute Weapon,* published in 1946.

Brodie did not think modern man had grown obsolete. He insisted that there was a choice. We could adapt to the new world of our invention, or we could destroy ourselves. Let us pause, he said, invoking an official truism, and remember that there has never been a military weapon that did not allow for a technological response, including a defensive one. There would be better weapons to counter this one. In the event, it was meant, he added, like the elephant gun, to kill elephants, not rabbits. We had to master a response, a deterrent, both offensive and defensive, and thereby master survival. To put it in a different way, human ingenuity and a dose of optimism were required "to give society the opportunity it desperately needs to adjust its politics to its physics."

Some people disagreed. Admiral Leahy regarded the weapon not as a bomb at all but as a spreader of poison. He had a point. And if the explosive and its poison were theoretically limitless, that is, total, then the scientists were right. To some of them, notably the Manhattan Project's director, J. Robert Oppenheimer, the nuclear weapon made military strategy useless. The onetime "merry, pixy" doctor had grown horrified by his creation. When he saw it work, he was moved to recall some words of Krishna, "Now I am become Death, the destroyer of worlds." German scientists, for their part, just didn't believe it was real: "Propaganda!" Truman for his part called Oppenheimer a "cry baby." But the bomb could not be uninvented. It is then all the more remarkable that the scientific golden age, and the concepts of progress and mastery, survived. America in 1946 did not pull back in revulsion toward Luddite certitudes. It kept going forward, with one foot in front of the other, just as Brodie had hoped.

Nevertheless, the country's leaders now found themselves trapped in another paradox of decision. They had possession of a weapon that could destroy all life on earth. Others would acquire it. Then what? The Truman administration decided two things, principally. It proceeded with development of better bombs, and it contemplated some way to limit the danger of what we now term nuclear proliferation. In other words, it went in two opposite directions simultaneously, as uncertain people are wont to do— expansion and limitation.

The first was straightforward, at least politically. The Pentagon was on board to expand and augment the arsenal. In spite of the costs, Truman found hardly any opposition from that quarter. Even stingy Louis Johnson was later called a "missionary for the H-bomb." Truman was heard to say that the country had gambled to the tune of a few billion and won. It was a feeling that appealed to his countrymen, to the aggressive worshippers of the experiment, or to, in the sad, reflective words of the writer Dawn Powell, "a Comic Strip public, a Buck Rogers, Li'l' Abner public, never outraged by folly or waste on such a gigantic scale but only by fear of a nation that dangerously prizes art and culture and brains—Russia—sharing and understanding it."

In the summer of 1946, a new round of testing occurred. Two bombs were detonated over the Pacific atoll of Bikini, looking, wrote Henry Wallace, "like the rapid growth of a tremendous, beautiful chrysanthemum." The journalist William Laurence, who observed the explosions both then and earlier in New Mexico, described them in a similar way:

> From the skydeck of the U.S.S. *Appalachian* some twenty miles away I watched the pillar of cosmic fire rise to a height of seven miles.... [T]he sight was awesome and spine-chilling. Through the haze I could see a boiling, angry, super-volcano struggling toward the sky, belching forth enormous masses of iridescent flames and smoke, and giant rings of rainbow, at times giving the appearance of a monster tugging at the earth in an effort to lift it and hurl it to another point in space. It was like watching the birth and death of a star, born and disintegrated in the instant of its birth.

He continued:

> The weight of the column of water lifted into the air was conservatively estimated at 10,000,000 tons. The spray and the foaming circle of water at the base brought the total weight of the water lifted by the energy liberated by the underwater explosion to well over 15,000,000 tons. Since the entire United States wartime fleet was somewhere around 11,000,000 tons, the power of the bomb was thus great enough to lift that huge fleet, more than twice as great as the combined tonnage of all the world's pre-war navies, to a height of about a mile out of the water.... And all this by the conversion of about one gramme of matter into energy.

And concluded:

> Before Bikini the world stood in awe of this new cosmic force which, concentrated in one rather small package, could destroy a large city, kill and maim hundreds of thousands and bring the surrender of an army of 5,000,000 without firing a shot. After Bikini this feeling of awe had largely evaporated and had been supplanted by a sense of relief unrelated to the grim reality of the situation. Having lived with a nightmare for nearly a year, the average citizen was only too glad to believe in any pipe-dream to regain his peace of mind.... He had been led to expect that one bomb would sink the entire Bikini fleet, kill all the animals aboard, make a hole in the bottom of the ocean and create tidal waves that would be felt for thousands of miles. He had even been told that every one of the 42,000 participating in the test would die. Since none of these happened, he was only too eager to conclude that the atomic bomb was, after all, just another weapon.

We now know that it was not. It was neither a tool nor a guarantee. Using it now, after the effects were known, would have been tantamount, Laurence wrote, to lashing out suicidally out of simple, mindless, primordial fear. Fear of sudden death is the most basic fear of all. What had been the agent of war's termination became our largest source of dread and damage, a great ticking time bomb.

General Marshall had a nice motto he liked to use: don't fight the problem, decide it. The latter part of the motto has also been rendered as "work it," which fits well with our definition of decision making as more proactive than reactive, pairing diligence and thoughtfulness with resolution. There are such things as quick, impulsive decisions, to be sure; but they are rarely good ones. Marshall used another phrase in relation to universal military training that could apply here as well: "The trouble was that we are playing with fire while we have nothing with which to put it out." It was tempting to relapse thus into fatalism, to declare that nearly every problem the country faced, including control of the nuclear problem, on which everything else depended, forced a choice between doing nothing or doing something we didn't yet know how to do. Deciding the problem in stages was the one alternative, and was what the Truman administration, in fits and starts, eventually did.

There were two aspects to control: domestic and foreign. At home the administration struggled to pry the hands, or at least one hand, of the military off the bomb by the rule of civilian control. Abroad it began an effort at the United Nations to establish an international atomic organization (the forerunner of today's IAEA) that was meant to become the principal depository, someday, of all nuclear materials. The first effort succeeded; the second failed. The reasons for this are more obvious today than they were at the time.

The debate over who would be in charge of nuclear materials at home began almost as soon as the Manhattan Project. It had been after all a joint effort between military and civilians. The question was a tough one. Some people preferred to keep silent about it, or to postpone it. Once the bombs were shown to have worked, this really couldn't continue much longer. Deciding the question needed a way to bring together the diverging biases and wishes of the military, the scientists, and the politicians. That was no easy feat amid a public mood that at times bordered on the hysterical over atomic espionage. In spite of all that had grown and proliferated during the war, America did not yet have a well-thought-out national security state, nor were Americans sure they wanted one. The country needed, in other words, a policy.

It did not take long before a clever Hill staffer called Charles Calkins hit upon the right slogan: military versus civilian. It was as simple and as obvious as that. Chances were, in the bring-the-boys-home mood of late 1945 and early 1946, that civilian would win. The scientists, some reluctantly, others with more enthusiasm, took the side of the civilians. In principle, and in spite of their recent success, many were opposed to military control of science. The antimilitary bias was ingrained, especially among returning veterans glad to be liberated from their commanders. It did not help that General Groves pursued his case by a love of secrecy, refusing to share information at congressional hearings and even interfering with the script of a Hollywood film, *The Beginning or the End,* released in 1947.

Calkins's boss, Senator Brien McMahon, took up the contest in a bill that proposed civilian control of nuclear materials. He had the support of most of the scientific community. As it happened, a few of them turned out to be rather shrewd political players. Two in particular, Vannevar Bush and James Conant, had achieved a measure of respect within official circles and outside them. People listened to what they had to say; both had performed yeoman's service during the war. Now they had prepared a plan for Secretary Stimson for overseeing the nuclear inventory. A later version made its way to Congress, and into a proposed bill called the May-Johnson Bill. Bush and Conant supported it, but according to other scientists, the bill didn't go far enough. They "rose in fury and smashed the May-Johnson Bill" in a campaign full of "fear and awe." To Henry Wallace, who would surface frequently in debates on this subject, and followed eagerly by his mostly young, earnest fans, there was nothing more important facing Congress: "The answer may determine whether our civilization and whether the human race itself shall continue to exist." To many congressmen, however, the whole subject was one of confusion and perplexity. Some admitted to voting the way they did on one or another of these bills just to get it over with.

McMahon's bill came next and satisfied most civilian opponents of the earlier bill. Many in the military, starting with General Groves, were unhappy, but they learned to live with it. They would have their say again, and win the argument, on the second front, international control.

Conant got to the point: "Our secret is an asset like a cake of ice on a hot day. I would be willing to trade our know-how, therefore, for a thorough exploration for even a short period of Russia's mining and industrial potential." It sounded simple enough. But this view, not surprisingly, was held by only a minority of opinion leaders, and certainly not by the majority of Americans. Even if it had not been—even if somehow a majority of Americans had supported a policy of sharing all with the Soviets for the guarantee, or even the promise, of a safer world—how many Soviets would have accepted the offer in good faith? How many agreed with their ex-statesman Maxim Litvinov that never again would the terrible weapon be used, least of all by a great nation that had grown war-averse?

Some people, notably Stimson, thought it was worth a try. Another was Wallace. He wrote to Truman in September 1945, "I agreed with Henry Stimson. . . . We have no reason to fear loss of our present leadership through the free interchange of scientific information. On the other hand, we have every reason to avoid a shortsighted and unsound attitude which will invoke the hostility of the rest of the world." A few Republicans besides Stimson—Clare Boothe Luce, for example—agreed with Wallace. It was true that the nuclear monopoly would last three or four years, at best—so said Bush and Conant. As for the generals, they held fast to Groves's and Forrestal's and now Leahy's line that important secrets should not be shared, and that disarmament without inspection was a fantasy; but they also must have known better. In any case the weapon's existence upset many of them less than its "startling efficiency."

Truman had to do something, so he turned to Dean Acheson and David Lilienthal, the ex-head of the Tennessee Valley Authority, and asked them to conduct a study. What would international control mean, exactly? What were the risks, the costs, the benefits?

The two men produced their report and almost nobody jumped. Their proposal for an international atomic authority at the United Nations was tentative. They were imprecise on the best way to sell it to the Soviets or to anyone else who might enter the nuclear business. But before anything more could be done, Truman took the advice of Byrnes and turned to Bernard Baruch.

In March 1946 the president offered Baruch the job of taking the Acheson-Lilienthal Plan to the UN and selling it there. It was not obvious that he welcomed the job. He said he did not but he didn't turn it down. Acheson and Lilienthal, however, regarded the choice as unfortunate. Actually, they were said to be "appalled" by it. Baruch was not a natural diplomat. He was old. He had no expertise or knowledge of nuclear matters (but then neither did they). Worst of all, they knew well one of the worst-kept secrets in Washington, which was that Baruch never did anything unless he took, and got, all the credit from start to finish.

The Acheson-Lilienthal Plan became the Baruch Plan. Acheson said the former had been just a "rough sketch" anyway. Baruch added that he was too old to be a "messenger boy" for someone else's work. In any event, their plan sounded fine but lacked the power of enforcement. True enough. But what did Baruch propose?

First he set a few ground rules. He asked the president what exactly he, Truman, had in mind. Truman said he wanted a genuine proposal, not a mere working paper, and that Baruch would be the one to draft it. It had to be enforceable, including provisions for sanctions.

We would be right to ask what Truman thought he was doing. He knew Baruch and his reputation for self-promotion. He may not have been very sanguine about the prospects for the report he had commissioned, and figured this was a way to place the onus on the Russians for a proposal they were bound to reject anyway. Who could say? For all Truman knew, Baruch might have pulled it off. In the event, he must have thought, "What a tall, esteemed, influential lightning rod!"

Baruch convened a small group of trusted helpers—"You know I never do any work myself"—and drafted a plan. It was not too different from the one that Acheson and Lilienthal had made, but, as promised, it included a special provision for enforcement and connected it to a staged process of implementation. Specifically, it offered to share American technology and repose American materials with the new UN organization—an International Atomic Development Authority—only if the Soviet Union first allowed full access to its own research programs, with inspection. While the latter took place, the United States could continue to stockpile bombs. Moreover, unlike the Acheson-Lilienthal Plan, Baruch's plan removed any prospect of a veto in the new authority. He said plausibly that the veto was irrelevant when millions of people could die in an instant.

Lightning rod indeed. The Soviets gave the proposal little benefit of the doubt and called instead for general disarmament.

Baruch and his plan brought even sharper hostility from another quarter. Henry Wallace attacked the plan in writing to Baruch and publicly. He charged that it not only sought to protect an American nuclear monopoly but also made concessions to the Soviet Union "on the installment plan, with each installment conditional upon Soviet good behavior during the previous period." It was not serious and it was dangerous. The only thing Baruch could do, that he must do, Wallace said, was to tear up his plan and start over by offering to share all we had.

Baruch took umbrage. Not serious? Dangerous? What Wallace was proposing was worse, akin to the Soviets' own proposal, which, Herbert Agar said, was "silly without being funny." Baruch might have reverted to advice given to him as a young man in the boxing ring: "Don't get mad while you are fighting. . . . You were getting a licking but you hung on. That's what you always want to do. You know how you feel and maybe you feel pretty bad. But you don't know how the other fellow feels. Maybe he's worse off than you are. . . . *To be a champion you have to learn to take it or you can't give it.*"

Only this time he did not. He called a meeting with Wallace and gave him a dressing-down, not for his opinions, which Baruch regarded as fanciful, but for his facts, which he said were plain wrong. Which facts he meant were not clear, but Wallace, he said, was poorly informed. The feud continued. "You have no monopoly on the desire for peace," he told Wallace. "I have given thirty years of my life to the search for peace." Wallace said simply, "Mr. Baruch has spoken. But he has not yet dealt with the central issue."

The Russians did, however, with their own successful nuclear test just a few years later. News that they had been purloining nuclear designs through a Canadian spy ring had broken back in February. Baruch, however, refused to give up, not yet. "I don't care what they call me or what they think of me," he said. "They may think I'm a senile old fool, but I'm not going to give the Russians or anyone else the chance to say that we did not explore every possible avenue in the search for an agreement." He asked Andrei Gromyko, at the beginning of Gromyko's long career in handling American officials, "Can't you see it's in your interest as well as ours to agree to this plan? Someday the Russian people are going to hold your government responsible if we fail to control the atom." Plenty of scientists figured the same. Gromyko's reply is unrecorded. But Baruch gave a hint of it when he took him to see a Joe Louis–Billy Conn fight. Observing the disparity in power and technique, Gromyko made the point: "Conn must wish he had the veto."

In June, Baruch had presented his plan to the United Nations in sacred language riddled with the cadences of Herbert Bayard Swope:

We are here to make a choice between the quick and the dead. That is our business.... This devilish program takes us back not merely to the Dark Ages but from cosmos to chaos.... Science has taught us how to put the atom to work. But to make it work for good instead of for evil lies in the domain dealing with the principles of human duty. We are now facing a problem more of ethics than of physics.

In the middle of September, after the Soviets refused to agree to the inspection provisions of his plan, Baruch declared the negotiation a failure. There would be no Baruch Plan put into action. It may have been for the best. The Bikini test had succeeded in July. "We should not ... throw away our gun," the president said, "until we are sure the rest of the world can't arm against us." By now many Americans as well as others had lost interest in the details of arms control. The British for one thought the former had been overly "bomb-minded," said Ernest Bevin, then foreign secretary. He added, "Let's forget the Baroosh and get on with the fissle."

However, we do not overlook Mr. Baruch, not because his plan had any real prospect for success, no matter whose name it went by. No, the more significant point about all this comes from its pulling back the curtain for the first time in the atomic age on the effort—the process, as later generations of arms negotiators liked to say—that would come to dominate the next half century of its history. Anybody studying the best way to strike a deal with a nuclear adversary, before or after they actually had the bomb, had to begin with Baruch. He set a precedent. It was stated well by one of his assistants, a man named John Hancock: "We believe we are firm in our good intentions." No negotiation on nuclear weapons could invoke such a statement ever again on such infirm ground. If Wallace's challenge taught

Americans anything, it was this: the nuclear arms race, and its diminution, had to be waged on the basis of actual capabilities, not of presumed intentions.

It is ironic to read the lines, and between the lines, of Baruch's memoirs where he describes his thinking. He championed himself a lover of facts. How else could a speculator make such a fortune? You had to have the facts at hand. Nothing could be worse than making a momentous decision on imperfect information. The memoir is full of such platitudes. So far as we know, Baruch lived by them. Woodrow Wilson called him "Dr. Facts." They were *his* armature, his source of certainty. They shaped his determination to get the best of any situation "like a surgeon," he wrote, sifting through the mass of facts to "operate coldly, clearly, and skillfully . . . free of emotion."

We will continue to encounter this personality, the Wall Street speculator with an eye to the future, an obsession with facts and capabilities, and a talent for argument and publicity. These were traits of Forrestal, and of his protégé, later adopted by Acheson, Paul Nitze, the man who later produced a scary document—called NSC 68—adding a year of maximum danger, 1954, to our list of annohistorical metonyms: "Victory Year" (1945), "Savage Year" (1950), and so on. The Baruch men outlived their progenitor.

"Dynamo." Henry Adams cast the term in the American setting half a century before. Adams's dynamo was an impersonal, unstoppable, consuming force to supplant intrinsic faith with extrinsic knowledge. It sometimes went by the name of progress. It overlaid, or intersected, mind with a mission—to do, not to be. In the American setting, it went further than creative destruction. Perhaps it neared the converse of Joseph Schumpeter's concept: not so much creative destruction as destructive creativity and a passion for means over ends, albeit ambiguously. At least this was Adams's depiction of it. It would come to equate disruption both with innovation and with demolition, akin to the man who decides there's nothing left to create, so he destroys simply because the will-to-do is still there, nagging at him, insisting on action, anyplace at all. Nuclear weapons may well have been the dynamo's logical culmination, now turning inside out, even against faith in knowledge itself.

By the middle of the twentieth century it had not come to a stop. Science and technology in fact accelerated; the space and atomic age, what Conant called the age of the Superblitz, had arrived. The century's inventive growth was staggering. Someday if the judges of history look back on what America did best during its rise to world power in a mere three or four generations, they will probably select the dynamo. In everything from internal combustion to the airplane to the cathode-ray tube to nuclear fission to the Internet, Americans were hardly alone. The contributions of others mattered. But Americans had a special talent for combination and utility, and for proliferation. Theirs was the so-called nation on wheels, and now on jet engines and rockets. They could take the best there was and make it work, promote it, sell it, consume it, idolize it.

It is strange to look back now at the marketing of the 1950s: atomic cafés, breakfast cereals, toys, "an atomic cocktail," and even a perfume called "GriGri...designed," its promoters said, "to replace the atom bomb with a dash of the inconsequential." These are somewhere between quaint and weird. It tempts our moral appetite to call them diabolical.

It was fitting that the atomic testing took place out west, with its surreal, vast spaces, a place for inventing "a new kind of fire" by somber men who had fled persecution from dense Old World cities for the open American desert, nomads reaching the promised land. They too were slapped by America, "like a blast or a storm," by the will-to-do, where human reason itself gave way to action. They could obliterate the land. They could change the weather. They had created, from such mastery, their own footprint, which would last for thousands of years, "a bit of near-eternity."

If Adams were alive in 1946 and still thinking about the dynamo, he might have been perplexed to see himself—and us—still alive and prospering, still spouting familiar lines like Dale Carnegie's in his 1948 book *How to Stop Worrying and Start Living,* which appeared a dozen years after his more famous book, *How to Win Friends and Influence People:* "Our trouble is not ignorance, but inaction." Adams may have said that the nuclear explosions did demonstrate a certain threshold, and a point of no return. The dynamo had proved brilliantly that it could, in an instant, destroy all. The rest of the century and the next represent, inasmuch as science and technology continue upon their usual course, an Indian summer. Who knows how long it will last? Perhaps until, as futurists have long predicted, there is little that separates human beings from the machines of their creation. Our own bodies will be full of gadgets, and the gadgets will have brains that come pretty close to our own, or surpass them, which may have been what Adams meant all along.

In truth the American dynamo was far from omnipresent in the middle twentieth century; Adams's dystopia had not arrived for everyone. Science and technology were still mainly about mastering nature first, then about mastering human life. Households in 1946 resembled more those of the first half of the century than those of the second. Most did not have automatic washing machines, televisions, or electric dishwashers. Many factories were automated but still employed millions of workers. Yet by 1950 more than 85 percent of American farms had electricity; in 1935 only 10 percent had, according to Frederick Lewis Allen. No wonder farm production grew by 25 percent during the 1940s while the number of farmworkers shrank by almost two million. These years also saw the proliferation of all sorts of chemical creations: detergents, cosmetics, fertilizers, refrigerants.

The war had been won in good part by American science, technology, and industry; they would not be quiescent. "Big Science" took hold during the war in the cohabitation of the Pentagon and the nation's major universities, with allies in industry and Congress. Eisenhower named Congress in his famous warning, then dropped it for fear of offending his party in an election year. Still, his target was the public power of the military-industrial complex, not technology or Big Science per se. He never stopped touting the importance of technical education, especially in the physical and natural sciences. The period after 1946 was a scientific golden age in America. Even science fiction got a boost.

Not all or even most of the scientific work to be done was military. Yet so much of it was, directly or indirectly through the cause of the common defense, and in competition with the Cold War rival. Unlike Adams's dynamo, its mid-twentieth-century descendant had a mission that was at once clear and composite: to defend the West (the civilizational one) and its way of life; to continue the incessant, determined march toward progress. Did the two-sided mission make it more menacing? Or more reassuring? Did the dynamo, now harnessed to national purpose rather than spiraling haphazardly in a rivalry of all against all, constitute an even greater advance of civilization? Or did it, in its own way, a way familiar in Adams's dystopia, signal another form of doom?

The nuclear age is a bit in this respect like today's globalization. We can criticize it, feel guilty over it, challenge it, ameliorate it, and manage within its confines as best we can, but we cannot fight it. It is with us whether we like it or not. The best our leaders can do for us is to "harness" (a popular word for the mastery of energy, from the age of horsepower, presumably) and exploit it as optimally as possible.

Such became the consensus among the nuclear priesthood, both military and civilian. They may well have been right. But their attitude did not dispel the qualms of men like Hersey or many of his readers. To some of them, perhaps, the explosion of a Soviet test weapon in 1949 came as an ontological relief. This was what many atomic spies said: they did what they did not to betray their country but to save humanity from another deadly arms race. After all, this had been the point of the Acheson-Lilienthal Plan: share the burden and the responsibility. Someday the world may come around to accepting cooperation as the only means for human survival.

That prospect was not so reassuring in 1946. Once the image of the mushroom cloud sank into their consciousness, many Americans came to regret and fear the advent of the nuclear age. They may have assumed the monopoly would not last; that may have been the source of the fear. Or perhaps they did not trust themselves with such power, however long the monopoly lasted. Few then would have seen the point of Arthur Schlesinger Jr.'s later verdict that the nuclear weapon should have been awarded the Nobel Peace Prize. Its power was still too raw. Schlesinger, who earlier had said that the subject of atomic weaponry was something out of a novel by Jules Verne, is no longer with us; we wonder if today he would endorse his own finding, as more nations seek these weapons. Someone, someday, is probably bound to use one again. It is remarkable nonetheless that nearly three-quarters of a century later Harry Truman still has that sole distinction.

Bernard Baruch wrote, "During my eighty-seven years I have witnessed a whole succession of technological revolutions. But none of them has done away with the need for character in the individual or the ability to think." Another Swopeian platitude, yet one that the postwar generation found it difficult to recall. Observing the "[s]haken, beaten, kneaded, scalded, frozen, suffocated, crushed" test pilots of the new era, the German, later Swiss, observer Robert Jungk asked, "Why do they permit themselves to be so tormented?" He could just as well have meant the American people as a whole. "No tyrant has condemned them to it. No regime wishes to extort confessions from them. Nevertheless they submit themselves to trials such as no torturer could surpass in refinement. And they do so of their own free will. For they have been told, 'You are our vanguard.'"

They had been uprooted. They had survived. They had an everyman president who, in spite of archetypical limitations, could stand up to anyone. They were going places, evidently. They had mastered the power of energy. They still may have feared where they were heading, because they did not know where that was, but they were going there fast, any and all contradictions tossed to the wind.

Chapter 5

Four Speeches

It is not suggested here that Buffalo Bill was a phony. He was born into a diminishing West, one that was already beginning to contrive its spectacles.

—"The Easy Chair," May 1946

The dynamo hit an object of its own making, someone else's, or both. We did not know what to call it at first. Eventually we settled on a name: the Cold War.

The idea was George Orwell's; Walter Lippmann got the credit, but he cribbed it from Baruch, who used it in a speech he gave in April 1947, which meant the term likely originated with Swope. He had used it in a draft speech about a year before, but Baruch took it out. Anyhow, it arrived on the American tongue and would remain there for the next half century. The war was declared, first and foremost, to be a war of ideas, which dated back in one form or another to the French Revolution. Others would date it even further back— to the very origins of civilization in the West, where liberty stood against tyranny, and where power alternately joined and vied with justice.

To say when it began means first saying what it was. What sort of conflict was it, primarily: ideological, political, socioeconomic, military, cultural? All of the above is correct, but gives us no better sense of when and why the war began, why it was "cold," how it was waged, why it ended (if it really ended or was superseded) when it did, and, perhaps most important, where it was fought. What were its boundaries? Or did it have real boundaries? Such questions boggle the minds of students; the rest of the world pays little attention, except when such wars become "hot." This is the primary fact about this phase or period of American history: it followed a very hot war. Some people may have said it was the logical continuation or the result of it, just as the Second World War was born of the failure to design a durable peace after the First. So too with the Cold War, just on a greater scale, with two of the principal victors now on opposing sides.

The United States and the Soviet Union (and Russia before it) had never been especially fond of each other. Nor did they have a chip on the shoulder with the other's name on it, as, say, the United States has had with France, or the Soviet Union would come to have with China. Their rivalry was not perverse in that sense. It was straightforward. Yet many Americans, at least (the Russians and other Soviets will need to speak for themselves), persisted in believing in the old storied rivalry. Some still do. The possibility of Russia and America today being allies or friends is as fanciful as ever. Why is this?

Arthur Schlesinger Jr. came up with a concise formula for it in the twentieth century: the Cold War, he wrote, "was the product not of a decision but of a dilemma."

There were and continue to be any number of people, including historians even more distinguished than Mr. Schlesinger, who reject this definition. The Cold War was started by a paranoid and wicked Joseph Stalin. Others, just as distinguished, have said, not at all, it was started by an insecure and simpleminded Harry Truman, who failed, unlike his predecessor, to deal properly with Stalin, paranoia and wickedness notwithstanding. The third member of the wartime triumvirate, Winston Churchill, for his part, was somewhat less culpable in all this, aside from the accounts of a few historians like Fraser Harbutt, or the torment of the Anglophobic Henry Wallace, who oftentimes charged the British with demanding more than their fair share, in nuclear technology, for example, leading him and others, such as the wartime American ambassador and later aspirant to the office of UN secretary-general, Gil Winant, to propose giving everything the British demanded to the Russians as well. The result in Winant's case was the decision by Roosevelt to limit or proscribe all nuclear cooperation, with both the British and the Russians, and following Wallace's case, as we shall see, a conservative attack upon the very idea of cooperation. This could have been anticipated back in the fall of 1945 on just this question, as there was no Soviet signatory, for example, to the Truman-Attlee-King declaration on peaceful uses of nuclear technology. But even as late as the spring of 1946, well after many people's hopes had dissipated, Lippmann returned from Europe to publish a *tour d'horizon,* the thrust of which was that the struggle was not between East and West so much as between the British and the Soviet empires, and it would be perfectly reasonable for the United States to play the honest broker, or just to stay out of it. Lippmann was a shrewd observer, but in this case he understood little about the Soviet Union, or about his own country, for that matter.

Well before Truman announced his doctrine in March 1947, then, the Cold War had been declared—in stages, or, in good old American fashion, on a case-by-case basis. The single date and the identity of the declarer remain unresolved. As we have said, the rivalry itself dated back a long time. If it, or a tense condominium between the two nascent superpowers, had not set in by the mid-nineteenth century (in Tocqueville's famous formula), then surely it had begun to take shape by the end of the First World War when the United States joined in the suppression of Bolshevik actions in Siberia. The refusal of the Wilson and subsequent administrations—until Roosevelt's in 1933—to conduct normal diplomatic relations with the Soviet Union followed. Then, during the Second World War, the United States joined the British in refusing the Soviets a say or a presence in the occupation of liberated parts of Italy. It was at this moment in 1944 that some said the postwar die was finally cast: the Soviet Union had survived; the Eastern Front had held; the question now was where the postwar lines in the east would be drawn and who would control the borderlands, following an assumption that there would be lines in the first place, colored "them" and "us" on a map and representing distinct nations as well as political philosophies, for the foreseeable future. The few Americans who served alongside Russians in combat—advising the partisans in Yugoslavia, for example—noted that the camaraderie had suddenly gone, almost as though an internal switch had been pulled in each one of them, sometime in 1943 or 1944. For a while their behavior was unfathomable. The hesitation and confusion over what to make of the rudeness of their soon-to-be former allies, however, was probably not reciprocated. Both may have wanted to live in peace. But the Soviets had perceived something else: the West was uncertain.

However, this was not yet a Cold War. No matter how fast postwar converted again to interwar amid the chaotic and frightening aftermath of World War II, some Americans refused to believe a third war was coming; but neither was a prolonged truce. Soviets, after all, did not speak, according to some people, in three dimensions. Theirs was a fourth, "and there was no stairway."

So a world rivalry did not yet govern American thought and action. It did not yet demand the remobilization of the American economy. Nor had "national security" come to be the baseline term invoked for passing bills, winning votes, explaining why this or that problem abroad mattered to Americans. It had begun to catch on in 1946, but we cannot say for certain whether the war really was on then. Some people resisted it, notably Wallace. He was pilloried for his views, which are nearly forgotten today except among the old left. But he was not a rarity, and his was not a marginal position. Rather, the burden was on the other side, led now by the president, to prove to the American people that they needed to sacrifice in order to win—or at least to survive—yet another war. The American people were not easily convinced.

The product not of a decision but of a dilemma? Not exactly. The Cold War in 1946 was not a product or even a by-product so much as it was a catalyst for understanding, and reshaping, a world that brought indecision and fear to the minds of people whose postwar reality was not what they had expected. It was brought forth by several choices on both sides, but the choices were not free. In fact they resembled efforts to transcend the dilemma that appealed to Mr. Schlesinger. Rather than transcend it, however, many of the questions reinforced it with additional dilemmas from the recent past. Namely, how would the defeated nations, notably Germany, be rehabilitated without falling into the trap of the last interwar period? Should Germany be partitioned? If so, where? How quickly or slowly should rehabilitation take place? How far should it go? What form should it take and who should gain by it?

Such dilemmas came to resemble the later infamous shorthand of "Catch-22." If Germany (or Japan, for that matter, although the problems there were different; Japan was not divided; this fate was left to its neighbors) rose again, would it not again pose a mortal threat to civilization? If it did not rise, or if it were held back, as the victors had so badly tried to do last time, would the result not be the same? Was rehabilitation, in other words, a question of calibration? Or did it involve something deeper, something more cultural?

Germany did recover, magnificently, but it was a different, partial, and temporary Germany, called the Federal Republic. By now Germany and Europe were divided. Some people must have felt relieved. "It is better," John McCloy, who became U.S. high commissioner there, wrote to himself back in July 1945, "to have a clear line of distinction and negotiate across that line. It has tremendous significance for Europe, but the other arrangement has more sinister and not entirely favorable considerations. . . . There are such diversities and lack of understanding that I cannot see how it can work out any other way."

By the end of 1950 Americans were fighting Communists in Asia, and NSC 68, the doomsday document mentioned in the previous chapter, set forth the drastic increase in military expenditure for approval by the president over the violent objections, followed by the capitulation, of his secretary of defense. The Cold War solved the German question by making it temporarily insoluble, at least by the Germans themselves. They would gain more time ahead of "playing their proper role," as the historian A. L. Rowse once put it, in Europe and the world.

This raises another accomplishment of 1946: the choices made during that year asserted propriety, rather than merely authority, as a central principle of international relations. The Cold War was not the product, therefore, of a self-evident balance of power. It was not the means to maintain that pernicious abstraction. It was not simply the old Bismarckian system of alliances and arrangements extended across the entire globe. Rather, it was a competition between those who thought it more appropriate to advance the cause of equality (whether or not by tyrannical means) and those who thought it more appropriate to champion the cause of liberty (whether or not by democratic means). To many of these people on both sides, perhaps even to a majority of them, it was a moral dilemma that could be resolved only by moral clarity and with that by the determination to ascribe immorality (or worse, amorality) to their enemies. But this was not the case in 1946, not yet, and certainly not to the main protagonists, who continued to quibble in their own hearts and minds over how far they should have pressed the other at Yalta. Most were determined now to find a way to justify what had taken place there and subsequently, not only to themselves but also to their idea of what the other side intended, and what they imagined the other side could expend. In the meantime, neither Europe nor much of what lay beyond it would be rebuilt as quickly or as solidly as the wartime idealists had hoped.

There was an interesting figure on the margins of American officialdom at this time whose ideas crept deliberately into the debate. His name was William Christian Bullitt. His public life was about as interesting as one could get for an American in the first half of the century. A rich boy from the Philadelphia Main Line, he saw his star rise early and fast. From Yale he took up journalism and became the scribe for Henry Ford's 1915 peace mission to Europe. The result was called *Bumping the Bumps with Ford*. This led to an assignment on the staff of Woodrow Wilson's peace commission in 1919 at Paris. A precocious and confident man with strong opinions, Bullitt spent much of the voyage there talking in Wilson's ear. Once the negotiations began, however, he lost faith in the president. The problem was Russia. Bullitt had taken it upon himself to visit Lenin, Trotsky, et al. and returned to Paris insisting that the new Soviet leadership be taken seriously, that is to say, given a place at the table. We don't know what Wilson's private thoughts were on this matter, but we do know that some others—starting with Georges Clemenceau—would not hear of such a thing. Nor would David Lloyd George or, for that matter, Winston Churchill, who was then leading an effort to nip the Bolshevik menace in the bud, which the victorious Soviets did not forget. Bullitt joined other young members of the commission, including Lippmann, who had helped to author several of the Fourteen Points, in resigning not so quietly. When he returned to the United States, Bullitt testified in Congress to the sins of the commission and of Wilson in particular. Mrs. Wilson said Bullitt's testimony was in part responsible for her husband's nearly fatal stroke. In the event, there would be no permanent peace.

Bullitt spent the interwar years wandering. He had already seen too much of the world and was not good enough of a writer to take up residence in Paris with the rest of the Lost Generation, even though Paris would always be his favorite place on earth. He married Louise Bryant, the free-spirited widow of John Reed, Bullitt's fellow journalist who wrote *Ten Days That Shook the World*. He coauthored a psychological study of Wilson with Sigmund Freud. He lived for a while in Turkey, then in Hollywood, where he tried his hand at screenwriting. By the time Franklin Roosevelt won the election, Bullitt again felt the itch to be close to power. He endeared himself to the new president and got appointed to lead the negotiations with the Russians over normalization.

As already noted, this was achieved in 1933, and Bullitt went to Moscow as the first American ambassador to the Soviet Union. The new embassy he established was known for some odd goings-on, including parties with circus animals—performing bears and the like. The members of the embassy staff he recruited nearly all became famous Kremlinologists: Loy Henderson, George Kennan, Chip Bohlen, Elbridge Durbrow, and the youngest and craziest of the bunch, Bohlen's close friend and future brother-in-law, Charlie Thayer, who after falling victim to McCarthy's inquisition wrote two excellent portraits of Bullitt's circus. (An even better-known rendition is found in Mikhail Bulgakov's *The Master and Margarita*.) Bullitt might have ended Thayer's career much earlier, for the latter had crashed the ambassador's favorite car, but Bullitt was, then at least, a more forgiving type.

Some of these officers, Bohlen and Kennan, for example, were among the first Americans in their profession to study the Russian language, history, and culture. They made the Soviet Union their life's calling. Bohlen described it as being as ineffable as "the act of love." But they had also known many anti-Communists. Bohlen, for example, was especially close to Isaiah Berlin, with whom he was said to have hatched the "non-Communist left." So they were also discerning, and sometimes hostile.

The latter feeling came quickly to Bullitt. He had shown up in

Moscow offering to construct a new embassy that would have been a replica of Monticello. He had all the credentials a friendly American needed—the man who had married Reed's widow, who had spoken up for Lenin, who had brought about normalization. But this was the time of the Great Purges. Stalin and company were not known for their gratitude or their hospitality, especially for a half-Jewish diplomatic entrepreneur from the headquarters of world capitalism. Bullitt was treated badly. His disappointment metamorphosed into betrayal and then deep hostility, which he nursed for the rest of his life.

Roosevelt meanwhile relieved Bullitt of his misery in 1936 by sending him as ambassador to Paris, where he became, it was said, a virtual member of the French cabinet and the close confidant to the premier, Édouard Daladier. He stayed through the fall of France and, as honorary mayor of Paris (he disobeyed orders to accompany the fleeing government), handed the keys to the city to the conquering Germans. He would return four years later as a volunteer enlistee in de Gaulle's Free French forces, rush to the now liberated American embassy, and deliver a speech from the balcony to crowds who cheered because they thought he was General Eisenhower.

Between these two episodes Bullitt committed a dramatic act of career suicide. He had, he thought, made himself indispensable to Roosevelt. He probably knew more European chancery gossip than any other American. It would have been expected for him to be given an even more important post—likely a cabinet position—following his departure from France. But Bullitt made enemies easily. Much of the British establishment mistrusted him for his open Anglophobia; almost from the day he arrived in France he had been pushing the line that the British and their masterless inactivity were to blame for the rise of Hitler. Isolationist opinion in the United States and elsewhere, namely from the mouth of America's ambassador to the Court of St. James's, Joseph P. Kennedy, mistrusted him for urging much greater levels of assistance, then intervention, on behalf of the French. He had burned his bridges in Moscow, and did not cease reminding anyone who would listen that the Russians were not to be trusted, even now that they were wartime allies, which could not have been welcomed by the White House.

There was more. Bullitt had chosen a rival. Sumner Welles was the undersecretary of state, an old Roosevelt family friend, and a man, like Bullitt, fond of drink. He was the de facto secretary, since Roosevelt had little use for the actual secretary, Cordell Hull. Hull too hated Welles. Bullitt presently conspired with him to blackmail the president into firing Welles, the cause being that word had spread of certain tendencies on the latter's part, which included, in one notorious episode, the propositioning of several sleeping-car porters on a train in Alabama. J. Edgar Hoover had looked into it and had plenty of evidence, and Bullitt told the president he was prepared to see that it appeared on the front pages of the papers unless his rival was destroyed. Roosevelt acquiesced but told Bullitt off. His career too was over.

The Welles-Bullitt affair deprived the United States of two of its most formidable diplomats in the middle of the war. Each had put a great deal of effort into mobilizing the bureaucracy to contemplate the world beyond the war and to plan for it. Students of policy history have found the "postwar planning" of this period to be one of the richest case studies of such activity. To his credit, Roosevelt encouraged the various planning committees in the U.S. government, perhaps on the belief that it gave people busy work, or on the presumption that the United States was probably going to win the war and he did not want to go down in history as another Wilson.

Roosevelt therefore was determined, if the public record is to be believed, to strike a postwar deal with Stalin. The details would bring controversy and Roosevelt knew it. Even Churchill, who struck his own bargain with Stalin, felt that Roosevelt gave away too much and probably resented the president's telling him of his privileged insight into Stalin's character, that he, Roosevelt, could "personally handle Stalin better than either your Foreign Office or my State Department. Stalin hates the guts of all your top people. He thinks he likes me better, and I hope he will continue to do so."

To this day Yalta is grouped with Munich as a metonym for appeasement, that is, weakness. There is some justification in that. Roosevelt himself said it was the best deal he could get, which was to say it was not the perfect deal he would have wanted. This was not widely known at the time. A majority of the American people supported the work of the conference—or what they were told of it.

There were some higher necessities: to ensure the Soviets entered the war against Japan, for one, and to gain their promise to make a viable United Nations, for another. Truman stood firm for the latter, a tribute to the recently dead Roosevelt. If the Russians balked, Truman said, they could "go to hell." He sent Harry Hopkins, on the verge of death himself, to Moscow to clinch the deal. According to most accounts, the discussions confirmed to Stalin just how muddled and self-absorbed the Americans had become so quickly; but the Soviets agreed to sign the charter.

In these aims, Roosevelt had counted on the full support of Sumner Welles, who had been, apart from Hopkins, FDR's most loyal supporter in seeking a modus vivendi with the Soviet Union. Welles later modified the view to say, accurately or not, that he had advised a "firmer" policy even before the invasion of Normandy, but Roosevelt had stalled; so an accommodation now had to be reached on pragmatic grounds. As head of the various postwar planning committees, Welles had been the architect of the accommodation. It cannot be proved, but it is certainly plausible that this fed Bullitt's hatred. Others worried too. Henry Wallace complained to the president back in December 1942 that dark forces—"certain bigoted Catholics and certain reactionaries," among others—were trying to take control of their party, and were moving the nation toward another war. Wallace later wrote, in May 1945, that the propaganda of such people would only lead to Communism's victory worldwide.

In three remarkable memoranda sent to Roosevelt in 1943, Bullitt laid out the reasons why the United States would find itself in conflict with the Soviet Union after the war. The images are familiar to anyone who has read George Kennan's Long Telegram, which appeared three years later: the irrepressible need to expand (Bullitt described it as a kind of miasma) and the desperate search for security through the subjugation of its neighbors. Soviets were "extraordinarily gifted" people, but they had to be stopped, preferably by some form of transatlantic alliance, beginning with the consolidation of power in Western Europe. Bullitt was consistent. Wallace recalled a conversation with him in February 1946, when Bullitt mentioned that "Stalin at one time was very affectionate toward me. At one time when he had had a little too much to drink he kissed me full on the mouth—what a horrible experience that was!" Bullitt

> spoke about the different people whom Stalin had shot— people who at one time were close to him. He said the Russians were like an amoeba, sending out pseudopods, surrounding that which they could digest and avoiding that which they could not digest. He then proclaimed that the proper policy of the United States was to put indigestible particles in their path . . . a Western European Federation.

Bullitt's successor, Averell Harriman, modified the image to an invasion of barbarians. We do not know what Roosevelt, and later Truman, did with this advice and how it affected official thinking. We only know that it went against the line that Welles and Roosevelt had been advancing and the one that Truman later reversed.

Peter Drucker once compared Roosevelt's management style to

that of Henry Luce, which he called classically Chinese inasmuch as it counterpoised rivals and left him unscathed and supreme. Roosevelt was otherwise claustrophobic. "If bombs fall," he'd say, "just take me out to the South Lawn." Welles and Bullitt were among its most prominent victims, which meant that when more bombs did fall (overseas), FDR had to rely upon lesser advisers. At Yalta, for example, he had to make do with Harriman and Leahy, with Chip Bohlen pinch-hitting as lead interpreter. Two months later the president was dead.

For Harriman, Bullitt probably did not have high regard. Bullitt was a snob, and to him Harriman, whose father was one of the richest men in the world, was nouveau. Bullitt's name and family wealth dated back to the eighteenth century. George Kennan served in turn under Bullitt and Harriman in Moscow. Kennan had the good fortune to wait until Harriman was on home leave before he wrote and sent his Long Telegram, described presently. It shocked some people. The army was said to be alarmed that the State Department was contriving to get the country into another war, at worst, and a typical cover-your-back move, at best, should war occur. Harriman didn't get the credit, although he later made sure, once the telegram had attracted so much fame, to tell everyone that he had encouraged Kennan to write it and even that he had specifically chosen to go on leave to allow Kennan some recognition. It's unlikely that this would have been the case otherwise. Bullitt would have sought and got all the credit, and Kennan probably wouldn't have minded.

Leahy, as we have seen, was a different breed: taciturn, loyal, guarded, protective, dutiful. His appointment to Vichy superseded Bullitt's, for there was no longer a government in Paris to which Bullitt was accredited, but neither man held it against the other. Sending Bullitt to Vichy with Marshal Pétain would have been unthinkable, and they knew it. Leahy returned to Washington to be Roosevelt's chief of staff, and continued in the post under Truman.

He and Bullitt met often. Leahy's diary notes the number of times the subject of their meetings, sometimes including Forrestal and usually over lunch, was the Soviet Union. It is not too difficult to imagine the line they took.

With Kennan sounding the tocsin about Soviet expansion and Leahy whispering in the president's ear, we can conclude that Bullitt, or his language and biases, at least, still had some influence. Bullitt became more and more interested, even obsessed, with the spread of Soviet power and influence in East Asia. He hoped the Chinese Nationalists wouldn't take their time to be defeated, after which, paraphrasing Walter Lippmann, the West should "encourage the growth of regionalism, and then lure the Russians into the swamp to drain their strength instead of ours."

He held other interesting opinions. Lunching with Kennan in October 1949, he told his former aide to be wary of independent India. "Build on anyone else you want," Bullitt said, "on the Moslems if you will, but not on the Hindus." Why not? He said Indians wasted too much food on their sacred animals. India therefore would never develop properly. "And intellectually, they were brilliant but unsubstantial."

This sounded to some like Bullitt's own reputation. When Truman became president, he offered his services, once letting Truman know he was off to Europe and would do anything there the president liked. Truman's staff moved fast to quash the offer: "He shouldn't ask him to do a damn thing. Bullitt is trouble. He'll just go parading around Europe saying he is a special emissary of the president."

One person who, curiously, took a liking to him was Henry Wallace. The two met often as well. "Bullitt is a vivid kind of person whose heart seems definitely in the right place but I would judge from looking at him that he probably has been drinking a little too much in recent years," Wallace recounted. He said Bullitt hadn't done enough manual labor in his life; that was another of his problems.

But he liked Bullitt's gossip, and his mind. The accounts Wallace gives in his diary are sometimes dismissive, but never hostile, and often intrigued.

The ghost, or at least the spirit, of William Bullitt is tempting to cast over the onset of the Cold War during 1946. It looked as though he dealt it like a curse, partly to show everyone that he had been right, partly to punish another ghost: Roosevelt's. Yet neither history nor even politics, especially in America, are known for the easy digestion of vague ghosts. Americans like things literal, with vivid words and symbols. It is said that every crisis generation finds its leader and its scribe, the man who gives a voice to the spirit, who puts it into words every citizen can understand. He was none other than Kennan, the man Bullitt first brought to Moscow, whose word was "containment."

The idea behind the Long Telegram, and Kennan's "X" article later, was simple and straightforward. The Soviet Union was formed upon a syndrome that covered a long-standing Russian imperial paranoia with an extra layer of millenarianism, another of historicist ideology, and still another with what the writer and outcast Freda Utley called "a kind of mystical masochism." There was one good way to deal with such a society and culture. Quarantined, or contained, it would turn in on itself and probably die. Then maybe it could start over again, reformed.

What would this entail in practice? Kennan didn't really say. It did not mean a new war, especially not preventive war. When one of his colleagues submitted a proposal for one, Kennan destroyed all its copies, carbons, and almost the typewriter platen. The fire he set in his wastebasket nearly destroyed his office. So what really was he talking about? "[I]n the fifty years I have known George Kennan," Joe Alsop later noted, "he has been more wrong than anyone else and more right than anyone else—and no one, including myself, has ever reliably deduced which was which at the moment of its expression." He had been ruminating upon the ideas for many months, probably years. But this moment was unique. Stalin had given a new speech. It shocked many people, though it probably shouldn't have. After all, Stalin was known for keeping abreast of American public opinion and knew that a portion of it had turned against his country. His speech certainly roused a few people in the State Department, and they asked Kennan, who had predicted Stalin's new line, to give his two cents. He did, in over five thousand words.

But what did Stalin actually threaten?

At the Bolshoi Theater on February 9, 1946, Stalin repeated the line that capitalist excesses had caused the Second World War. His country had been dragged into it, but had passed the test. That it did was testament to the achievements of Communism during the preceding years. Now the world had changed. The Soviet Union would launch another five-year plan that included rearmament. Arms mattered more now than other priorities—consumer goods, for example. Could the wartime alliance continue into peacetime? Could Communism and capitalism coexist? Could another new world order be devised? He doubted it.

Some Americans who read the speech the next day called it a new declaration of war. Secretary Byrnes treated it as the dropping of a gauntlet; there was no more point to cooperation, or even the appearance of it.

How had things come to this?

Let us recapitulate. The Big Three—Churchill, Roosevelt, and Stalin—met for the first time all together at Tehran in 1943. The main topic on their agenda was war strategy, but Stalin opened a discussion about the next phase—that is, assuming their strategy succeeded. He drew lines on a small map, but Roosevelt put him off, saying it was premature to discuss such things; Roosevelt had an election coming up in 1944, and there was still a war to win. Like his generals, Roosevelt touted the curious American preoccupation with keeping political matters separate from military ones.

At Yalta the following February, this would not do. They discussed the postwar arrangement, and they agreed, notoriously, on another division. In April, Truman came to power. Loyal in public to FDR's liberal legacy (and to the watchful eyes of Eleanor and Harry Hopkins), he nonetheless treated the Soviet Union less gingerly. He told Harriman right away that "the Russians need us more than we need them."

At Potsdam the following July, the leaders were meant to seal the deal. Germany had been defeated. Truman met Stalin and, briefly, Churchill. Midway through the conference the British people defeated Churchill's party. He was replaced at Potsdam by Clement Attlee. Now the Big Three looked a couple of measures smaller. The only member of the original trio was Stalin. Truman treated him to a performance of Paderewski's Minuet in G, which Stalin liked. Truman also "liked the little son of a bitch. He was a good six inches shorter than I am and even Churchill was only three inches taller than Joe! Yet I was the little man in stature and intellect! So the Press said. Well we'll see."

There at Potsdam the Americans raised their flag in Truman's presence. It was the same flag that had been raised over the Capitol on December 7, 1941; it had made its way to Rome for the liberation of that city; now it was in Berlin; it would travel on to Tokyo. We can imagine what Truman felt. He said that he was tired; both Churchill and Stalin were night owls; he rose early. Finally, during a discussion about Yugoslavia, Truman's composure broke:

> I felt that I had heard enough of this. I told Churchill and Stalin that I had come to the conference as a representative of the United States to discuss world affairs. I did not come there to hold a police court hearing on something that was already settled or which would eventually be settled by the United Nations.... I told them frankly that I did not wish to waste time listening to grievances but wanted to deal with the problems which the three heads of government had come to settle.

I said that if they did not get to the main issues I was going to pack up and go home. I meant just that.... Stalin laughed heartily and said he did not blame the President for wanting to go home; he wanted to go home too.

That was the Potsdam Conference, what Byrnes called "The Success that Failed." Had American and British armies, instead of the Red Army, occupied most of Eastern Europe, there might have been more to discuss. Truman did his best to look and sound able, but he was new at this business, and it showed. He was uncertain, ambiguous, and contradictory. He had said he would get tough with the Russians, but he still attempted—sincerely, we must presume—to deal openly and constructively with Stalin. The Soviet Union would feel the brunt of his hasty cancellation of Lend-Lease, but there would be no large loan as had been offered to the British.

Truman was now the *demandeur*. Harriman had said the president thought he could get around 85 percent of what he wanted. As it happened, the three agreed on a provisional arrangement for Germany under their mutual occupation and to expedite the end of the Pacific war with, at last, Soviet participation. Truman also told Stalin he had a big new weapon, and Stalin told him to use it well. Right as the second bomb was dropped on Nagasaki, the Soviet Union entered the war against Japan. Stalin kept his promise. The loose ends of the three conferences were not yet tied, however. Stalin had agreed to free elections in Poland and elsewhere. These did not happen. He had agreed to a combined occupation of Germany. This did happen, but it would later break down over reparations payments, prisoner repatriation, currencies, trade, movement among the various sectors, and so on. There were also the politics.

Back at Potsdam, deep in what became the Soviet sector, the Allies must have had a hint of the world to come. Stalin put it best: whoever controls the territory determines the way of life there. His case was simple, really: to the victors ought to go the spoils. Sole

American possession of the bomb did not make him any more ostensibly halfhearted in what he said was his own neighborhood.

The division of spoils would take another couple of years to sort. Because sorting was more often than not tense, even hostile, a hot peace, or a cold war, would supplant the wartime alliance. At first the hostility was symbolic, political, and, to use a favorite contemporary term, "propagandistic." Not for long. By 1949 the Soviet Union would have the bomb. The Baruch Plan lay stillborn. The nuclear powers ventured on to deter one another without an international intermediary, or a higher force, to govern them. Yet by 1950 their rivalry would bring bloodshed in Asia.

There had been other disputes in Iran and the eastern Mediterranean. The former led to a crisis in mid-1946 when Soviet troops refused to depart from what is now northwestern Iran and respect Iranian sovereignty, which they had promised to do at the Tehran Conference in 1943. Russian tanks were seen just twenty-five miles from Tehran. They had to be compelled to pull back. The new United Nations stood on principle: small nations could not be denied a voice against big ones.

The Mediterranean dispute was more complicated. Greece had fallen into a nasty civil war to which a formidable Communist movement was a party. Success there, combined with the popularity of Communist parties in France and Italy, especially, threatened, some said, to turn part of the Mediterranean into a Red zone. Communist parties also did comparably well in elections in Belgium, Denmark, Finland, and Norway.

At the same time the Soviets were pushing hard for a rewriting of the Montreux Convention and to allow themselves a joint defense with Turkey of the Dardanelles, which others said was a first step toward converting Turkey into a vassal state. It was a fanciful idea, but it raised doubts. Stalin could also be ambiguous. When asked how much farther he would go, borderwise, he said "only a little further." Not surprisingly the British—who still depended heavily on freedom of access to the eastern Mediterranean and on to Suez—were alarmed by the events. For its part, the United States sent the remains of the recently deceased Turkish ambassador (whose jazz-obsessed son, incidentally, would make his home in the United States and go on to found, among other things, Atlantic Records), back on a warship—the USS *Missouri*—straight to the Bosphorus.

The British later dropped a bigger bombshell when they informed the State Department that they could no longer underwrite a military presence in the eastern Mediterranean, Communist threats or not. Greece and Turkey would henceforth be left to their own devices. The British were in effect passing the torch to the Americans. How did the Americans react? According to one officer then working in the bowels of the State Department:

> The sudden spark set off a dazzling process which within fifteen weeks laid the basis for a complete conversion of American foreign policy and the attitudes of the American people toward the world. . . . For decades massive historical caravans had been observed moving slowly toward predictable destinations: Great Britain toward loss of Empire and inability to maintain the balance of power in Europe and order in Asia; Western continental Europe toward instability and weakness; the United States toward economic and military pre-eminence in political isolation; and the Soviet Union toward a fundamental challenge of Western civilization.

This and China, which had by then also lapsed into a civil war, were tests, Truman said. It was not that the United States sought to supplant the British or anyone else. Rather, it was the duty of the United States to stop the Soviets; let others make of it what they wanted.

Hostility was furthered by the series of foreign ministers' conferences that followed Potsdam. They were meant to finalize the various peace treaties. They turned out to be for the most part futile exercises, as the Soviets succeeded in linking every question to their own demands. At the first conference, at Lancaster House in London, the British foreign secretary, Ernest Bevin, tore into Molotov for obstruction and bad faith. Bevin, the former docker and trade unionist, a "bullying, capricious, sasquatch of a politician," had dealt with Communists in his unions for years; he had expelled most of them; he spoke like a man who knew much from experience.

Alas, Bevin had little liking for Byrnes either. To him Byrnes was just another slick politician who, though like Bevin new to the job of diplomacy, had done little homework; what little he had done he kept mostly to himself, or got in the habit of sharing with the Russians before the British or, for that matter, his own president.

After London came Moscow, in December. The results were just as thin. The Americans and the British had grown even further apart. Some said this was Moscow's plan all along. Reports from the Soviets about the meeting implied that great things had been accomplished there.

Finally, Paris. Bevin again was the star of the show. Byrnes did most of the talking, but Molotov again got nearly all he wanted. Harold Nicolson saw

> Molotov and Vyshinsky stride across the stage with all the consciousness of power; Byrnes and his [American] delegation walk slowly and sedately with all the consciousness of great virtue; and then in trips little Attlee, hesitates on finding himself on the stage, tries to dart back again into the door through which he has come, and is then rescued by an official who leads him across the stage with a hand on his elbow. A lamentable entry.

A better summary cannot be found of British resignation in the summer of 1946.

This led to the induced birth of the Truman Doctrine. In March

1947, Truman delivered his speech to Congress pledging American support for these putative frontline states, and then for any state that was menaced by Communists, even if said Communists were citizens of said state.

Congress backed its president. Little more than twelve months before, the American people for the most part had been opposed to the "get tough" policy toward Russia. Truman, however, had slowly begun to turn. By the following year, they had been sufficiently frightened by what he had said, and the stark language he had used to say it. Rather than force them into their own resignation, this time he stiffened their collective spine. Senator Arthur Vandenberg, who had once been a leader of the isolationist wing of the Republican Party, led his party to Truman's side. He had not really been much of an isolationist anyway, he said, rather an "insulationist." Security was his obsession.

Insulating the nation—keeping it and us safe—had now become the great mission of government. How to do it—proactively and reactively—and to pay for it were another matter.

The recapitulation requires some revision. Truman too had passed through a few stages. He began to act "firm." He dressed down Molotov. He said the Russians had to be taught a few manners so that they, like the Germans, would learn to play their proper role. He had listened to the "get tough" crowd, especially Harriman, Leahy, and, by the beginning of 1946, Byrnes and Vandenberg. But he did not close the door to cooperation. Perhaps he thought the Russians were as undecided as he was. Hopkins said they were; so, even, on occasion did Forrestal. Perhaps Truman felt sorry for insulting them one too many times, or encouraging them to equate his Missouri attitude with his true feelings. Then he opened the door a bit wider. He tried his best at Potsdam, but his advisers—apart from Stimson and, to a lesser extent, Marshall—caused him worry. His government's strategy was still a blur, and its politics were matched badly to its rhetoric. It came to project and reflect Soviet malevolence but wanted to avoid war, and probably presumed that the Russians did too, or that they were not ready to fight. So Truman turned, again, to close the door, drafting his famous "I'm tired babying the Soviets" statement, so that by the second month of 1946 there was just a small crack left.

Into it stepped the large figure of Winston Churchill.

Westminster College is a small school in Fulton, Missouri. Churchill, now out of office, had been invited there to receive an honorary degree. He picked up another in Florida, spent some time resting in Palm Beach, and also went to the Roosevelt homestead at Hyde Park to pay homage to his friend the late president.

Fulton on the day Churchill spoke was festooned with balloons, banners, crowds. Churchill joined the rear of the procession of professors in their black robes; his own was scarlet. The procession marched to the accompaniment of an organist who played "O Come, All Ye Faithful." A student read a prayer: "There can be no peace save in the hearts of men. . . ." Truman sat there, in his own black robe, off to the side. Then he spoke: "This is one of my greatest pleasures and privileges since I became President of the United States. Mr. Churchill is one of the great men of our age. I know he will have something constructive to say." Churchill rose to the podium, fixed his reading glasses, and began his speech, titled "Sinews of Peace."

He outlined the state of the world as he then saw it, in March 1946, a world dominated by the United States and at the same time endangered by the persistent ruin left in the wake of the recent war. Out of this ruin the Soviet Union would reemerge and challenge the West. Then, about two-thirds of the way through, he stated the famous line: "From Stettin in the Baltic to Trieste in the Adriatic, an iron curtain has descended across the Continent."

There was an outcry in the country. Recently demobilized men were not happy to hear Churchill's clarion call. Stalin declared him a "firebrand of war" and added that Churchill was not alone. The British government denied they had been behind the speech. Dean Acheson was ordered by the State Department to skip a dinner in Churchill's honor and instead had an embassy lunch with him, where Acheson's wife told the former prime minister, referring to painting, that his "palette is keyed too high. Your work would have more depth if it were toned down." Mrs. Acheson, as it happens, adored Churchill and thought well of his Fulton speech. Many others, however, were lukewarm, if not hostile. Some said it "might wreck the United Nations"; that it frightened people; or, if these things needed saying, "why couldn't *we* say [them]? Why can't the United States speak out for itself?"

Byrnes said the speech had "nothing to do" with the United States. But the country demanded to know whether Truman had seen it beforehand and whether he agreed with it. He answered no to both questions. Truman told Wallace that Churchill had sprung it on him, and that he did not foresee another Anglo-American military alliance venturing against the Soviet Union. The first, at least, was a lie. Churchill said he showed the president the speech on the train on the way over, and the president said that "it would make a stir."

What of the second? The speech had followed Stalin's; followed Kennan's Long Telegram; followed the first foreign ministers' conferences; and coincided with the Iran, Greece, and Turkish crises. Still, the country had not accepted the existence of the Cold War, and this included—at least in public—its president. Byrnes put it oddly: "There is no iron curtain that the aggregate sentiments of mankind cannot penetrate."

Aggregation, penetration. From Bullitt to Kennan and now to the American people, the images held, but their cumulative effect on public opinion was uncertain. The speeches were menacing, yet some people may have considered them a grand service rendered in the name of clarity. They were worth the strain and sacrifice, even for Churchill, who joked that "Uncle Joe" would no longer be sending him so much caviar. To his credit, Truman let others do the sounding. He may have learned this from Roosevelt, and perhaps from the example of Woodrow Wilson. You cannot take a country to war without consent. Consent takes a while to form, especially when a president holds back and allows public opinion to coalesce before he champions a new direction. Or we may give Truman too much credit. Nobody can really know if he knew, or even if he thought he knew, what he was doing by accompanying Churchill to this event. Nobody can really know, for that matter, if he digested what he had read on the train. Time and again (as we are about to see), Truman had to deny he'd read something following a public outcry.

For now, he continued to vacillate. In March he had said, "Before we were trying to keep her [the Soviet Union] in the war, now we're trying to keep her in the peace—and it's an entirely different thing," but that it all "would be settled pretty soon." To his staff he could sound almost nonchalant about the Russians; his usual comment upon seeing negative reports was "That's not so good, is it?" Then he would move on to something else. Finally, in July, he asked to see a list of Soviet agreements and violations.

Had something changed? Truman told Clark Clifford to prepare a report. Clifford turned to his own assistant, George Elsey, the young man whose Harvard graduate-school career (in history) had been interrupted by the war, and asked him to assemble something. The resulting Clifford-Elsey report was probably meant for a sub rosa existence. Admiral Leahy had not been asked to prepare it, and was critical when it was done, declaring, "It ought to come right out and say the Russians are sons of bitches!" Byrnes was resentful that the State Department had not been asked either. He had shunned Clifford. What agreements? Byrnes asked. Why, there were probably several that Harry Hopkins made that he kept to himself.

The Clifford-Elsey report, delivered finally in September, went directly to the president, who ordered all copies destroyed. For it confirmed what had by now become the Washington consensus: the Soviets had to be challenged and contested. Truman himself had at last been persuaded of this; he still was not ready to share his certainty with the public. Clifford, for his part, later telling himself that this document laid the foundation of what would become the Truman Doctrine, and all it entailed, went against the president's orders and saved a copy—which he leaked in 1966 to the journalist Arthur Krock. But Elsey, citing a Washington adage, had the last word: "No one signs a paper that he writes, nor does he write a paper that he signs."

So, yes, something had changed. One man who noticed was Henry Wallace. His views on relations with the Soviet Union were well known. He had, as we have read, long supported clueing them in on the nuclear experiments. His line was straight. He was no Communist or fellow traveler (although people in his orbit certainly were). He was convinced, by both logic and common sense, that if present hostilities continued there would be war with the Soviet Union. The only people who could possibly gain by this, he said, were the British. America, however, had everything to lose. In any event, if it was going to happen, better that it do so as soon as possible.

The debate exasperated him although he may have welcomed having it. Back in January, for example, he attended a dinner at Joe Alsop's. Alsop, whom Gore Vidal aptly called the Baron de Charlus of Georgetown, was the best-informed reporter in town and, according to Wallace, much used by the government. His role as court scribe notwithstanding, Alsop liked to challenge his guests; his dinners were known for broken tempers and sometimes other things. At this one were a few old New Dealers, including Supreme Court justice Hugo Black, Ben Cohen, and Grace Tully, as well as Wallace and a Mr. and Mrs. Gaud. Mr. Gaud and Alsop stood on the "get tough" side of the party. In fact, Gaud said, the United States should "kick the Russians in the balls." Wallace replied:

I said I thought the Russians were entitled to free access through the Dardanelles; that they had been promised this in World War I.

Gaud said this was "crap";

I replied that his statements were "crap. . . ."

I said to Joe, "In other words, you look on Russia as a young man and think that he ought to declare his intentions regarding the young lady. You assume that the young lady has no intentions of her own at all."

Ben Cohen took somewhat the same slant. . . . Alsop called his statements "a barrel of horse-shit."

It really had come to this.

In Germany, the tension among the occupying powers had grown so intense that General Lucius D. Clay, soon to become military governor, insisted that something be done. "We all might as well face the facts," he said, "and we know now that the information given to the Germans indicates certain discords and lack of unanimity among the Allies. There have been certain recent charges of the German Communist party that the western zones are harboring Nazis and Fascists." What had become a de facto reconsolidation into two principal sectors came to take on a formal character. In the spring Clay and Byrnes had discussed merging the British and American sectors into a single one. It would be called Bizonia. Byrnes then discussed it in Paris in July; it was accepted by the British and formalized in December. Also at Paris, Molotov had spoken forcefully and Clay insisted there be a response. The State Department thought otherwise, and held up matters for so long that Clay threatened to resign. Byrnes then conceded and told Clay that he would come to Germany in September and deliver an important speech.

Byrnes kept his word and delivered it at the Stuttgart Opera House on September 6. He made sure to accentuate the symbolism. Byrnes and Clay traveled in Hitler's old train car with its marble bathtubs. Clay saw that the route taking them to the opera house passed rows of troops, armored cars, and large crowds. Byrnes brought along the two best-known senators from the Foreign Relations Committee, Vandenberg and Tom Connally, who sat on the stage with Robert Murphy, Clay's political adviser from the State Department and a man known to be close to Admiral Leahy. Clay himself sat way in the back so, he said, he could gauge the audience's reaction.

Given what Byrnes said, it was unsurprisingly favorable. He paid homage to the Germans' desire for self-government, peace, and prosperity. So far as he was concerned this needn't be at anyone's expense, but if it were, so be it: the time had passed to allow anything to obstruct the German-American interest, with or without others. He pledged to help the country keep from becoming any other country's pawn. He said that American troops would remain in Germany for as long as necessary, that is, so long as anyone else had troops there. This last point Byrnes had wanted to remove from the speech, but Clay made him keep it in. He ended with a short homily: "The American people want to help the German people to win their way back to an honorable place among the free and peace-loving nations of the world." That was followed by "The Star-Spangled Banner," which brought Clay and Vandenberg and perhaps a few others to tears. "Thus the effort to rule Germany by unanimous agreement of the representatives of the four occupying powers failed," concluded General Clay. "As this failure became evident, vital decisions had to be made in Germany."

Byrnes had accomplished his mission. Or so he may have thought. For just a few days later he and his Stuttgart speech would be upstaged by a very different one back home.

Henry Wallace was now the last holdout in the administration. He had been agitating about Russia for as long as he or most anyone else could remember. At the end of July he sent the president a very long letter on the subject. At last he decided he'd had enough. On September 12, he walked into Madison Square Garden and delivered what is only possible to describe as a frontal attack on his own government. He charged it with everything from provoking a war with the Soviet Union to collusion with British imperialists to furthering a world arms race. Again, the public demanded to know what Truman had understood about the speech ahead of time; again, he demurred; again, he lied. Wallace had visited Truman before delivering the speech and, by his account,

> went over [it] page by page with him.... Again and again he said, "That's right"; "Yes, that is what I believe." He didn't have a single change to suggest. He twice said how deeply he appreciated my courtesy in showing him my speech before I gave it.... The President said that Secretary Byrnes' speech of September 6 had been cleared with him over the telephone and then it had been sent back to Washington for minor checking. He said also that he thought it must be a pretty good speech because neither the British, the French, nor the Russians nor the Germans [sic] liked it.... The President apparently saw no inconsistency between my speech and what Byrnes was doing— if he did he didn't indicate it in any way.

Truman would later concede that this had taken place, but denied the "page by page" bit, saying that Wallace had merely let him glance at the speech at the end of a conversation about a number of other subjects. Moreover, Wallace had modified significant parts of it on delivery. But Truman had not been blindsided. In fact, he had given a press conference just a few hours before Wallace spoke:

Question: Mr. President, in a speech for delivery tonight, Secretary of State—I mean Commerce—Wallace [*laughter*] has this to say, about the middle of it, "when President—"

Answer: [*Interrupting*] Well now, you say the speech is to be delivered?

Q: It is, sir.

A: Well, I—I can't answer questions on a speech that is to be delivered.

Q: It mentions you, which is the reason that I ask, sir.

A: Well, that's fine. I'm glad it does. What was the question. Go ahead. Maybe I can answer it. [*Much laughter*]

Q: In the middle of the speech are these words, "When President Truman read these words, he said that they represented the policy of this Administration."

A: That is correct.

Q: My question is, does that apply just to that paragraph, or to the whole speech?

A: I approved the whole speech.

Q: Mr. President, do you regard Wallace's speech [as] a departure from Byrnes' policy—

A: [*Interrupting*] I do not.

Byrnes certainly disagreed. The poor man on press duty back at the State Department, Assistant Secretary Will Clayton, tried his best:

Can you say whether the Wallace speech was cleared with the Department?

He replied it was not cleared with him.

Was it cleared with Secretary Byrnes?

Clayton did not know.

Have you heard from Mr. Byrnes?

No.

Do you intend to talk with the President?

No.

Are you going to talk with the Secretary?
No.
Do you have any comment?
No.

There was the suspicion, given what came next, that Truman knew exactly what he was doing in this instance, although it carried a big risk. On the margins of his copy of Wallace's speech, according to a secondhand account, was the comment "This will make Jimmy sore." Byrnes told the president that he had already said that he had wanted to resign and postponed it for the peace treaties. Now there was no way he could stay any longer. "You and I spent fifteen months building a bipartisan policy," he wrote to Truman. "We did a fine job convincing the world that it was a permanent policy upon which the world could rely. Wallace destroyed it in a day."

One day later Truman demanded Wallace's resignation.

That this took place after Truman waited for Wallace to take the initiative and resign—and when he did not, wrote him one of his impulsive letters, only to have Wallace return it—need not detract from the conviction that one or two men would, or must, go. Wallace left the government and ran against Truman in 1948. Byrnes was replaced presently by General Marshall.

Four speeches and two sets of memoranda, Bullitt's and Kennan's. Each one a testament to choice and to certainty. But throughout 1946, Harry Truman still had not decided what to do about the Soviet Union. "Nobody," an editorialist at the *Christian Science Monitor* wrote, "seems to be sure what is going to happen. And few are sure what should be done, no matter what happens." This was true for Truman, and for the majority of his advisers, who were said to be not so much divided among themselves as divided within themselves over the Cold War until the summer of 1946. For all that Stalin set in motion a new division of the world, it was not so much his determination to resist and confront the West, led now by the United States, as it was the "general irresolution" of the same to grapple with him. A dilemma, possibly. But a decision? Surely not.

Chapter 6

Poujades

Small religious sects that appear among the desperately uneducated sometimes appall us by the intellectual squalor which they reveal, the superstitious ignorance, the compulsive frenzy which seems diseased.
—"The Easy Chair," June 1946

Pierre Poujade, who gave his name to an ism, Poujadism, was a bookseller from a town in the Lot Valley of France. In the early 1950s he led a small tax revolt that snowballed into a national movement that has since become an ideology akin to populism but with a darker, more reactionary tinge. "Poujadism" now describes a popular movement that seeks on the one hand to bring down the elite that is ruining the nation and on the other to be left alone but not to leave others alone.

America had experience with this tribe. From the nineteenth-century Know-Nothings to the twentieth-century nativists to the twenty-first-century Tea Party, Poujadism has been a semipermanent feature of the country's politics. The traits are similar in each incarnation: the tone and the terms of reference are geared toward the lower middle class even if some of the adherents are not; the reactionary tendency—some historians have preferred to call it the paranoid style—bases itself upon threats to the country from abroad as well as from within, however formless they may be to the rest of us. There are the usual suspects: immigrants; preachers of strange ideas, especially religions; bearers of strange physiognomies, that is to say, the nonwhite races. Often, and more frequently in the twentieth century following the growth in the power of the federal government, these threatening populations were seen to be in league with the cloistered and the powerful, whose ranks were said to include fifth columnists, traitors, sellouts, and fellow travelers.

Poujadists are as endemic to American political culture as advertising and money. Over the long run the country has found a way to tolerate them—the two parties are still too big and rich to be taken over or defeated by them—but at particular times and places they have seen success within the political system, mainly by shaping the tone of politics, mastering its language, and forcing it to pay homage. The late 1940s to early 1950s was one of those times.

Today we call this the era of McCarthyism. But there was more to it than the witch hunt led by a fanatical and self-destructive senator and his small band. Some members of the band and some of its own fellow travelers—Bobby Kennedy and Richard Nixon being two of the better known—recovered easily from the experience, and in fact, at least in the case of the latter, wore it as an opportunistic badge of honor.

Why then? Why in America?

The usual answer is the Cold War. Arthur Schlesinger Jr., soon after ending his army service in 1945, was helped by none other than Whittaker Chambers to write an article for *Life* magazine about the threat of Communism in the United States. Chambers, he recalled, had written a nice review in *Time* of the book (*The Age of Jackson*) that Schlesinger somehow had written while he was off in the war. He picked Chambers's brain after promising that whatever he gleaned therefrom was off the record. He talked with Chip Bohlen and a few others, but evidently not with Joseph McCarthy, who was about to win an election against Robert La Follette Jr. with, Schlesinger has noted, the support of local Communists. Challenged to explain, McCarthy said that Communists have their civil rights too. All this led Schlesinger eventually to conclude that Soviet Communism might pose some threat *to* America but not *in* America. He stated the *bien-pensant* view about such people: that they were deluded and sometimes delusional but not really all that dangerous. Unfortunately some of them, and their enemies, were bloody persistent.

This verdict, like Dean Acheson's description of McCarthyism as the attack of the primitives, is not sufficient to explain the phenomenon at midcentury, nor is the diagnosis of paranoia as a permanent feature of the American body politic that goes into remission or flares up as per the opportunistic talents of individual politicians and wings of political parties. All this may be true, but it is, again, insufficient. It cannot pardon the excesses of this particular witch hunt, or diminish the tragedy of so many lives and reputations destroyed. So we must ask again, why and why then? The source of the tragedy is easy to identify; by now it is a familiar one in these pages: fear. But fear of what, exactly? Revolution? War? Change? A foreign ideology? The Democratic Party? Loneliness?

We need to draw a bigger circle around fear. It was not the Cold War, or Communism, or Korea, or the persistence of the welfare state, or the atomic bomb, or the military-industrial complex alone. It was all these things, combined in a generational moment: the mood right after the war was akin to a vast hangover of fear. The country was weary; standards had fallen; it wanted to go forward, but it could not, no matter how much it tried, shake the fear that it had lived with for so long. "I live in an age of fear," wrote E. B. White at the end of 1947. "The Age of Anxiety," as W. H. Auden called his poem, was above all one of pervading fear.

The Know-Nothings and the nativists remind us that fear, broadly speaking, was not only self-referential, fear of fear itself, but also antagonistic—that is, fear of its opposite, swagger, or of higher knowledge. That others might have more of it and use it against you. That your own swagger, which may be effective, is just a ruse that you made to survive. Yet acting differently from what you longed to think and believe was not only disorienting but also frightening because it meant that something was awry with certainty. Something had gone wrong. We were not sure what it was, but, barring a better solution, it had to be personalized and vilified. The fear had to be conquered, lanced, repulsed. Send back the foreigners, or keep them out to begin with; identify and persecute the fifth columnists.

> And the intensest form of hatred is that rooted in fear, which compels to silence and drives vehemence into a constructive vindictiveness, an imaginary annihilation of the detested object, something like the hidden rites of vengeance with which the persecuted have made a dark vent for their rage, and soothed their suffering into dumbness.

Those classic lines from George Eliot's *Daniel Deronda* tell us all we need to know about why McCarthyism became so ugly. Fear is absolute, insatiable, boundless. It surfaces over and over in the writing of our short period. A typical sample from Norman Cousins (1945):

> The beginning of the Atomic Age has brought less hope than fear. It is a primitive fear, the fear of the unknown, the fear of forces man can neither channel nor comprehend. This fear is not new; in its classical form it is the fear of irrational death. But overnight it has become intensified, magnified. It has burst out of the subconscious and into the conscious, filling the mind with primordial apprehensions. . . . Where man can find no answer, he will find fear.

Bruce Catton (1948):

> America did the most colossal job in history and came out of it with an inferiority complex and a deep sense of fear.

Arnold Toynbee (1948):

The present Western fear of Communism is not a fear of military aggression.... The Communist weapon that is making America so jumpy (and, oddly enough, she is reacting more temperamentally to this threat than the less sheltered countries of Western Europe) is the spiritual engine of propaganda.... Communism is also a competitor for the allegiance of that great majority of mankind that is neither Communist nor Capitalist, neither Russian nor Western, but is living at present in an uneasy no-man's-land between the opposing citadels of two rival ideologies.... Yet the fact that our adversary threatens us by showing up our defects, rather than by forcibly suppressing our virtues, is proof that the challenge he presents to us comes ultimately not from him, but from ourselves.

Vance Bourjaily (1947):

What pain, then, and how bitter; what hollow, mordaunt dances, what grim destructive hornpipes, what macabre Arabesques. When we know our final folly, we find our final answer, we know, know, know, for certain that the cats do not exist. That is the great fear, that is the arch fear, that is the mad fear, that there is no fear.

The generation of Americans that succumbed to fear, as we have said, was the generation that survived the Depression and the war. They were the ones who worried, and feared losing life, livelihood, and limb, or of being buried alive, one of the worst imaginable fears—and one that now haunted the entire country thanks to John Hersey and the terrible weapon he described. This was still, on balance, a pious generation, some of whom had been raised on the usual fears propagated by religion. It was also the first or second generation to be liberated from Victorian practices of physical punishment dealt upon the child. Twentieth-century children were punished in another way—psychologically—and it was considered shameful for parents if their children showed fear. That did not make for a great solution. So in 1946, timed perfectly for the baby boom, there appeared Benjamin Spock's *Common Sense Book of Baby and Child Care*. It sold in the millions and was translated into dozens of languages. It's hard to name a more influential how-to guide for rearing children or for managing fear.

Spock conveyed a more pleasant message. It invoked the binary images of the child: the bogeyman and the paradise; the shadow and the light; the pit and the sky; obscurity and clarity. And he said, do what you must to keep them separate; to insulate the good; to keep, above all, from seeing the bad in the good, from confusing one with the other. This was his message for children and for parents. It is all right to feel afraid; it's not your fault; and if you try, with a bit of encouragement and expertise, you can find comfort from your fears. You can insulate yourself. And you can and should do the same for your children.

Later editions of Spock's book added a few correctives to what critics, by the time the sheltered and spoiled baby boomers became teenagers, decried as a dangerous "permissiveness." By then, however, the effects had set in. It may still be too soon to tell what they were on the baby boom generation; its full history has yet to be written. But among the baby boomers' parents, one aspect was evident: America was full of anxious, fearful people, doing all they could conceivably do to hide or smother their fear, to insulate their children from it, to wish it away, and to dream of a safe, secure, and better world.

This response may have been more properly called comforting than permissive and wasn't anything new, but this generation took it a step further. Its fear became a fear not of progress but of history, of not wanting to see it repeated anytime soon while also fearing the unknowns of the future. It wanted somehow to freeze things as they were, or as they imagined they might have been, at some time before everyone's lives were dominated by fear. Most people could not remember when that was. It was not when some of them were born, during the Red Scare of the previous postwar period. It was not when they were children, during the Depression. It certainly was not when they were teenagers and young adults, when some said the world might come to an end, when panic—think of Orson Welles's 1938 *War of the Worlds* broadcast—became such an easy thing to foment. It fit a familiar pattern. It was still there, primitive, immoral, and it had to be tamed or denied.

Discipline against fear straddled the line of the individual and the group, between perceptions of power and powerlessness. Individuals could be afraid. Society must not be, lest it give in to panic. Yet social repression in the name of social stability can make some people even more afraid, or at least more anxious. Anxious individuals, Freud had written, transfer their anxiety back upon society in an outward direction, in the form of aggressive fear. They then recoil inward, on the hunt for subversives, threats. Then the cycle repeats itself.

Each time, though, it carries a different manifestation, and in practice the boundary between fears directed inward and those directed outward can be hard to discern. What about the Reds under the beds? Were they internal manifestations of an external threat, or the reverse? This generation's fearmongers, our own Poujades, had different targets and different methods from his, but their sources of resentment were similar. They were not just scared. They were scared and small-minded. They knew at some level that many people in many places around the world were much worse off than they; at the same time, though, many of them were (and are) opportunists of the first order.

As we'll learn in the next chapter, Americans had a rough time adjusting to the postwar in any event; the American dream didn't kick in for another few years. But most people had life's basics. Most of all they still had their democracy. "Democracy," Bruce Catton has written, "means the end of all fear." Does it? What if some

Americans feared what the war had done to them? What if it had destroyed their capacity for democracy? How could they recover it? Did they want to recover it? Fear was America's enemy, to be sure, but it did not fight alone or for itself, when it had become afraid, to an extent, *of* itself. Given that, could the country and its democracy endure another war, especially if they won?

Fear hit back with a vengeance, in the name of American democracy. Good taste, good manners, civility, gentility declined and deteriorated. High government officials attacked one another in the press; unions fought industrialists; farmers complained and withheld their products from markets; people sounded petty, angry, nasty. It was the climate of George Orwell's *Animal Farm*, which was finally published in the summer of 1946 after having been rejected by a number of publishers, including T. S. Eliot at Faber & Faber. He told Orwell that his "pigs are far more intelligent than the other animals . . . so that what was needed . . . was not more communism but more public-spirited pigs."

There were, alas, a few traitors among us. The public-spirited may have tolerated them once; their brains were put to some good use during the New Deal, but no longer. They had infected our most cherished public institutions like a virus. They were in our schools and universities, our churches, our newspapers, our film, radio, and theater companies, even in our army, and at the highest levels of our bureaucracy—starting with the State Department.

Security in the State Department during the war was poor. This was not necessarily for nefarious reasons—although we now know there were a few spies at work—but was mainly due to the generally disorganized, confused, and quick expansion of what had long been a sleepy bureaucracy. Slippages will happen, and they did. It was just a matter of time before Congress began investigating, and not much longer before breaches of security were conflated with disloyalty. The congressional apparatus, led by the House Un-American Affairs

Committee (founded in 1938 but with antecedents going back to 1918), was well in place, as was the executive apparatus, led by J. Edgar Hoover's industrious Federal Bureau of Investigation. It was even known to tap the phones of lawyers in the Justice Department, and induced Ronald Reagan to be a secret informant. Truman was neither the first nor the last president to kowtow to Hoover or to accede to his inquisition, however much he may have hated it.

Indeed, loyalty checks of one kind or another had been going on since 1942 as a wartime necessity. In 1946, Truman ordered a review of them, which resulted in the creation of a new commission with more powers of investigation and enforcement, and by early 1947 a new Loyalty Program. He never said there was anything wrong with this; he merely said that it had been hijacked by politics.

In the summer of 1946, Byrnes, testifying in Congress for the State Department's annual budget request, was inundated with demands for evidence of disloyalty. He said the department was doing all it could. Congress was not satisfied. It gave State and several other departments new powers to dismiss suspected officers. State did not make much use of these powers, and so was singled out again. It had not done enough. Waiting for the disloyal to act and get caught was too risky, and the administration had already shown itself to be incapable of stopping the traitors in time. The thing to do was to investigate everyone in advance. Once they were cleared, they and the country could feel safe.

The hunt would culminate with Senator McCarthy's waving sheets of paper in the air; with the Hollywood hearings in 1947; and finally with the Alger Hiss trials and their revelations, from 1948 to 1950, when Hiss and his nemesis, Whittaker Chambers, assumed the roles of martyr and avenger. The testimony might have been comical had the effects not been so dire. We hear, for example, a Hollywood studio boss say during congressional testimony that he would be happy to add a few more names to the list of traitors if the committee so desired. Lest anyone doubt the truth, "you'll find a hammer and sickle on their rear ends," he said.

These episodes were not, as Truman once had the poor taste to describe them, a mere distraction. For now the culprits, or victims, were less prominent. There was, typically, a "Mr. Blank" who for unknown reasons began to be tailed by two FBI agents in the summer of 1946. They followed him, talked to his friends, neighbors, and coworkers, photographed him, showed the photos (one of him with a female colleague crossing a street) to his wife, and so on. About a year later he was fired, no reason given. He was not allowed to know it nor to resign or appeal. He lost his savings and nearly his house, but found another job in 1948. He was lucky. There were many stories like this and many worse. By the time the hunt was all over nearly a decade later, thousands of people had lost their jobs; some lost much more.

Poujadism's effects, even at this early stage, were not measured solely in livelihoods. They also cheapened the culture. "About 90% of USA needs to be rescued from vulgarity," the young writer William Gaddis wrote to his mother from Panama in 1947. "Doubtless the most critical time in history." Was it? Who said what was vulgar? What was necessary?

It is interesting that so many Americans read newspaper comics—they accounted, for example, for a majority of the Hearst Corporation's income. Yet during and even after the war, heroes like Superman (born in 1938) were less alluring. Readers, according to the historian John Lukacs, were more interested in simple escapism or plain "shiny and tacky" triviality. (They also were more interested in astrology, for some reason.) As for the news business, certain practices augmented triviality. Henry Luce, for example, in his quest for middlebrow homogeneity, devised the system of "group journalism." Writers were not the same people who did the research. The researchers, usually women, compiled lists of facts. The writers, usually men, assembled them into stories. The "result," noted Peter Drucker, then getting his journalistic feet wet, was that "the writer does not really understand the facts, and the researcher does not really understand the story."

Readers and readership were debased, for neither the first nor the last time. John Gunther, who surveyed typical readers of the country's largest-circulation newspaper, the *New York Daily News*, has quoted some of their opinions:

> Russia shows by its spy activities in Canada that it badly wants the atom bomb, so I say give the bomb to Russia the same way we gave it to the Japs. . . . Churchill was right. F.D.R. was the best President England ever had. . . . If we taxpayers were consulted, there wouldn't be one U.S. soldier on foreign soil. . . . We should announce in plain words that if ever again a nation attacks us every man, woman and child in that nation will be condemned to death. . . . As soon as I see a war looming, I am going to take a plane to Cuba post-haste, and then to South America, and I'm never coming back.

The simple story: fights with Congress, fights over the Russians, fights against the now jaded legacy of FDR. The statements also speak to the American love of simplicity, which is hard to distinguish—at least in many newspapers—from a fixation with triviality. Triviality is an anodyne formulation of the actual obsession in popular culture, which is with the easy and digestible and addictive. The obsession is not especially American; the country did not have a monopoly on tabloids. But its size, the volume of its voice, the seduction of its image, and the propensity to repeat down to the lowest common denominator give a formidable place to such trivial pursuits. Americans in the 1940s were no less passionate to "expose," to vilify, to celebrate, to scandalize, to curse, to worship, and, most of all, to resist the impulse to leave most matters and other people well enough alone. Poujadism was its own talisman. The exhaustive, trivial tendency extended from the daily crime report to the sports pages to politics. There are the same urges, the collective passions of a democratic people, as Tocqueville would have said: the mass primitive culture of a democracy in heat.

Lowest common denominator—all three words matter, especially the middle one. The malefactors of triviality often will say that they are just giving the public what it wants. What could be more profitable, more honorable, more democratic than that? What is so wrong with it? But we know the idea of a homogeneous public is a half-fiction. In fact the contents and their placement are determined by a small minority of opinion leaders, often self-selected, who profess to simplify, exaggerate, circulate, and magnify in the public's name. They follow and lead the public mood, and profit therefrom. They prompt people to fear, not necessarily out loud, but sometimes subtly, through their selection of reporting and language, in order to dish out a paradoxical feeling of comfort in the perverse guise of a tar-and-feathering or a bloodletting. Satire, on the other hand, is really the only way to combat and undermine Poujadism. Satire rarely sells.

American fads are good to study because there are so many of them and they rise and fall so quickly. They are as competitive as any other aspect of national life. Who is up and who is down has been the national sport for a long time. Accordingly, McCarthy rode a wave of mob passion. He latched on to the great fear and made it work for him. No longer were people so concerned that democracy could prevail. Now it was simply down to us versus them, down to fear. He had as much to do with promoting the fad of a witch hunt as it did with promoting him.

We could claim that triviality is a placebo for indecision—or for the fear of decision—when decisiveness proves too scary or difficult; or we may depict Poujades as just another crop of boosters and competitors, who are, again, as old as the Republic. Neither explains fully why McCarthyism became so all-consuming, and so nasty, or, apart from the international setting, which was an obvious and important conditioning agent, why it happened exactly when it did. Americans after the war should have been magnanimous, peace-loving, tolerant, thoughtful, and decent. What accounts then for the meanness? The petty, angry, malevolent, and malicious echo chamber? Was it a national exorcism, where citizens needed such people in order to feel virtuous? We would be presumptuous to reach that verdict on a mere suspicion. This in turn recalls the historical bromide, popular among some twentieth-century historians, that American freedom has always depended on some degree of oppression, as though the nation's creed were so bifurcated and dialectical. It is a convenient explanation for why some Americans are always searching for and finding an enemy; when one recedes, another takes its place. This is difficult to prove or even believe. A more convenient and simpler explanation for divisions in 1946 is the first one. It came from politics and the peculiar mixing of probity, chauvinism, and caprice which makes real decisions difficult but quick choices easy. When in doubt or fear, moral exhibitionism usually works to bide time.

It is often said of populists that they are merely the lowly born out to find and humiliate someone lower than themselves: purveyors of "the socialism of fools," as anti-Semitism was once called. In this instance, however, some of the McCarthyites had a point. There were spies in the U.S. government. There were attempts by the Soviet Union to recruit and exploit friendly sympathies of Americans and others among America's friends abroad, just as Americans and their friends attempted to do to the Soviets. There were consequences too. It was no accident that the Soviet Union succeeded in exploding its own nuclear weapon in 1949; the atomic spies played a role. Even a hint of truth made people more afraid.

Fear is at the root of Poujadism. The reactionary tendency is not so much a failure to manage fear as it is, especially in America, an alternative means of offense presumed to be a defense. The difficulty with fear when mongered by Poujadists was that the threats were rarely self-evident. You could not tell a traitor by looking at a face; there were not obvious external markers. You had to probe, cajole, blackmail, scorn. For this reason—its duplicity—this reactionary movement was generated internally by those who may have feared some quality in themselves, perhaps more so than had other reactionaries. Recall how quickly the nation's institutions had begun to change. Truman had integrated the armed forces and established the U.S. Commission on Civil Rights. Racial and ethnic divisions certainly persisted and may even have been exacerbated by wartime and postwar disruptions, but now it became convenient to fear even more insidious enemies that had infiltrated society without our knowledge. Alienation had met new potential. Different enemies were easier to fear and therefore easier to hate.

There was this other side to the Poujadist reaction. It came from what we might call a form of Manichaeanism that prefers simple, adverse choices: good guys and bad guys, separated (ideally) by a line on the map, another frontier. When the frontier no longer held, the fear turned inward; the bad guys lurked at home. The simpler and the starker the map, the more necessary it was to believe they were there. This is what happens to a society that lives by its fears, whose fears and therefore whose purges must be, in Acheson's classic phrase, "clearer than truth." As he and Vandenberg told Truman, the American people would never support the sacrifices needed to wage the Cold War unless they were truly scared, as Acheson said he had been when he returned to government and his fears took the place of worries. It was a devil's bargain: fear is a hard emotion to control once let loose. But it is a rare leader who can withstand a fearful public demanding action.

The American brand of Poujadism was not perfectly synonymous with populism, therefore. It was anti-elitist in a familiar, Know-Nothing way, but also boorish, trivial, pandering, petulant, angry, and highly patriotic. Its aggression was as much outer- as inner-directed: it is almost impossible not to regard the tenacity and brashness of Poujadists as the product of tremendous self-doubt or even self-hatred, very deeply buried and concealed by a thick layer of disgruntled audacity. How much these people take their cue from more reputable leaders is also unclear. Would Joe McCarthy have thrived as easily in a country led by a less cantankerous and insecure president? In 1946 the country had yet to experience the worst excesses of McCarthyism; they lapsed by the more confident middle 1950s. The collective psychology of Poujadism is complicated. We can only conclude that indecision cloaked by resolute pique can be as contagious as the base resentment upon which Poujadism feeds.

Chapter 7

Coal and Steel

But though we are a very sick society, we are not a dying one. The slugging match will not turn into a knife fight. Social discipline will reassert itself, the productive system which ended the war at a pitch beyond anything the imagination had conceived will begin to produce goods.... The convalescent people will resume an adequate minimum of decency, honesty, and honor.

—"The Easy Chair," July 1946

The "Arsenal of Democracy" was a moniker coined during World War II by another Frenchman, Jean Monnet. Monnet had a knack for getting to the source of power, and for knowing the ways of Americans. He spent his young adulthood wandering around North America selling cognac for the house that bore his family's name. He went on to learn the nuts and bolts of finance in the United States. There he formed friendships with American empire men such as John McCloy and John Foster Dulles. Monnet cultivated a reputation as a Frenchman the Americans could trust, so much so that "The Battle Hymn of the Republic" was played at his funeral at their request. Monnet knew and liked Americans. He became the point man for Allied purchasing during World War I. He resumed the job during World War II, making sure that those fighting fascism got the planes, guns, and other matériel they so badly needed. After that war he and his network of collaborators channeled American largesse to France, and to the rest of Europe, and sought to transform all three in the act.

Today Jean Monnet isn't well known, at least not in America. Others have received credit for the phrase he left in the mouth of

Felix Frankfurter, knowing the influence the latter was said to exert upon President Roosevelt. Instead Monnet is known by most people—or, more precisely, by most Europeans—as the father of the European movement. It began not with a flag, an anthem, a currency, a parliament, or a number of bloated ministries, but rather with a very simple idea: that France and Germany, if they were not fated to make war upon each other, had to integrate. Integration meant adding, or preferably multiplying, the number of economic ties between them. This began after World War II, by necessity, with the two industries they depended upon most: coal and steel.

The idea was not original. Monnet's innovations were mostly operational. He had a sixth sense for getting things done. It was not complicated, though it could look that way. The talent came mainly from a blend of insights into the ways of power, and persistence in getting the right people to listen. Monnet once said that he was willing to undergo any amount of humiliation or frustration to see his ideas take root. His character was uncommonly strong in this way.

Truman's was not. As we have seen, the president was not a patient man, and he hated slights. He had the good sense to absorb them, some of the time. We note the photograph of Truman selected by Dean Acheson for display in his memoir: the president's back facing the camera, one arm behind, palm open as if holding a gun, pressing into the bend of his taut lower back; a pose, Acheson wrote, that was "eloquent of the man."

Truman was not known for his eloquence either. Acheson had been generous. The president was, however, known for his backbone. It could be strong, yes. It was almost never supple. But it somehow needed reinforcement—the press of the open palm posed a question. It was not a backbone made of steel, iron, or any other strong metal or amalgam. It did not gird, in other words. It needed girding, a buttress. Made of what? From where? That it eventually came to reside in Acheson's brain was not necessarily ironic (although it does nicely explain the inclusion of the photograph), but this was still in the future. The photograph was taken during deliberations over what to do about Korea in the summer of 1950. Acheson, head cocked and topped by a white hat, faces him watchfully like a sheriff.

Four years earlier, Truman had been on his own. His buttress was the act of contention. When challenged, especially in a way he regarded as unfair, his backbone stiffened, as he liked to say, hard as a cob.

Monnet's plan was in another vein. The merging of the French and German coal and steel industries in what Monnet called a community, and overseen by a High Authority—over which, in turn, he would preside—was its keystone. The Coal and Steel Community, and the cooperation and confidence it brought, would underwrite a larger political and eventually cultural association as its beneficiaries would over time develop supranational allegiances. The backbone, in other words, was external to the man and the idea: it had objective value; it projected strength outward, above and beyond itself.

The moment in America went by the name of "reconversion." The image was straightforward enough: what had been a wartime economy needed to redirect or reorient itself to peace. But the chosen term, with its spiritual undertone, was one that a man like Monnet may have liked. Truman, so far as we know, did not. He knew a good deal about the previous state of affairs from his time in the Senate, as we have seen. Where production was concerned, he knew the tricks and where many skeletons were buried. As far back as the middle of 1944 he had sponsored legislation in Congress to plan for reconversion. He knew how much these industries meant to the economy, how much they had grown, how powerful they had become. Now he was president, and reconversion came sooner than expected, in part because most people who had not known about the atomic bomb presumed the war would last at least another year. Truman would choose the pace and extent of reconversion, not they. Soon after taking office he issued a twenty-one-point program. It was not enough.

For as much as the structure of the American economy—and of American society—would undergo great change during the next decade, it did not redirect or reorient itself singularly so much as become the field for powerful interest groups to wage battle over the future direction of the country during what Alonzo Hamby has termed "an attempt to govern by the principles of New Deal liberalism in a conservative age." The battle was probably bound to happen, most historians would say; but it happened then, and it happened on Truman's watch. He may have been happy to play it by ear and let the economy rearrange itself on its own time; if he had had any grander plans, he did not make them well understood. He was not only vague but also occasionally incoherent on the subject, but he would be forced into a succession of corners and would react.

Or so he may have thought. Because the question of reconversion was not so much about how far and how fast, but was more basic: how much to preserve of the old ways, how much to restore, and how much to reinvent. It was, as Hamby has stated it, a political question over the role of industry in the economy and in society, the role of government, the relationship between industry and labor in a post–New Deal America. Much of that was up in the air in 1946.

There are one or two more facts to remember. One is that the war was won, according to many Americans, by the country's vast productive machine—more vast than anyone had thought possible right away, even Monnet, who had been one of its biggest cheerleaders, having trouble persuading his American colleagues during the ramp-up to war that all those airplanes could be built, and then some. We shall return to this point in chapter 10. The second is that the production machine worked so well because all its sectors came together in the name of wartime solidarity. There were a few threats, a few near misses, but no giant wartime strikes, at least not on the scale of what would follow. There were no major pay cuts. In fact, workers were earning more than ever, on average, and more people were employed than at any other time in recent memory. But this production effort, this system, had been reengineered to supply the war, and now the war was over.

The wartime managers were divided over what to do. Some said everything should go back to normal, to a prewar way of doing business—or really a pre–New Deal way—without much regulation, many controls or taxes. Others said that was impossible. The economy was now too big, and there were too many cross-dependencies. The war economy had been good, very good. Some forty-five million Americans were employed in 1940; five years later this number had risen to sixty-five million. Median family income was about $2,600, more than double what it had been before the war. Yet the concentration was stark. Take military contracts: as early as the summer of 1941, a mere fifty-six corporations had around 75 percent of the dollar value of all contracts. Meanwhile, the average price of food in 1943 was some 47 percent over what it had been in 1939, and this had been *with* price controls.

Reconversion would take time. Producers and consumers, and the many people who fell somewhere in between, however, sought to use the mission of reconversion to further their own vision, or lack of vision, of what the American economy should do and be.

Already back in 1944, members of Congress went to battle over the shape reconversion would take. There were, for example, two contending bills for unemployment compensation. Americans had known this was coming. One year earlier a majority of respondents to a Gallup poll, nearly 60 percent, said that unemployment would be the biggest postwar problem. Only 13 percent said peace. Now on the Hill the fight was over who should determine rates of compensation, the federal government or the states. In this case, the states won. It was the New Deal fight all over again: states versus feds, price controls versus wage controls, industry versus labor, the country versus both unions and big business, farmers versus housewives, and big business versus the government.

No one view in the end would prevail, not entirely. There would be no victory—not for business, not for labor, and certainly not for government, including the president, who waded into the middle of a giant mess in about as thoughtless a manner as a president could.

His plan at first was to demobilize everyone right away; terminate the war contracts, also right away; close or reconfigure the production plants back to a civilian economy; keep prices stable, and wages too; end all other controls; and do whatever else was necessary to stabilize incomes and purchasing power. Simple points, clear-cut yet ambivalent: reconvert immediately to a peacetime economy, but put the consequences, including the pain, on hold.

The first part came quickly enough. Some $35 billion of wages were threatened by the cuts in wartime spending. More than two million civilian jobs were lost by the end of August. Two billion dollars of war contracts with General Motors, for example, were canceled, and GM fired 140,000 United Auto Workers. These were consequences of quick, firm decisions.

No wonder people worried. They had the so-called reconversion jitters. Would it work, whatever "it" was? What if it did not? Then what?

Reenter Mr. Baruch.

At the end of 1943 he too had begun to agitate for planning the postwar economy. He also warned that doing so could still impede the war effort; it would take discipline, a dispassionate mastery of the facts. So he pulled his team together and they produced a report that appeared in February 1944. Among other things, it suggested a plan for the redistribution of war surplus, for which Baruch would recommend the capable Will Clayton as administrator, as well as investments in medical care for veterans, unemployment insurance, job placement, and retraining.

Baruch plunged ahead with his usual tough-sounding optimism. He told Henry Wallace that there would be no recession after the war. It all came down to confidence, still in abundance. It's not certain that Wallace shared that view, but he did know one thing: "The old boy is still a clever operator, apparently placing a small bet on the possibility that I might one way or another eventually be in a position of some power."

There was another name, another power, on people's lips that became the lightning rod of reconversion. This was the Office of Price Administration, or OPA. It had been charged with managing wartime prices and rationing. It was obvious that it would need to be dismantled at some point. A battle ensued over when that point would come. OPA finally went out of business at the beginning of 1947, but its dissolution was a long-drawn-out affair, accompanied by much hand-wringing. In any event, nearly all price controls were already gone by the end of 1946.

Getting rid of OPA had been popular, briefly. Farmers in particular had hated it during the war—it kept their prices down—and farmers, especially big farmers allied with the transportation industry, gained a reputation for being one of the more recalcitrant interest groups. During the war this and other lobbies became better organized and, some said, more opaque. So too, others said, did their antagonists, principally OPA. Congress voted to kill it, but Truman vetoed that. It lingered on, until finally it was gone. Some farmers, at least, were happy. John Gunther talked with one of them:

FARMER— . . . Who killed OPA?

REPORTER—The President vetoed it.

FARMER—I thought he was for it.

REPORTER—He was and he says he's just begun to fight for it, but he wanted more price control so he killed what there was. He blames Senator Taft. . . .

FARMER—How's that? I thought Taft was against price control.

REPORTER—No, he says now he's for price control.

FARMER—I've missed a lot during the harvest. Whatever happened to that fellow Bowles?

REPORTER—He quit.

FARMER—But I thought you said the Administration was just beginning to fight for price control. Isn't Bowles for price control?

REPORTER—Sure, but he recommended that the President veto the price control bill and then he quit....

FARMER—We've had a whopper of a wheat crop.

Taft was Senator Robert Taft, son of the president and bastion of his party, "Mr. Republican." We shall return to him later. Bowles was Chester Bowles, then an eager New Dealer, a rich advertising man from Connecticut who later made a name for himself as one of the first idealistic casualties of the briefly idealistic Kennedy administration. Fifteen years before, he looked very much the New Frontiersman ahead of his time, earnest yet personable, in the jaunty way of the WASP, but also by his happy confidence invoking a nostalgia for the New Deal at the moment when its days looked to be numbered. "Bowles operated," Tris Coffin has written, "with all the enthusiasm of a small boy digging a hole." He now was head of OPA.

Bowles relished taking on his fellow Yale man, the mighty Taft, known for his self-importance and, at least in public, humorlessness. Bowles was one of the people (Dean Acheson was another, as we'll see) who knew the right way to get under his collar. Coffin has described one of their confrontations, in April:

Senator Taft said dryly, "How can you hold prices down when wages go up?"

The witness asked patiently, "Can I answer?" There was a roguish, schoolboy look on his face.

Democratic Senator Murdock said angrily, "Give the man a chance to answer."

Bowles explained, "All through the thirties wages were increased. Costs went down and profits went up."

Senator Taft stopped him sharply. "Lots of people are going out of business these days."

Bowles argued back, "There are fewer bankruptcies now than ever before."

Taft bit off his words impatiently. "Bankruptcy is going out of style. They just quit. . . . You did not answer my question."

Bowles replied good-naturedly, "Obviously, I am never going to satisfy you."

Senator Bob Wagner of New York, the old progressive fighter, was slumped in his chair. He watched the exchange through partly closed eyelids. He was sick and tired.

Chester Bowles could not save OPA. He had plans of his own, namely, the Connecticut governorship. He got out in time and Truman bore the brunt of OPA's demise. He had told people he would never remove price controls while there were still shortages. Then he did. The laws of economics applied their full force. A "reckless group of selfish men," as he called them, withheld supplies, in this case of beef and pork, to raise prices by curtailing demand. Restaurants stopped serving steaks, or just closed. Sam Rayburn, Speaker of the House, would take to calling the upcoming midterms in November the "beefsteak election." The name stuck. Truman for his part found an easy enemy:

My young infantryman gave his legs and would still give his life for this glorious country of ours. My young conscientious objector was and is willing to do the same thing. . . . [T]hese greedy industrialists and labor leaders who are now crying beef and bacon made no sacrifice, gave up nothing to win the war. . . . You've deserted your President for a mess of pottage, a piece of beef—a side of bacon. . . . You've decided that the Office of Price Administration should be a goat and a whipping boy. You've decided not to support price control although price control has saved your bonds, your insurance policies, your rent—in fact has kept our economic structure sound and solvent.... I can no longer enforce a law you won't support, botched and bungled by an unwilling Congress.... Therefore I'm releasing the controls on meat and will proceed to release all other controls in an orderly manner as soon as I can.... Tell 'em what will happen and quit.

This is what happened: Average rent went up, in some cities, by 1,000 percent. The price of butter went up by 25 percent. The price of steak, as we have read, went up as well, in some places almost doubled. There were fewer cheap trolleys and subways, no more ten-cent Sunday papers. Soldiers were seen selling "Welcome Home" signs, begging for a place to live. It was no wonder that Mr. Levitt found so ready a market for his new identical, prefabricated houses built on their tiny lots in former potato fields. By 1950 there were some two million new houses, many paid for through the GI Bill. Yet it was no surprise that soon after the demise of OPA, many people wanted price controls back. Some people feared for the future of free enterprise. Prices wouldn't stabilize fully until 1949. So said those who again could find a nickel beer, an affordable sixty-cent steak dinner, a standard batch of groceries for under four dollars, and pie à la mode for a penny.

Wages did not keep up. In fact they did the opposite. The average manufacturing worker got $47.12 per week in April 1945; by July 1946 this had fallen to $43.07 while the average price of consumer goods rose by 11 percent. Tris Coffin met a welder who told him that his take-home pay had declined by $15 per week—this when he spent $10 per week on rent, $25 on food, $8 on clothing, $2.50 on medical expenses, $3.29 on insurance, $2 on the dentist, $6.30 on income tax, 66 cents on Social Security, $1 for a telephone, and $1.50 on utilities; and there was a tonsil operation for his child, which came out of his savings. His total weekly expenses: $60.25. His wage: $66.

Truman took some measure of pride in what he had done, on paper. The country had a balanced budget in 1947, he said, and a surplus the following year. He eventually brought down the public debt by some $28 billion. But something was amiss. The economy may have been going in the right direction of prosperity, but many Americans, including politicians, did not necessarily notice, given how far the economy still had to go. Recall that back in 1945 the government had to raise $243 billion in loans and $179 billion in taxes. The Employment Act of February 1946, which created the Council of Economic Advisers, would go on to have a big effect, said Secretary of the Treasury Fred Vinson, but it brought neither full employment nor peak production. It was, by Truman's own admission, a holding tactic. Prices continued to rise, which some people, like John Snyder, who succeeded Vinson, figured would solve the problem.

The problem, though, was psychological as well as economic. The war had enhanced the assertiveness of workers, not merely in the United States. Related to assertiveness was querulousness: "Rosie the Riveter isn't going back to emptying slop jars." Labor/management committees had only just gotten off the ground, without much durable success. Some efforts to solicit and incorporate "suggestions" for "improvement" were laughable. A few people distrusted the committees as a socialistic body. Others feared they were an attempt by industry to co-opt and emasculate labor. These really were, at the time, measures to improve war production. Not many people said they would survive, no matter how well or how poorly sold.

Who were these workers? They were no longer the workers of the Great Depression and the New Deal. No longer the masses. They were properly patriotic and established members of the middle class. This was how most regarded themselves, and still do. Whether this was due largely to prosperity, to security, or to the war cannot really be known; it was due to some combination of those things. Suffice it to say that the American worker was not a separate class or species. He was just "another American citizen who wanted to know what the score was," and such people, like most members of the middle class, are known above all for their tenacity, even brutality, when their status is threatened. There is not much to insulate them from the thing they dread most of all: falling into poverty, or being treated like someone who has. If anything, the war reaffirmed the paradoxical self-perception of the typical worker as someone deserving of respect while at the same time feeling free to disparage those of both higher and lower rank. In fact, during and right after the war, the most fervent opponents of strikers were veterans; but that did not last long.

Who was big business? Had it not been decimated by the Depression, or gone into permanent hiding? Wasn't it residually fearful of a run on its profits and practices? Indeed many remained scared, or were even more scared, of the specter of socialism. Some corporate memories were long. The first progressive Roosevelt—Theodore— came into office promising that no harm would come to big business, and he proceeded with his trust-busting. It hurt some trusts but was not fatal. That wasn't very long ago and neither was the Depression. There was a good deal of residual mistrust and a deficit of faith and confidence in the powers of the all-mighty industrialist. Many people retained their skepticism even after industrialists signed up as dollar-a-year men during the war. The businessmen celebrated as entrepreneurs, individualists, risk takers, and heroes had given way to the organization men with their charts, experts, and the like.

Meanwhile, workers remained fearful of unemployment and inflation, while businessmen worried about the workers. Both groups may have wanted a pause and a recovery, and both might have sought less of an us-versus-them public image, a new debate between growth and redistribution, and more of a practical guide on how to get by and get ahead in the new circumstances, however loath they may have been to admit it.

As for the war itself, it had been sold like a stock, and the public now demanded a dividend. Many people owned that stock, and somehow the dividend had to match expectations. Baruch, who knew a thing or two about the stock market, had warned of that. Rising prices would accelerate inflation. The value of the dollar would fall. Savings would disappear. Taxes would become more burdensome. The people would become angry. Baruch confronted the president, who said he was not all that worried about what he called a "bulge." Baruch disagreed: "There's no holding it." Surely not, Truman said: "Ain't I the boss?" "No," said Baruch. "In this matter, no one is the boss; the laws of economics are." He concluded with one of his bits of park-bench wisdom: "There is only one way to avoid inflation and that is not to let it start." As for the stock market, well, "[w]ith rare exceptions, stocks are high because they are good, and stocks are low because they are of doubtful value."

Social solidarity had a diminishing quality, at least at this time. It would return, just not yet. Barriers remained, starting with the layer of hostility that lay near the surface of economic life. It was tied to mistrust and suspicion: of wartime bosses and profiteers, and of the country itself, which may have still needed or wanted a firm guiding hand to tell it what and what not to do. There were fears of all these things, with good reason. Many people also realized, though probably less consciously, that the fears predated the war and so were smothered by it, and were allowed therefore to fester. It was true that there had been a recognition of the value, even the necessity, of good planning, and that the government, with the right discipline and good faith, and more than some direct involvement of the private sector, could act productively and openly—that is to say, democratically. But for some reason or some set of reasons, this faith, however meager, was now in jeopardy.

The president had been thinking along similar lines. He told the country back in January that "1946 is our year of decision. This year we lay the foundation for our economic structure which will have to serve for generations."

Others may have had that idea. Now that the war was over, it was perhaps time for unions to compensate for their wartime restraint. Nineteen-forty-six would see the largest strikes in recent memory. Although most were settled, they would continue off and on until the end of Truman's presidency.

The president did his best to look and sound nonchalant amid the discord. He received visitors, accepted presents, journeyed about the country. "We are having our little troubles now—a few of them. They are not serious. Just a blowup after a let-down from war." They wouldn't last long, he said. He might try to steer a middle course, to play the role of honest broker. After all, he was a Democrat, wasn't he? Weren't they his constituents? His base?

Some base. Strikes hit nearly every major industry: coal, railroads, oil, rubber, automobiles, lumber, electricity, meatpacking, steel. There was even a tugboat strike in New York that stranded British war brides on the Queen Mary, which meant that some were unclaimed by their suitors. A mere three months after V-J Day, the United Auto Workers demanded raises equivalent to what they had been earning during the war, but adjusted for inflation and a peacetime work schedule. This meant, for example, that General Motors would need to give their workers a 30 percent raise. The response was predictable—refusal, then walkouts. The strike, involving some 177,000 GM workers, lasted for 113 days. It would be hard to overestimate the impact of this strike given the central place of the automobile industry, and of GM, in the pantheon of American prosperity.

This strike was, however, comparably tame. So was the great steel strike in January and February 1946, which lasted twenty-six days and affected over one thousand companies across thirty states. The president dragged both parties to the White House—Big Steel, represented by Benjamin Fairless, and the steelworkers, represented by Phil Murray—and banged their heads together until they came to a compromise. The workers got their biggest raise to date.

Much of that was down to the businesslike manner of Murray, a Scottish immigrant who was respected, even beloved, by the rank and file of his union. Murray had, "it would seem, only one thing to fear." This was his former mentor, protector, and boss—we are tempted to add the adjective "the legendary"—John L. Lewis.

In April the coal miners followed suit. Four hundred thousand of them went out on a strike called by Lewis. Roosevelt had managed to parry him during the war, using every ounce of that president's legendary charm and deviousness. Truman had very little of these; and whatever else he was, Lewis was popular, powerful, and probably fearless. It is hard to imagine that he had much respect for Truman either. Truman reciprocated:

> He is a Hitler at heart, a demagogue in action and a traitor in fact. In 1942 he should have been hanged for treason. In Germany under Hitler, his ideal, in Italy under the great castor oil giver, or in Russia now he would have been "eliminated."

The strike lasted through May and resulted in millions of tons of coal lost. In this case, Truman decided to fight. Some people may have thought that "Big John" impressed Truman. That was doubtful. As with Stalin and General MacArthur, this president relished standing up to a bully, or being given the opportunity to be seen doing so. In private he may have felt differently; we do not really know. During the coal strike, the government intervened to manage the mines while negotiations continued over the course of the summer. Side agreements were reached, and the sides muddled through. But in November, Lewis called a new strike, and because the government was now managing the mines, the strike was against it. Here Truman stood firm. He did more than that, by his account: "There was only one thing . . . to do when he called his strike by indirection and that was to take him to a cleaning. . . . He is, as all bullies are, as yellow as a dog pound pup. . . . I had a fully loyal team and that team whipped a damned traitor." Lewis was found guilty of contempt of court and fined $10,000; his union was fined over $3 million. "The White House is open to anybody with legitimate business," said the president, "but not to that son of a bitch." The coal strike was over.

This was not the sum of labor troubles, however. Back in May two railroad union leaders, Alvanley Johnston, grand chief of the Brotherhood of Locomotive Engineers, and Alexander F. Whitney, president of the Brotherhood of Railroad Trainmen, threatened a strike. Truman wasn't worried; he knew them, and even had counted Whitney an old friend, but no longer. He greeted them at the White House with one of his curt, the-buck-stops-here remarks: "I brought you gentlemen here to discuss with you the emergency of a railway strike. I think you should call it off." Whitney asked if the government would break the strike. Johnston suggested the president might not have all the facts and would welcome a discussion. Truman interrupted him: "Yes, I do understand it. I know all about it."

The two agreed to postpone their strike for a few days, but no compromise resulted. So on May 23 the strike came. The railroads stopped. There were runs on gasoline and food. Much of the country was on pause. Truman had already called the two men back to the White House. Whitney insisted that the strike must go forward. "Well then," Truman said, "I'm going to give you the gun."

It was one of the largest railroad stoppages in American history. Truman chose severe action. He announced that he would draft railroad workers into the army and order them to work. Republicans on Capitol Hill, who were no fans of the strikers, bristled. Taft said, "The idea of drafting men to work is the most extreme form of slavery." The Republicans then repudiated the president, voting against his measure. Truman appeared at a press conference in a neat blue suit with polka-dot tie. "Do you agree with Whitney that you have signed your political death warrant?" he was asked. He had no reply. One question followed after another. He tried to stay calm, then could no longer. He said this was an emergency and he had taken emergency action. That was what presidents were supposed to do. If that meant he had to "deputize" workers, so be it.

The crisis benefited one person close to the president: Clark Clifford. He fought a battle of his own against the White House's designated labor envoy, John Steelman, an Alabama college professor who prided himself on being conciliatory. To Clifford, Lewis and the other labor leaders had thrown down the gauntlet and made the dispute personal. Truman had little to gain by meeting them halfway, or anywhere, really. Like a good staffer, Clifford perceived this as, and depicted it to be, a challenge not only to Truman personally but to the office of the presidency. Challenging Steelman, he pushed for a confrontational position. Truman's own temper probably decided it. Clifford was now the so-called point man. He sat down to draft Truman's response to the railroad strike.

To the many detractors who snickered at Clifford's Hollywood looks, the moment could not have been better scripted. Truman's own draft was full of spleen: the labor men had "flouted, vilified, and misrepresented" his administration. Congress? A mere bunch of "Russian Senators and Representatives" who were "weak-kneed" with no "intestinal fortitude." The solution? "Let's put transportation and production back to work, hang a few traitors, and make our own country safe for democracy." Clifford avoided such language, but not all of it, in the speech Truman gave on May 24. It said the strikes were akin to the attack at Pearl Harbor.

Truman was scheduled to address Congress in joint session the following day. Clifford worked with FDR's old speechwriter, Sam

Rosenman, on two versions of his address: a tough version, and a mild version in case the strikes were settled in time. Steelman meanwhile continued talking with the labor leaders, without much progress. Clifford went with Truman to the Capitol, carrying both versions of the speech. The president began reading the tough version. Suddenly Clifford got a phone call from the Statler Hotel, where Steelman was. "We have an agreement!" Clifford rushed into the House chamber, walked over to the Senate secretary, Les Biffle, with a note, and Biffle passed it up to the president in midspeech.

Truman looked at it, paused, and smiled. Then he read the note to the joint session. "The House chamber erupted in cheering—longer, louder, and more sustained than anything he had experienced before or was ever to experience again in Congress." So remembered Clifford, who got a nice promotion. One or two members of Congress accused Truman of staging the entire thing. But so far as we know, he did not.

There would be more struggles with labor, and even more industrial seizures (like that of the steel mills during the Korean War, for example, which was overturned by the Supreme Court). There would come the Taft-Hartley Act of 1947, which passed over Truman's veto. Yet labor's power was on the ebb. It was unlikely again to cause as much disruption or achieve as much notoriety as in 1946.

What did the big fight mean in the end? We are tempted to say that it was another episode in the grand three-way struggle of capital, labor, and the government, with the government, in the shape of Truman's backbone, asserting itself over the other two. This was true, but only so much. It was about something else, something different. This fight did not reverse the basic New Deal arrangement; that would not happen until the late 1970s and early 1980s. It was not about the welfare state per se—or the American version of the postwar push throughout Western Europe for a much larger peace dividend to honor all that sacrifice. The American people might have repudiated Truman for any number of reasons, but he was not Winston Churchill in 1945, and the American electorate was not about to reject him in favor of someone who promised a permanent welfare state. Truman may well have wanted to give them at least some of that, but reconversion was not meant to be so drastic. Books like James Burnham's two classics, screaming of statism, corporatism, and conflict, made a splash in the public mind; but Truman was no ideological warrior for or against Keynes or Hayek. Nor was he a visionary like Monnet, or as shrewd. He thought and acted on a more basic level. He coasted, until challenged, when he resisted in favor of what he said was right. His administration accepted many of the premises of the welfare state and did not deny the power or the import of the New Deal. His Fair Deal, announced in 1949, proposed a few big things like national health insurance, but decided few big questions. It was eloquent of the man.

His challengers and critics asserted something similar, coupled with an insult: that Truman was unfit, unwise, or just plain out of his depth, all of which he was, to an extent. There was the state of the American economy and its implicit social contract. The war was so big, so demanding of labor and resources. It was not enough to win the Four Freedoms; some Americans sought a grander, nobler, fairer society. Truman could not possibly have delivered that in so short a time. His enemies, starting with John Lewis, smelled his indecision, which they took to be weakness, as fighters are brought up to do. What they did not count on was the president's resoluteness. Roosevelt's methods were gone. For now, dissembling was not Harry Truman's métier; self-righteousness and self-possession were.

It was ironic that consensus became the ultimate result. To this day, those historians who wrote during the 1950s and into the middle 1960s are called the consensus school, residing up on "a promontory of American self-satisfaction." At some point between the end of Truman's presidency and the winding down of the Korean War, the beginning of a consensus did emerge: an anti-Communist mission backed by a forward posture abroad and a mild welfare state at home, except in defense, where it was somewhat less than mild. This probably would also have happened had Dewey won in 1948. Even the Taft wing of the Republican Party, had it come to power then or later, would have had to accommodate itself to the consensus in some fashion. But consensus did not come from nowhere; it did not forge itself. So how much credit ought we to give to the pitched battle with the unions and the corporations of the early Truman years? Did it in fact perform as a release to allow a stronger consensus to emerge? Or did that happen in spite of the bitter fights Truman and his enemies waged? We could also ask the question about the economy. Nearly every war is followed by a postwar recession. Did the one in 1946 need to be as bad as it was? Might it have been worse? How do we find the right measurements to advance the cause of consensus? Or was consensus merely the default position?

The Fair Deal did not answer these questions. They would take another decade or so to work out; or maybe they just were eclipsed and shelved again by Cold War prosperity. Another, apparently fortuitous boom postponed and papered over a bevy of unmade political and economic decisions. Consensus nevertheless dominated the Cold War years, not just in America but also, and just as importantly, in most of its allies. Having persuaded every administration from Truman's to Carter's to underwrite the postwar prosperity of Western Europe, Monnet must have appreciated it, but he did not take it for granted as some of his American friends may have done. As the Cold War wore on, few of them would challenge the primacy in coal (and later oil) and steel; they were more interested in butter and guns. The surfeit of one made possible a debate over the right balance of the other. Whether it could also be a fair balance was something that Truman never really resolved. Like Hamlet, he was a bit (maybe more than a bit) egocentric. His backbone, he may have imagined, held up the country's; or maybe what he really needed was to liberate the backbone, and the ego. He and his ego did prevail over those arrayed against them in the dark days of 1946; but they were also lucky.

Chapter 8

New York City

The historian in me should have come awake in the almost monotonously beautiful countryside of New York.

—"The Easy Chair," August 1946

Many of the New Deal's best and brightest migrated in the 1930s to Washington, D.C., which had been readorned with proud neoclassical buildings, wider avenues, and brighter suburbs. During the war the migration continued, particularly from Wall Street as lawyers and bankers discovered a passion for public service. But Washington was a pale competitor, or really no competitor at all, at least in culture, to New York.

There are other cosmopolitan, polyglot cities—Chicago, for example, with its boosters and its immigrants—but Chicago was still of the heartland, superimposed upon the wider nation. It was and in a way still is the last great American city. New York is something else. New York did not look around its hinterland but inward and upward. For all its capacity to generate brilliance and treasure, and to lure so many talent seekers, it consumes as much as it produces, including "reputations, many of them fraudulent." It lives for those who seek to live well, and to gain all the means necessary to do so.

New York was alluring but, to some, no doubt bewildering, the repository, real and imaginary, of all the flora and fauna of midcentury life found in the tales of Joseph Mitchell: rivermen, cops, barkeeps, old families and gypsies, rats, clams, and whiskey-sellers. It is the world's microcosm, "a Constantinople, a great Bazaar." It is all-American, therefore, so not really American at all, even perhaps "a European city," as James Bryce once called it, "but of no particular country."

It is said that decadence is the handmaiden of high culture, at particular times and places. Paris and the other cities had given way to New York in the forties. Think of Vienna in 1900, Paris in the 1920s, Berlin in the 1930s, Rome in the 1950s, or London in the 1960s. The 1940s belonged to New York. The shift had begun more or less in the 1920s, slowed during the Depression, then began again after the war. New Yorkers could almost smell the scent of the city's renewed splendor. The foundation had been laid; the structure was already in place. A couple of decades earlier New York became such a capital for cultural exiles, especially African Americans and midwesterners; theirs and others' movements exploded the city's population. But in the 1930s one trend went in reverse. Hollywood attracted artists as well as their entourages; but just as wartime Washington never stood a chance of overtaking New York as a cultural magnet, Hollywood (we shall return there in our final chapter) succeeded by only a fraction. New York remained the growing mecca, attracting the cleverest provincials and enriching the locals, the purveyors and the consumers of cultural capital. So too with the other kind of capital, the liquid kind. The rich in America like to buy or bankroll vehicles of culture: studios, radio networks, newspapers, sports teams. But the most upwardly mobile, in the traditional sense of class, at least, have preferred to "support the arts," paying for museums, ballet and opera companies, galleries, literary journals, and Broadway plays. What is interesting, then, about these cultural brands is that in twentieth-century America they had their own geographic nucleus, which was not the imperial capital (Washington, D.C.) or the nascent entertainment capital (Hollywood), but rather the capital of the world.

Everybody who was anybody, the cliché held, went to New York. Its population in 1940 stood at nearly seven and a half million;

by 1947 it had risen by several hundred thousand more, which placed it at the top of the population table, not just of cities but also of states—third in the nation, not counting New York State—and of countries, exceeding forty-one out of seventy-five.

The traveler John Gunther, from whom these figures come, visited New York after having toured much of the rest of the country. As we see elsewhere in this book, he was partial to statistics. His New York selection is suggestive of his interests and curiosities. The shops featured "anything from Malabar spices to stamps from Mauritius to Shakespeare folios. A stall on Seventh Avenue sells about a hundred different varieties of razor blades." The city

> houses no fewer than 36,000 different industrial concerns.... Manhattan alone employs more wage earners that Detroit and Cleveland put together; Brooklyn more than Boston and Baltimore put together; Queens more than Washington and Pittsburgh put together.... New York uses about 34,500,000 pounds of food a day, 98,000 tons of coal, and 4,000,000 gallons of oil ... has more than 43,000 elevators (about 20 per cent of all in the country), which carry about 17,500,000 passengers daily ... has more trees (2,400,000) than houses, and it makes 18,200,000 telephone calls a day, of which about 125,000 are wrong numbers. Its rate of divorces is the lowest of any big city, less than a tenth that of Baltimore, for instance ... [and it has] 33,000 schoolteachers ... and 500 boy gangs.

New York was never cheap, but just after the war it was possible for an aspiring writer, artist, or composer to set up in a hotel, eat, and survive. There were the boîtes, the watering holes: Bleeck's, the Blue Angel, Lüchow's, Spivy's Roof, Ticino's, Tony's on 55th Street, the White Turkey. They gave shelter and sustenance to many who headed there to seek their fortunes, their dreams. There was this expectation. We quote from Vance Bourjaily's *The End of My Life:*

"Wait until after the war," Benny said.

"After the war," Freak said, firmly, "we will go on a party."

"We'll go on hundreds," said Benny, gloomily.

"But one special party," Freak insisted. "Right after we get back. In New York. We'll get an apartment and fill it with women."

"And liquor," Rod said. "All kinds of liquor."

This was it: New York also was aspirational, a quality and mood as old as America. "Making it" there had a precise meaning. It suggests—now anachronistically—the line in John F. Kennedy's inaugural address about what you can do for your country. Setting up in New York wasn't a civic gesture in itself; many people who did were just as keen to see what New York could do for them. Nevertheless, fame and fortune were more a means than an end. Would-be New Yorkers sought, and decided, to make a bigger mark.

They needed New York to gauge their talents. New York evidently needed them. It did not have a monopoly on high culture; it never has had one. But to understand the literary culture of the country at midcentury, we really must begin and end with a New York standard. It was not just brash or thrusting, then, not vainglorious, myopic, exclusive, or singular. It was all these things and something more. It was absorbed in itself, self-regarding, self-improving, and occasionally self-defeating (as with, for example, the shooting star of Truman Capote). Fame had such an effect on people. The culture of the city sapped and surged energy at the same time. It was prudent and brave. It sought preponderance, even predominance, but its culture was never universal. It mixed with Hollywood, for example, but never embraced it. Gore Vidal spent some time in Hollywood, and eventually went nearby to die, but California to him was more a curious object of anthropological attention—a template for understanding the past ("Screening History," as he called it in the book with that title)—than the fountain of creativity and lust that New York had been in 1946.

New York's position at the cultural center of the country was less spatial than conjunctural. It had to do with the midcentury transfer or migration of European culture to the West along with so many European exiles. True, some of them—Christopher Isherwood, Aldous Huxley, Thomas Mann—made their way to California, but New York was a more natural inheritor. New Yorkers did not see it that way—they were progenitors. The New York art and publishing markets were happy to supplant those of Paris and London, as were the fashion houses, although their position was shorter-lived. Paris and Milan would recover soon enough. There was, however, no lost generation of Americans packing up for Paris this time. Berlin lay in ruins. It would be rebuilt, but it would not regain its status as a world cultural capital until the 1990s. London was now the capital of Austerity Britain. This generation's Hemingways went to New York.

Literary or high culture in America is a mixed business, however. America has a low culture, someone once said, and she ought to promote it. It tends not only to emanate in waves from Hollywood or the thousands of radio stations that broadcast (the term is apt) their sounds to the populace, but also to gather in clusters of like-minded creators. That is, most culture does not usually take the shape of the ink blot, spreading, merging, and coagulating. Artists live and work in "colonies" or hubs that are archipelagic and tend also to be insular, growing by hunch more than by choice or plan. New York was such a colony.

Being insular—that is, self-referential—also included the recent past: "1919! 1919!" exclaimed Delmore Schwartz of the *Partisan Review*. "It's 1919 over again." Victory this time was less enthusiastic. There were celebrations, as we have noted in chapter 1. They were tempered, however, by the different entry into the war, different from previous wars, when many Americans went proudly off to earn their bit of glory; but not this time.

The aftermath was different too. This postwar generation, again, could not be lost, for the appellation was already taken. Worse, they had to recognize the earlier generation as a predecessor and model, and the intermediate period of the Depression as having laid a layer of topsoil upon social distance. The new war sealed it and separated it. This postwar literary generation lay on the other side of the separation, also self-conscious and distinct, and distant, even untouched, by its predecessor, yet at the same time not permitted or tempted to imitate it. A journey from belief to alienation was no longer possible, because this time around, alienation also was passé. So they turned further inward, became critical, restless, impatient, and jaded in another way, in a way that said they had never been disappointed, that they still sought to live well, but that they also never expected much from anyone.

This much is evident in some of the writings of the period: in Bourjaily's *The End of My Life* (1947), Norman Mailer's *The Naked and the Dead* (1948), to an extent in James Gould Cozzens's *Guard of Honor* (1948), and in the works of other, now obscure writers like John Horne Burns and Alfred Hayes. The jaded idealism that appears in their books is almost always a mask, and a poorly drawn one at that. They sound cynical, but they are not. The problem they had was in not really knowing what lay behind their own mask. They were at once "terribly aware" and aimless, muddled. The reaction to that paradox was natural. We have seen it already several times in our story, from the waffling of Harry Truman to the wandering families of veterans to the quixotic bellicosity of the labor unions. The individual felt, and was, lost—true—but this was not the source of the problem, the last target of displaced and somnolent idealism. No—it was something else. It was, simply, the system.

Today we are so used to hearing the term that it glides past our consciousness, but we usually understand it as political, institutional, and ideological in the language of the late 1960s. Here it means something related but different—a system of human nature, that is, an ecosystem. America in the interwar period was still in most ways a country of individuals, and of individualism. Americans still believed in that particular ism. They still do today, but they also treat it more hopefully than empirically; that is, individualism is a wish, an aim, but not a fact of life to be taken for granted. Rather, the system, however defined, is. The Great Depression set that up. The system—pockmarked, vengeful, perverse—touched this postwar generation in a way that their predecessors had not experienced. How to subvert something as vague as a system, especially when some of it resides in all of us?

It is a slippery target, hard to hit. Let us take a figure of the earlier generation, John Dos Passos. The critic John Aldridge has reminded us that Dos Passos's first novel, *One Man's Initiation: 1917*, published in 1920, appeared again in 1945 with a different title, *First Encounter*. Dos Passos attempted to bridge the difference by also reminding us that his generation saw the earlier war through rose-colored glasses, then played their disillusion to the hilt. What to do now? He was not sure. But he did know that they "would not be writing books like *One Man's Initiation*. . . . [W]hat he may or may not have sensed was that, because of these differences, they would also have little patience with anyone who [did]." He had, in a way, recognized great literary success and a great failure. His country had disappointed him, and he had disappointed himself. He had also grown too big, or felt too small, in New York.

It was not 1919 all over again, precisely because people like Dos Passos were still around. The world the veterans met promoted itself as the same, or nearly the same, as the Lost Generation had met on their return—a world desperate for normalcy, desperate to be left alone and not to be asked to do too much, and a world that, in turn, demanded a great deal. A world with less hope to give yet one that demanded, and reaffirmed, more in the sacrifice of friends, comrades, family, youth, simplicity, health, spirit, and autonomy. Some turned back—some, like Philip Rahv, who cofounded the *Partisan Review* with

William Phillips, back to the great moderns. He sought, like any modern, to create a new cathedral, less by destroying the old than by supplanting it with his own creation, one of the most fashionable New York magazines of the day, in homage to and in imitation of its predecessors, especially European. For their part, European travelers to New York—among them Albert Camus, Le Corbusier, Cyril Connolly, and Simone de Beauvoir—were intrigued, jolted, and bemused. Now Europe was no longer the beacon or the principal treasure. American literary culture had again declared its independence, and this time Europe had migrated to it.

Phillips and Rahv had a rival on their home turf: Harold Ross's *New Yorker*. The *Partisan Review*'s tone was intelligent, engaged, ideological, and sometimes monumental, in the modernist sense. It is no surprise then that the magazine had a rather short tenure in fashion. The *New Yorker* is still here. It was none of those things; rather, it was clever more than intelligent; postmodern *avant la lettre* rather than modern. According to Aldridge:

> The influence of *The New Yorker* magazine on the values and attitudes of this generation of writers will probably never be accurately estimated.... The code ... is evident in everything they write.... It is a code based on a fear of all emotion that cannot be expressed in the whisper of a nuance. It depends for its existence upon a view of the world as a vast cocktail party where the very best people say the most frightening things about themselves and one another in a language which the servants are not expected to understand, where the most tragic confession of personal ruin is at once diluted by the ironic titter in the speaker's voice.

The *New Yorker* had had a good war. Its circulation rose from 172,000 to 227,000. It made the transition from prewar to postwar with a boost. Its appeal to the upper reaches of the middlebrow was just about right. It skirted rather than succumbed to postwar cynicism. *Partisan Review*, by contrast, nearly succumbed and then reemerged with a cause—anti-Communism. Its style and code would migrate by the middle 1950s back to Europe or to the academic margins. The *New Yorker* would stay put. The writers it championed, the Updikes and Fadimans and Mailers and Matthiessens, emerged as the familiar postwar generation most people know. Theirs was a fluency, an easy way of storytelling or criticism, with just the right amount of pique, stretching mores but not going too far. They had made it in just the right way. They would come to dominate New York's literary culture well into the 1970s.

The *New Yorker*'s own portrait of Mailer, back in 1948, hinted at the trend. "We'd heard rumors that Mailer was a rough-and-ready young man with a strong antipathy to literary gatherings and neckties," wrote Lillian Ross, "but on the occasion of our encounter he was neatly turned out in gray tweeds, with a striped red-and-white necktie and shined shoes, and he assured us that he doesn't really have any deep-seated prejudices concerning dress. 'Actually,' he said, 'I've got all the average middle-class fears.'" She went on to describe her subject as "a good looking fellow of twenty-five, with blue eyes, big ears, a soft voice, and a forthright manner," who was set to earn around $30,000 in royalties. His success with *The Naked and the Dead* did not unnerve him. After all, he had enrolled in Harvard at sixteen, done his war service, written a couple of books, each in a few months. *The Naked and the Dead* took him sixteen. "I'm slowing down," he told Ross. She wrote, "He thinks *The Naked and the Dead* must be a failure, because of the number of misinterpretations of it that he has read." Mailer explained:

> People say it is a novel without hope.... Actually, it offers a good deal of hope. I intended it to be a parable about the movement of man through history. I tried to explore the outrageous propositions of cause and effect, of effort and recompense, in a sick society. The book finds man corrupted, confused to the

point of helplessness, but it also finds that there are limits beyond which he cannot be pushed, and it finds that even in his corruption and sickness there are yearnings for a better world.

Perhaps the contrast is overdrawn. Mailer says all the right things here, does he not? He pays homage to displacement. He almost mimics it. He raises the possibility that his success and the success of his ilk are the result of painless imitation. They rode the trend, in other words, but, like our empire men, they did not set it.

If not, then who did? The *Partisan Review*? Yes, to an extent, but it would be undone by the consensual 1950s. Other writers were not, but instead were undone by the failure to ride another wave: Burns, Bourjaily, Hayes, Robert Lowry. Some, like Burns, were briefly in vogue. Only very recently have they been rediscovered, thanks in good measure to Vidal, whom we may classify together with them but who, because of his own special origins, his versatility and knack for publicity, avoided their obscure fate. It was Vidal who described these years as a golden age, not only of American power but of American culture, centered on New York. It was Vidal's own happiest period, he said: New York "was as delightful a place to live in as to visit." One of his favorite local characters was a writer, also later forgotten: Dawn Powell.

She was, he recollected, "our best comic novelist ... always just on the verge of ceasing to be a cult and becoming a major religion," yet "rather like a Civil War cannon ball" with her "familiar round face with its snub nose and shining bloodshot eyes." Powell came from small-town Ohio. She set up shop in Greenwich Village in 1918, married an advertising executive with whom she had a disabled son, and never left. She had modest success, but her diary tells of constant struggle: health, money, work. Until Vidal promoted her in the 1980s, her novels had ceased to sell. He regarded her as "America's only satirist," which was about the highest compliment Vidal could give. She returned the favor, noting him as a "Luciferian-looking young man.... Very gifted, brilliant, and fixed in facility as I am." Yet, she wondered, "the trouble with being a clear, sharply cut, extraordinary individual with a rich articulate gift is that no characters can equal the author himself, whose muscular skill directs most complicated interplay of plots, guides contrapuntal themes with suave, veiled power and a doom-like rhythm that compels and lulls."

To both Powell and Vidal, New York combined the vital and the infuriating. Vidal left it for Hollywood and then Italy. Powell remained, drank heavily, and died from cancer. Both spent a good deal of time sniping at the men Powell called "somberly riding geniuses—the clumsy, overweight jockeys on the delicate Arabian steeds." That is, the writers touted by the *New Yorker*, and Mailer specifically. Vidal disparaged Mailer, whom he claimed to like. He called him "a Bolingbroke, a born usurper...a public writer, not a private artist...bold...loud, [with] brighter motley, and...more foolish bells." Powell's satires are written in this way; through her bloodshot eyes she saw to the core of nearly everyone and reconstructed their character as best anyone could, a slash-and-burn writer whose prose sings with empathy, however hard it may be to diagram. Vidal too looked in the mirror every now and then and acknowledged, though he did not attain, the greater whole. His own memoir is called *Palimpsest*, which is about as honest an image as there is for the life he led and the books, essays, and plays he wrote. Once again, he deprecated his own tendency first in others. About John O'Hara, for example—a writer already of some stature who adjusted well to the wartime mood and concocted some memorable and emblematic characters (Joey Evans of *Pal Joey*, for example)—Vidal wrote:

> In many ways, Mr. O'Hara's writing is precisely the sort Santayana condemned [in Somerset Maugham]: graphic and plausible, impertinent and untrue...the naturalistic tradition....

> Like so many of O'Hara's novels, the book [*Elizabeth Appleton*]
> seems improvised.... To be effective, naturalistic detail must
> be not only accurate but relevant. Each small fact must be fit-
> ted to the overall pattern as tightly as mosaic.

The mosaic of New York was loose, not tight. It was not a cloud
of confetti, yet it landed closer to the spirit of O'Hara's stories than
to the classically naturalistic novels of Zola. Powell wrote in this
vein; Vidal toyed with it. Those genuine naturalists who literally
stood apart, that is, in the provinces, tended to be otherwise type-
cast. J. F. Powers, as fine a Method actor as any, only that his métier
was the written word, kept away from New York. He had not fought
in the war but spent part of it locked up in the Sandstone Federal
Penitentiary in Minnesota as a conscientious objector. He preferred
Chicago and referred to the two cities as partaking in some form of
combat. Today he is still known as a "Catholic writer." Shirley Jackson, who kept to Vermont, saw some of her best work published in
the *New Yorker* but was not of that city or its culture. Despite her
own literary rehabilitation she is considered slightly too strange to
be so celebrated.

New Yorkers may have felt that their time at the top of the class
was short, that their window of opportunity was brief, their freedom compressed. Or they may have suspected this without quite
knowing it, which could have almost meant self-censorship. William Phillips, for instance, said of Alfred Kazin, "Alfred insists so
much on sincerity when he's talking to me that he makes me feel
insincere." On the other side was James Agee, also a sincere man,
who "felt this chill and withdrew." His dalliance with the *Partisan
Review* set was brief. O'Hara's characters also are inflected with sincerity, sometimes perceptible, sometimes sought. This was the
curse of Year Zero: a promise of rebirth, of making the new day the
first day of your life but knowing, somewhere, that this was not
really possible, or that it was possible, just not likely. Theirs was a

cautious rebirth, if that were an option. They had survived Year Zero. Now they were in Year One; life from now on would be different. This was the trope that was common in Europe, at least. In some places, notably in Germany, it was also called the "hour of the women," where the wartime victimhood of some women was contrasted with the shame of some and the heroism of others, even now, as they gathered the rubble to rebuild their villages, towns, and cities. Back in New York, however, a condition of rebirth was less straightforward, for there had been less destroyed in the first place.

This brings us to two additional New York art forms: on the stage and the canvas. Both Method actors and abstract expressionists relished the total immersion that also stood apart, placing or suggesting a new distance from meaning. Was this the end or the means of cultural renewal? Was it also the result of surviving the war comparably unscathed? What were the outlines of its freedom? Was it a type of freedom that is the opposite of survivor's guilt? That is, was it another lazy, default sense of superiority bred of luxury, a luxury that itself served only to delay or mask the moral duties of the artist?

Another *New Yorker* mainstay, Mary McCarthy, issued an easy dismissal, according to William Barrett: "The language of our current American drama has forsworn literature; as written, it could hardly be read; and as spoken from the stage, could hardly be heard. The famed Method acting, which had become a kind of sacred fetish among the professionals, was really a training to teach actors how to mumble."

Most plays during the war in fact had been of the escapist genre and had little to do with the war or with Method acting. One or two that dealt with the war were, in the words of theater critic Wolcott Gibbs, quoting George Jean Nathan, "mechanical and doughy as an Automat pie." Yet according to Gibbs, Broadway had a good war as well. The 1944–45 season saw ninety-five openings, which exceeded in number those of the previous two years. "It was all wonderful," he concluded, "but the unfortunate fact remained that the best plays had to do with such strictly nonmilitary personnel as an enchanted rabbit, a Norse matriarch, a pillar of Boston society, a neurotic cripple, and a colored daughter of joy."

Paucity was not so simple. It was not that people wanted to forget the war for the sake of forgetting. Escape involves more than amnesia. Rather, it was that audiences asked playwrights to draw dark contrasts. Audiences, even New York audiences, Gibbs noted, did not want complexity for its own sake. The war demanded contrasts, in other words, and although audiences would rather not be reminded of all that was taking place over there (they had enough of that from the newsreels), they still craved a decisive tone. This is one interpretation. Another is that the old familiar genres just felt better. Rodgers and Hammerstein's *Oklahoma!* revived a 1931 play in musical form, which included excellent choreography. It was the Broadway hit of the 1943 season, with over two thousand performances to 1948.

Beneath the surface, however, a shift took place, even in the musical. The 1946 production of *Annie Get Your Gun* saw Ethel Merman offer what we might say was a small paean to Method acting. Gibbs appreciated her "gift of suggesting a wide range of emotion without perceptibly altering her expression—her leer is wonderfully suggestive but practically immobile; laughter disturbs her face only for an instant and then usually in only a rather chilly parody of amusement; and love for her, at least in *Annie,* is expressed by a look of really terrible vacancy."

If so, this would be a logical end to reinvention. The means are less clear-cut. The Method actors who founded the Actors Studio in 1947 broke away, but did so by the mastery of means, the blending of the internal with the external. The roles they played did not displace them from themselves or their audiences but, paradoxically, took what resided inside themselves and put it out there for all to see. It may have been a method of courage, or it may have been, just as well, a departure for departure's sake, as if to say, *We are now different. We act differently. We stand apart.*

"Everyone knew that the theater was never going to be the same again." These were the words of John Latouche, a lyricist and a popular New York figure, ventriloquized by Vidal: "Brando's changed the whole idea of what an actor is—the way Barrymore did before the war." For her part, Powell regarded the Method actors—in their previous incarnation as members of the Group Theatre—"like publishers, regarding the author and his work as nasty stumbling blocks between them and the public, and if they could only brush aside this horrid obstacle and act (or publish) freely without the barrier of writers' words, everything would be fine." No matter. What counted was "the feeling." Here the Method actors actually allow for more continuity than other literary genres, maybe because of their unusual place vis-à-vis more mainstream entertainment. Eugene O'Neill, a prewar figure, came out with *The Iceman Cometh* in 1946. The setting was prewar, as in pre–World War I. He wrote it right before World War II. So too did the Actors Studio link the prewar with the postwar theater, for the Studio, as we have noted, emerged from the Group. Tennessee Williams's *A Streetcar Named Desire* came in 1947. Brando had rejected a part in O'Neill's play; he accepted one, fortuitously, in this one.

A similar continuity happened with music. Latouche promoted a young composer and conductor, Leonard Bernstein. Latouche's zest, his exuberance, so much like his city, drew him to Bernstein, and was prescient. Bernstein's debut at Carnegie Hall "was the talk of the season, and a few months later his music at the Met for [Jerome] Robbins' ballet 'Fancy Free' was the next sensation." In 1946 Bernstein was in London, where he sold out the Royal Albert Hall. The *Times*, he noted facetiously, called him a "real Wagnerian conductor."

The visual analog to such continuity masquerading as rupture, we could say, was abstract expressionism. It has come to posterity as a by-product of the atomic age, of the need to protect, perhaps to hide, to lurk beneath the psyche by drawing it outward, at full volume, like Brando's rendition of Stanley Kowalski with his capacity for doing without thinking, casting forth emotion without any need for translation. This was Willem de Kooning, William Baziotes, and Jackson Pollock (said to be the model for Kowalski), splashing his paint across the canvas in a hysterical trance. Most such innovations, we could say, give themselves over to caricature, but how else do we come to remember and understand them? As visual adjectives grappling, DeVoto-style, for the certainty of strong verbs? Or do we think of them fatalistically, a progression, or a regression, away from representation, as if to say that the old modernists and then the war gave them little choice in the matter? They had to keep clearing away, uncovering, and then covering up in a dual mission of accommodation: not merely to Pollock's "painting out of the unconscious," but also to striking their own kind of balance between being individual, introspective creators and residents of a vibrant, all-consuming cosmopolis. A leading guide, almost a guru, to the art world of New York in these years, Hans Hofmann, preached the value of perpetual movement. Perhaps it was just that simple. To him, movement in all its variety underwrote, uncovered the essence of all that art and life were and ought to be. The art critic Jed Perl's verdict on Hofmann and the abstract expressionists could just as well apply to most artists in this milieu, after 1946 at least: "New York was a magnificent symbol of the new American prosperity, and even though the artists often regarded themselves as being out of step with a consumer society, their extravagant images could be seen as symptomatic of an era that—in spite of the Korean War, the Cold War, and the threat of the Bomb—felt to many like a time of expanding possibilities.... What was clear to just about all the artists was that the ball was in New York's court. The grand old themes now belonged to Manhattan."

It has been said that civilization itself is representational, that is, it is a reflective expression that achieves logical coherence only upon decline. Empires and their imperial culture do not usually pause to reflect as they rise. Few renaissances occur to people in the moment. Civilization represents, in both meanings of the term—representative and representational—both rise and fall, as in the "dialectical drama" or "extravaganzas" that Perl has set "at the core of Hans Hofmann's teachings." Put differently, somebody once said (the identity of this observer is lost) that the best sign of an empire's power and prestige is the quality of the coffee: if its power is waxing, the coffee is usually dreadful; only when it is about to collapse can one get a decent or even an excellent cup, for the quality of most things is relative to what came before, when luxuries of taste had not entered our experience and consciousness so easily, and before we had developed the right language to describe and demand them. All that, in turn, required the relative power and prosperity of noblesse oblige.

Sadly, no one documented, Kinsey-style, the quality of the coffee in New York at midcentury. From its art, theater, music, and literature, however, we gain a mixed picture. It may or may not have been dialectical. The culture of the city and the world it represented was sharper: its juxtapositions had become more personal. There was too much guilt for clarity—not merely survivor's guilt, but also a murkier feeling that the war was somehow America's fault, or that it had not entered the war, nor exited it, with an entirely clean conscience. Now another war, or something like a war, was appearing on the horizon. Unlike their counterparts in Europe, for whom the postwar era signified a new optimism and survival meant again that all they represented was not extinct, many American artists entered their golden age with an eye fixed over their shoulder.

The effect was to make some people weary: at having little to oppose that was concrete, including morals—previous generations has already done that—and at the possibility, or the probability, that troubles would continue, that it could all happen again, only that now, as the Second World War was to the First, it would be much worse; weary that the story was not over, but ought to have been over a long time ago, before they had even walked on the stage.

To Vidal the culture of the fantastic interim was not proud or decadent. It was not coincident with American rise or decline. It was uncertain, and this meant, again paradoxically, for some a sense of freedom and energy that recalled the 1920s and would come again, briefly, in the 1960s. Yet unlike their counterparts of those two decades, American artists in the mid-1940s were not exuberant or clamorous; their art was. They were for the most part, and against our recollection, timorous, not quite innocent but conscious of having lost innocence, and not quite prepared to see it gone. They were worldlier than their parents but not yet worldly. Their expression resided somewhere between a recollection of idealism and a gesture: genuine, in a guarded fashion. Guardedness was related to the above-mentioned frustration with political isolation and the unresolved pre–Pearl Harbor debate over intervention. Culture was perhaps a way out, an escape, as it often is or is described, although here too it was more a simple gesture of freedom. There also was a nostalgic premonition. Right after the war, artists felt free to create in a way that many had not remembered feeling for some time, and would not feel again. Why?

New York at midcentury stood somewhere between model and metaphor, between utopia and the future. It had become a mature city; it was no longer a boomtown. Its maturity resembled that of the European capitals some imagined it destined to supplant: a city that never slept, with neighborhoods of every shape and color, a boundless ambition with a circumscribed scope that clung to itself. This was the United States before it acquired the discipline, the so-called consensus, of the superpower; before it became the permanent underwriter of European peace and the world's crusader elsewhere; before the transatlantic fad of existentialism; before *tier-mondisme*, revolutions, and counterrevolutions; before the resurgence of the culture wars, with their tyrannies of ideology; before the attack of the primitives from Washington; before the resurrection of Babbitt from coast to coast. New York in 1946 was free and still self-consciously American. Its mind was open to the world but not possessed by it. Its spirit was blithe without being fantastical. It saw itself perhaps as a cosmopolitan compromise between traditional radicalism and innovation, but it too remained uncertain. "[W]hat did I have to hold on to?" William Barrett asked:

> A few memories of a handful of intellectuals in the milieu of New York City years ago. . . . It's a small world, as they say; and this one was a tiny bubble within the larger currents of American society. Yet, marginal as its existence might seem, it might not be without some significance. The microcosm reflects the macrocosm; the smaller world is a mirror of the larger one. And smallness here may have the advantage that within a narrower compass one may perhaps see more sharply defined the issues that are crucial to the larger life of the time.

Vidal was right. It was a wondrous time to be in New York. There was a blurring of limits, and a boon to the imagination. Indecision here meant lack of boundaries, and a special, fleeting liberty. The city and its culture had power and influence but not yet too much responsibility. It could produce, consume, and reproduce at will, without worrying about overstepping the mark or being condemned to insignificance. It looked carefree but was extremely busy doing the things it wanted to do, which began at perpetuating its own sounds and its own recent, as well as remote, images, sensations. Its leading figures had found, in some way and very briefly, a clue to taming fear. So we leave Vidal and his beloved Dawn Powell with a pair of typical observations on this topic. She, on a visit to Staten Island in May 1954, saw

[a] tall, distinguished looking white-haired lady mov[ing] down the walk, lightly leaning on a slender cane—a living reminder that Staten Island had its old wealthy aristocrats just as its broken old mansions proclaimed.

He recalled her description, about a decade earlier, during the war, of the sight of a man on Fifth Avenue and 55th Street about to jump from a hotel room window:

Look at the jewels, the rare pelts, the gaudy birds on elaborate hair-dress and know that war was here; already the women had inherited the earth. . . . Civilization stood on a ledge, and in the tension of waiting it was a relief to have one little man jump.

He concluded, "I know of no one else who has got so well the essence of that first war-year before we all went away to the best years of no one's life."

Chapter 9

Gaze Homeward

Just how deep or just how honest is this growing Western passion for the past? . . . Somewhere in this pumped-up saturnalia on behalf of retail sales there must be a few people who know what really happened.
                                        —"The Easy Chair," September 1946

America's long obsession with democracy was Henry Wallace's obsession. He gave it the romantic tinge that many uncommon men loved—the opposite of the tinge that Truman, the least romantic of politicians, gave to it. Idealism is a form of romance. Wallace was an American romantic. He could be sentimental, especially about nature, and about Franklin D. Roosevelt. Nothing was the same for him after FDR died.

Roosevelt had picked Wallace in 1940. Wallace's people filled the convention at Chicago in 1944, but this time Truman got the place on the ticket. Truman told Wallace that he was unhappy, never so much as at this moment. "You know, this whole matter is not one of my choosing. I went to Chicago to get out of being Vice President, not to become Vice President." Wallace was courteous. "Harry, we are both Masons." He offered his support. Truman acknowledged that he "was not a deep thinker like I was and he needed my help."

Wallace was also prescient: Truman "is a small man of limited background who wants to do the right thing. . . . [H]e is a small opportunistic man, a man of good instincts but, therefore, probably all the more dangerous. As he moves out more in the public eye, he will get caught in webs of his own making."

It was only a matter of time before they broke with each other. But that was just what Wallace allowed. He took his time, then he sprang.

Both men were midwesterners, although Wallace, from Iowa, was a different sort than Truman, from Missouri. The latter leaned south, the former north and west. Truman once said (with "a big grin") that Wallace had been "the best damn Secretary of Agriculture we ever did have." He may have believed it, but whereas for Truman farming meant aches, failure, and loss, for Wallace it was the stuff of innovation and the future. The hybrid seeds he bred and sold made him a rich man. Mainly, though, there was the stark difference in disposition. Truman, it bears repeating, was flamboyantly direct and blunt. Wallace was a walking daydream. Conversation with him took place on a nebulous plateau. Forrestal called this "Wallace's global stare."

It made Wallace a hard man to like, unless you were an acolyte. He barely knew senators, even though he'd presided over the Senate as vice president for nearly four years. He welcomed admiration: Senators Claude Pepper and Robert Wagner, for example, may have looked up to him and recognized him as their natural leader, as did most remaining New Dealers. But he was, in the literal sense, aloof. And he had not gotten there on his own: his father had had the job of agriculture secretary before him, under Warren Harding and Calvin Coolidge, so his stature was inherited. His name was already associated with the romance of rural progress and at the right moment in the country's history, when the average person would be hard pressed to name most cabinet members—certainly not the secretaries of state, treasury, or war, the three (the final one rechristened as defense) whose names would most come to mind during the second half of the twentieth century. During the first half few people had heard of them. But people did know the names of the secretaries of agriculture, interior, labor: Henry Wallace, Harold Ickes, and Frances Perkins were not quite household names during the New Deal, but they came close. Apart, briefly, from Ickes—more on him in chapter 12—Wallace was the only one left.

The war was not good to Wallace. He fought much of it at home in turf battles, especially with the secretary of commerce, Jesse Jones. Roosevelt kept Wallace at a distance. He gave him a few important responsibilities in supply and production. At one point he sent him on a long visit to China, where Wallace got interested in persuading the Chinese to acquire American tractors. As the New Deal left receded in wartime influence, or had begun to lay its best cards on the First Lady, the de facto head of the idealist, "progressive" wing of the Democratic Party (a position she would retain for life), Wallace's star faded. Truman retained him as a cabinet member, secretary of, of all things, commerce. Wallace raised the Jeffersonian flag against Truman's, against, in essence, Andrew Jackson's. He raised it at Madison Square Garden against the specter of a military-industrial conspiracy itself having been raised against an enemy, Soviet Communism. The enemy was not imaginary, though the conspiracy was, but no matter. Romance demanded simplification and exaggeration. Anyway, Wallace had a point: Hadn't America won the war? Wasn't Eisenhower's "crusade in Europe" over? How many more crusades were to come? For how long?

Wallace may have been sublime, but his followers, among them more than a few oddballs, were visible and charged. They adored him. To their ideal he dedicated his May 1942 address, "The Century of the Common Man," a dedication he would repeat in the title of a 1943 volume of essays and in his diaries. To others—such as General Charles de Gaulle, who concurred with the epithet—the war guaranteed the century would be thus. To Wallace it did not, and he worried. His problem was not one of inspiration but, like Truman's, of persuasion. Like many idealists, he disliked chitchat, disliked individual common men but revered them in the abstract. The mystical bent of "Farmer Wallace," as Alice Roosevelt Longworth called him, went even further. He had a bond with the land that was holy and visceral. He was a follower of the Russian savant Nicholas Roerich and Roerich's son George. Letters to the father addressed "Dear guru" were intercepted and published alongside forged ones by Wallace's enemies in 1948, giving ammunition to those who saw him as a seditious egghead. This Wallace was not, but he was a spiritual man—a dreamer, to be sure, and one in love with the abstract and the conceptual, but also at root a scientist who was satisfied only when he saw the abstract made real. Those who served under him recall him as a first-rate administrator, disciplined and able. His fault may have been not that he was too dreamy but that his aloofness came in automatic reaction to having the high expectations he placed in others dashed too easily. He sounded like an ungracious, self-important prophet. "Progressives," he pointed out, "are splendid critics but very poor builders."

Back in 1946, he still was tolerated by Truman, probably to appease the remaining New Dealers in his party. This did not appease Wallace. He waited through the summer and then, as we saw in chapter 5, pounced in the fall. By the end of September he was gone from the government.

The big straw for Wallace, as we have already seen, was the atomic bomb. The scientist in him knew the American monopoly was short-lived. The politician, perhaps the statesman, knew that it would tear apart the wartime alliance unless something was done differently in the new circumstances. To Wallace the answer was clear: atomic know-how had to be withdrawn from the calculus of rivalry, and that meant sharing it with the Soviets. This was a stark difference from the president, even before Truman had commissioned the Acheson-Lilienthal study. The challenge for those who took Wallace's position was not to sound like Soviet apologists, or worse. They said America's atomic monopoly exacerbated Soviet insecurity, which in turn justified Soviet actions in its presumptive sphere of influence. This was a weak argument, even for Wallace. He conceded that the Soviets may have had ill will toward us, or toward others, but why give them due cause? Preserving peace trumped the need to prove a point. Getting tough with them would only backfire.

Either they would become our permanent enemies or they would, for now, regard us as in cahoots with the British to deny them their proper postwar place in the sun.

Wallace chose instead to accentuate capabilities. We could not script Soviet behavior, especially Soviet behavior close to home. This was not our concern, so much, he said, as the effect a certain arms race with the Soviet Union would have upon the United States, its way of life, its security. In his long letter written to Truman in July 1946, he spoke from and about the homeland. The homeland was safe. It was powerful. It was, finally, beginning again to prosper. Why behave like insecure Soviets? Why throw out a fistful of self-fulfilling prophecies? But for argument's sake, if we are really so sure that the Soviet Union presents so large a threat, why not conquer her now, while we still can? If not, he wrote, then the

> facts rather make it appear either (1) that we are preparing ourselves to win the war which we regard as inevitable or (2) that we are trying to build up a predominance of force to intimidate the rest of mankind. . . . [Preventive war] is so contrary to all the basic instincts and principles of the American people that any such action would be possible only under a dictatorship at home.

He found no support from the president. Instead Truman leaked to the press word that Wallace wanted to give the bomb to the Russians.

There was more to Wallace's dissent than a roundabout effort to show he was not trying to program the Russian mind. To the extent that he held foreign prejudices, these were not so much pro-Russian as anti-British, in the usual midwestern way. Nearly every time he referred in his diaries to Winston Churchill, for example, it was to disparage Churchill's attachment to the British Empire, his desire to perpetuate it, his influence over Roosevelt. Wallace held little hope for Churchill's new successor, Clement Attlee, "a rather mousy little man who speaks without spark." No, the British were more or less all the same, "very likeable people but it seems to me their whole attitude inevitably leads to causing the other peoples of the world to feel inferior and fearful and therefore willing and anxious to strike out in a violent way as soon as they think they can do so with some chance of success. The United States is the only country which has gotten away in a big manner with resisting the British." So it ought to be. The country—his country—must look to and after itself, and the world would be grateful.

A curious exception to this was the novelist Roald Dahl, to whom Wallace took a liking while Dahl served in wartime Washington with His Majesty's Secret Service. It was said to be because Dahl resembled one of Wallace's sons. They would walk together often, ponder the future, and agree to disagree. With Dahl and, as we have read, with a few others, notably William Bullitt, Wallace could be solicitous in spite of strong disagreements.

Truman had been less so. "Wallace is nothing but a cat bastard." We can guess what he wrote in the letter demanding Wallace's resignation, the one he had to recall from him soon after sending it. The public line later would be that he had nothing against Wallace, really, but feared that he would be misused by those making up his entourage, which included some dangerous people. He needn't have worried. Wallace got a tiny portion of the vote in 1948. He did not pose a threat. He never convinced the American people that he was the one to keep them safe and, in a more basic way, to bring them the tranquility they needed.

Perhaps Wallace had been fortunate. A man so aloof could hardly have been a good president; a critique so pure could hardly have remained untarnished in power. His place in history is that of the noble loser. He could have done worse.

Looking back to Wallace's generation, we realize that the Jeffersonian vogue of the New Deal years was less a paradox, as it looked on the surface or in retrospect, than an adventure in statism. It was not the antithesis of the laissez-faire of the Roaring Twenties. That decade wasn't so much laissez-faire as it was Hamiltonian, according to the historian William Leuchtenburg, who has reminded us that Calvin Coolidge, after vetoing a farm bill while denouncing it as an improper intrusion of federal power, went on to raise the tariff on pig iron. This was the classic American political economy: some are in favor, others not. There was not much of a hidden hand if you looked carefully.

Truman was torn between twentieth-century Hamiltonians and Jeffersonians, depicting himself, and the government, as an "umpire" between interest groups in a way that was consistent with being a loyal New Dealer, or so he said. But a real diffusion of power back to the states? Certainly not. Jefferson, after all, was the first imperial president. Some people who speak of Jeffersonian democracy really mean Jacksonian. For unlike Jackson, Thomas Jefferson was an elitist and as abstract-minded as they came. The new vogue was of a different flavor. It was conservative, Poujadist, reactionary in asserting the will of the people and their entitlements over the moral paramountcy of the common man. Earlier populism too had been infused with romance and idealism. This may be seen in the murals commissioned for New York's Rockefeller Center; in the popularity of John Steinbeck; in the ambassadorial appointments of Claude Bowers and William Dodd, both biographers of Jefferson; in Bullitt's quixotic attempt to construct a Monticello at Moscow (although he persisted in keeping a portrait of Jefferson above his desk at Spaso House); and in the career and fame of Henry Wallace. How else to explain popular book sales? The historian Charles Beard's books did not do as well as journalist William Shirer's *Berlin Diary*, which topped the bestseller lists, Ambassador Joseph Davies's *Mission to Moscow*, or war thrillers like William White's

They Were Expendable or John Hersey's *A Bell for Adano*. This last one even won the Pulitzer in 1945. Then there was the biggest bestseller of all, Wendell Willkie's *One World*. All this was in the very recent past.

Now there was instead the bloody-minded tendency of the Truman administration to slash. Even as late as 1950, Louis Johnson at the Pentagon continued to reduce the size of the armed forces, right up to the eve of the Korean War. He slashed manpower, slashed the number of weapons systems, slashed the funds spent on training, on what we today call combat readiness, but he did what he was asked to do. He fought waste, inflation, and deficits; he forced through the unification of the armed forces. He left them confused, myopic, and desperately weak.

There was also, paradoxically, the new language of the day. "National security," for example, had become a mantra as early as the fall of 1945. It may be heard in the contrary fears of men like Forrestal and Baruch of a new mood of isolationism—or what they called isolationism—gripping the nation, which reminded them of the previous postwar, now the interwar, period. It may be heard in the transmutation of isolationism that now took place. It had split between traditional isolationists who, in George Kennan's words, "hold the outside world too unimportant or wholly wicked and therefore not worth bothering about, and those who distrust the ability of the United States Government, so constituted and inspired as it is, to involve itself to any useful effect in most foreign situations." Kennan counted himself in the latter category. Still others, like Beard, who had become virulently anti-Roosevelt, turned to the former, to "refined nostalgia."

Beard, as we'll see in our final chapter, sought a tabula rasa in which America could be free and safe. He imagined that it could exist if only Americans stopped bothering themselves so much abroad. He turned homeward and urged them to do the same, to cast the devils and "giddy minds" from their midst; to leave in peace;

to recall a time with more generosity and less cynicism—a time when strangers offered one another a job or a meal, when Americans may not have been so clever but were at least sincere, when they were less complacent, less solitary, more pacifist, protective, defensive. Now they were these things, yet they were also more fatalistic about the outside world, especially after Hiroshima.

"Oh, won't it be wonderful after the war / There won't be no rich, and there won't be no poor.... Why didn't we have this old War before?" So went the ditty over in Britain. Americans knew better. The Depression had taken care of that. They had survived interrupted, negated childhoods; they could hope for better in their dotage, but they could not take it for granted. They could more easily switch priorities—say, for example, to the local economy. Come home, build here; you don't have much to lose. All there was to lose, more so as the 1940s gave way to the 1950s and 1960s, was time. Your attention would be thinner and shorter, but you would be all right. You had the will to survive, and to thrive, here at home. Your will came from the heart more than it came from the head. Foreigners got it the other way around. That's why they were envious of America.

By now we have gotten to know some uprooted and rerooted Americans. They even resurrected the national calling card. Their country was once again America, no longer just the United States. They clamored for home and all its pickings—the comfort of familiar roles and institutions; the union boss, the symphony orchestra, the public school, the parent-teacher association, the Social Security Administration, Ford and GM. Security is known, as George Packer recently reminded us, by the preservation of these and so many others, and it is seen in the principal organs of information and opinion: the nation's great newspapers, then enjoying their own golden age of mass consumption. Take, for example, the *Chicago Tribune*, in the description of John Gunther:

[M]ore than a mere newspaper . . . it is a property in several dimensions, a domain, a kind of principality . . . aggressive, sensitive in the extreme, loaded with guts and braggadocio, expansionist, and medieval. . . . It is, like Russia, big, totalitarian, successful, dominated by one man as of the moment, suspicious of outsiders, cranky, and with great natural resources not fully developed; it has a strong nationalist streak, a disciplined body of workers, a fixed addiction to dogma, hatred of such assorted phenomena as the idle rich, the British, and crooked bourgeois politics, and a compelling zest to fight for its own. . . . Every *Tribune* employee has his teeth cleaned free twice a year.

Only the *New York Daily News* sold more papers, and it was a tabloid.

This is how to understand the homeward impulse in America. It was a feature of public opinion but, as Lukacs has argued, more of popular sentiment. Opinions can change at the drop of a hat, especially political opinions, and especially those concerning foreigners. One day the majority of Americans are pro-British and anti-German; another they are pro-German and anti-Soviet. But national sentiment runs deeper. It is more continuous. In mid-twentieth-century America it was protective, whether by isolation or by intervention, or, again to invoke Vandenberg's convenient term, by insulation, by any means necessary.

That sentiment recalled the dormant isolationism of the prewar years, but not quite. Wallace did not count himself an isolationist. Many of those who once had done so by now had caught the anti-Communist bug. In any case, isolationism had long been Eurocentric. Few isolationists had similar feelings about Asia (and even fewer about Latin America, which most people regarded as the United States' "backyard"). Some prewar isolationists became Asia-firsters and outright interventionists. They would go on to lead at the turn of the decade the who-lost-China crusade. Wallace offered an alternative with what once had been called the school of Peace

Progressives. It was not quite the one-worldism of Willkie either. It was not, in other words, an idealist bit of globaloney (the term was Clare Boothe Luce's). But it was romantic and, in Wallace's case, came to border on the mystical. Was insulation so unrealistic? What was wrong, really, with an America shorn of alliances and crusades, tilling its own garden, bettering itself and its people, upholding the freedoms of its citizens and its institutions, having a decent respect for the opinion of mankind? For a center-right country, or one that was about to become so, was such a position so bad?

After all, it was Truman's own position, evidently. Throughout 1946 he resisted the giddy minds; he kept Byrnes in place longer than he should have; as late as 1949 he brought back Louis Johnson. They sought a peace dividend and limited liability overseas. Beginning with Byrnes, they started out equivocal but became more rigid in their dealings with the Soviets. However, they had not really thought through the implications or the costs of that half-reversal. Byrnes may have imagined he could have worked out his own private modus vivendi with the Soviet Union, but Truman was not the type of president who could allow this. Byrnes's days were numbered, and for somewhat different reasons, so would be Johnson's. He resisted for as long as he could, but he was torn apart from within the Pentagon and eventually from without by a much superior infighter, Dean Acheson.

The most famous Cold War document from this period after Kennan's Long Telegram was NSC 68, which we have already encountered. It was a magnificent piece of policy entrepreneurship, sold behind Truman's back to nearly everyone (except Johnson) who mattered in the upper reaches of the bureaucracy, and then foisted on Truman after it was too well known to ignore. The nominal author was a onetime banker named Paul Nitze, one of the most adept bureaucrats ever to emerge from Wall Street. He augmented a fortune there as Clarence Dillon's golden boy. Inspired by the writings of Oswald Spengler, he took courses in sociology at Harvard, returned to Wall Street, then was brought by Forrestal, his mentor at Dillon Read, to Washington. Nitze, along with other later Cold War luminaries such as Robert McNamara, Walt Rostow, John Kenneth Galbraith, and George Ball, spent the war in relative safety figuring the best sites for American airplanes to bomb, and then surveying the damage. Later he became Kennan's number two on the Policy Planning Staff at the State Department. When Acheson took over as secretary, Nitze moved up to number one.

Full of the noir language that some people embraced by the late 1940s, NSC 68 offered itself as a blueprint to save human civilization. We cannot know how seriously its proponents took that aspect of it. Nitze's copy of Spengler's *The Decline of the West* is not dog-eared. The spine is stiff. Apart from his name written on the title page, there are no notations. Nitze may well have been the type of man who took good care of his books, but that is immaterial. NSC 68 was not a realistic plan. Indeed it was just a harder rendition of the sentimental impulse, only ostensibly outer- rather than inner-directed. When Dwight Eisenhower came to office in 1953, one of the first things he did was consign it to the archives and start all over again with a planning exercise that ended up rejecting nearly every one of NSC 68's premises. Still, it had done its job. It was not a blueprint but, in Acheson's word, a "bludgeon." Bludgeons do not wield themselves, even ones so well made they speak, as Acheson again put it, "clearer than truth."

Still, Truman resisted. He put NSC 68 in his drawer. It may well have stayed there. But the invasion of South Korea by the North in the summer of 1950 made that impossible. Now he approved it. He had almost no choice.

This was another reminder that in spite of all that had taken place during the previous three years, Truman had not bought in fully to the Cold War as a military or militarized conflict, even as late as early 1950. He did largely as he was told up to then, but he, like Kennan, and perhaps with a Wallace-induced caveat, refused to countenance a leap from a basically ideological and political conflict in Europe to a military contest worldwide. Kennan insisted to his dying day, in fact, that his doctrine of containment was not meant to be understood in that way. The amoeba grew only from the Urals to the Atlantic and possibly as far south as the Mediterranean. It did not swim. Let the rest of the world fend for itself. Truman and possibly even Marshall were of the same mind. The latter, as noted, spent most of 1946 in China, where he concluded that the Cold War could not be won in such a place, not least by the United States, and probably not by anyone else who hadn't a firm grasp of Asian nationalism or other isms, let alone politics or topography. The guiding axiom of the era, again, became one of mastering capabilities, not intentions. Who could say how far the Communist menace would go? Who could place such arbitrary limits on containment? Better to gather more facts, then wait and see.

American power and the American way of life did not cotton to self-imposed restraint. Restraint was left to others, self-imposed or otherwise. This was the lesson most people learned in the last war: it had to be won from the inside out, by sheer capacity. Politics abroad would fall in line. The Berlin Airlift (1948–49)—in which the United States laid down a deterrent through the middle of Berlin and vowed, and acted, to defend it—worked. Acheson's perimeter speech (1950)—in which he implied that the United States would not act to extend its reach in Asia beyond a line that placed Korea on the other side—did not.

The events and decisions of 1946 through to the signing of the North Atlantic Treaty in 1949 appear in retrospect to have followed a logical path that, all the way to 1989, unfolded as a Churchillian drama, with dark beginning, muddled middle, and triumphal end. It would be presumptuous of us to reject that type of narrative now out of hand; someday it may well be the accepted story of the Cold War, once all or most of the facts are known. It would be inaccurate now to say that this was how it was perceived at the time, at any point during this chronology, except perhaps in the imaginations of a few people (perhaps, just perhaps, Kennan) only at the very beginning and then again at the very end, more or less, around 1986. Certainly this was not how it looked forty years earlier from the American homeland.

In fact the choices were more circumscribed as the terms of reference expanded. John Lukacs has described it as a great inflation, whereby "[b]eyond and beneath the inflation of money and of materials there exists an inflation of communication and of words: in sum, more and more of everything, meaning less and less." As veterans and others redirected their attention to civilian life, some imaginations stagnated, except when threatened. Americans had become, like it or not, enforcers of order at home and abroad. They preferred not to debate the effects this had on their freedom, and on their capacity—preferably acknowledged as incapacity—to doubt. Their doubt, in turn, made their own society into another microcosm of the Cold War, suspended uneasily between the risks of power and chaos. Finding the right path between the two had to begin, they said, at home.

The historical point here is typical. We usually don't get the whole point of the story until it's over. But the Cold War as it came to be understood was a different kind of war, or so it was said by nearly everyone who spoke about it. There was a relative timelessness to it, a sense, by some in the West at least, that peaceful coexistence could last indefinitely. Soviet influence had to be resisted when it stepped over the line, but to many Americans, especially American liberals, the matter for debate was marking the lines themselves—where and how firmly to draw them—rather than the principle or the existence of a semipermanent global antagonist who at the same time, it could be argued, accentuated all that was worthy about the American way of life. Wallace objected to the binary formulation and to the policy, and his objection threw him to the margins of American public life. America was no longer an idealist nation, much Cold War rhetoric notwithstanding. Idealism, even romanticism, would return every few years, but never in the heart of the country's leaders, at least, arguably, until Ronald Reagan took one of the biggest Cold War gambles any had ever taken. For now they were nearly all tough-minded pragmatists. Even the Kennedys, as idealistic as they later pretended to be, were brass-tacks men.

Herbert Hoover might have agreed. The disgraced Republican president had not been heard from much during the war years. Americans who thought about him may have presumed him cocooned high up in the Waldorf Astoria, nursing the grievance of having been misunderstood and unloved. The presumption was correct—partly.

Like his fellow Iowan, Wallace, Hoover sounded a voice in the wilderness, and he was busy. It is interesting to note that Hoover, back in the Harding administration, had been Wallace's father's great opponent when Hoover was secretary of commerce. Now Wallace *fils* held that position, and Hoover, strangely, got along much better with the president, now Truman.

A little more than a month after becoming president, Truman telephoned Hoover, whom he had heard was visiting Washington. He rang directly to the Shoreham Hotel. The conversation went something like this:

"Mr. President, this is Harry Truman." . . .

"Mr. President, I don't know what to say." . . .

"Mr. President, I want to talk to you. If I may, I'll come right up there and see you." . . .

"I couldn't let you do that, Mr. President, I'll come and see you . . ."

"That's what I figured you'd say, and I've got a limousine on the way to pick you up."

Hoover arrived presently to the White House. Truman said to him:

> Mr. President, there are a lot of hungry people in the world, and if there's anybody who knows about hungry people, it's you. Now there's plenty of food, but it's not in the right places. Now I want you to—

The next thing Truman knew, Hoover was crying: "I saw that great big tears were running down his cheeks. I knew what was the matter with him. It was the first time in thirteen years . . . that anybody had paid any attention to him."

Hoover remembered the encounter somewhat differently, but he took the assignment to investigate the needs and requirements of a foreign aid program. He had done this before: in 1914 he led an emergency relief mission that became one of the largest ever recorded, lasting until 1923 and extending some $5 billion of food and assistance to war-torn areas. He also led the relief of the Mississippi Valley after the Great Flood of 1927. People called him the Great Humanitarian, the Great Engineer. We would more accurately call him a great internationalist, just as Wallace in his more enthusiastic moments might have been called a great globalist. Both also were passionate American nationalists. Hoover's reputation took him to the Harding and Coolidge cabinets and then to the White House. Then everything came to an end for Herbert Hoover. He was blamed for the Depression. He had become a political untouchable.

Truman granted him rehabilitation. In 1946 he reassembled his mission, visited some thirty-eight countries, and gave Truman the report he wanted. He would then be asked to chair two commissions on the reorganization of government. Hoover was back in somebody's good graces. Meanwhile he devoted much of his time to writing a detailed masterwork on the sabotage of the American dream by Franklin Roosevelt and his followers, the first of six planned volumes. He had been writing off and on since 1934. He tried and failed to win the Republican nomination in 1940, delivering an address that drew from his book, but somebody fiddled with his microphone, and he was not heard. Now he would aim to be read.

Hoover too turned introspective, inward. His magnum opus shows him to be every bit as romantic as but less mystical than Wallace. There is the same special American civilization, under threat less by foreign powers than by the misguided and cynical politics of its own government, in this instance by the prevailing internationalists of the Democratic Party, whom Hoover equated with the wrong sort of fellow traveler. There were plots to be sure, and he condemned them as deliberate—that is, decisions, planned and executed. Yet whereas Wallace drew a line between those now serving Truman and those like himself who had once served under Roosevelt, Hoover saw the rot settling in from the start with the latter, and for precisely the opposite reason. Roosevelt was a statist, a collectivist, an empire builder. He did not have the cunning of Churchill or the sadism of Stalin, but he was not, when it came down to it, all that different from them. This was not, however, his worst problem.

To Hoover, Roosevelt had been a dangerous innocent. He had misjudged the country's primary enemy, the Soviet Union, by commission and by omission. It had sought and obtained secret agreements and misunderstandings. These were followed by those made by Truman, to no better result. It is interesting that in 1964 Hoover removed the following sentences from his memoir:

> There ensued a period of about two years after the war during which [Truman] was groping with these entanglements. At times in this period he apparently still had some confidence in Communist Russia's fidelity to their commitments. Also, statesmen in the Western Democracies were slow to realize what had already been taken under control of the Kremlin.

Perhaps Hoover had been grateful for the aid assignment. Or perhaps, in the passage of time, he came to realize that Truman had acted more from confusion than from malfeasance.

For his part, Wallace had contended that the United States could, by an act of will, preserve its neutrality between the British and the Soviets. To balance its overreliance upon the former, it had to bend over backward to accommodate the latter. Hoover saw no such political triangle. Britain and the Soviet Union and every other power in the Old World could do as it liked. The United States could offer humanitarian assistance, advice, and well-wishes, but no more. This was not because America had no interests that extended beyond its shores but rather because it no longer shared or never did share the values and culture of those other nations. He upheld the doctrine of the two spheres—Old World and New World—and refused to accept that their three-centuries-long division had come to an end. America could, and must, resist them abroad. Just as important, it must resist their pernicious ideas—starting with collectivism and socialism—at home. If not, Americans would drive the nation to ruin. He, Hoover, must do all he could to stop it. Like Wallace, he failed.

Chapter 10

Preponderance

I chanced to see an advertisement by a tire manufacturer which announced forthrightly that his 1946 tires were the safest and toughest ever made.
—"The Easy Chair," October 1946

H oover and Wallace faced an even bigger obstacle than the assorted political opponents to their calculated desire for retrenchment. It was preponderance. It went to the core of the American spirit. It rested on an axiom about power. When in doubt, it says, grow. Whether or not he actually said it, the Confederate commander Nathan Bedford Forrest got the credit for inventing it in battle: get there firstest with the mostest. American security, and its way of war, has long been based upon this simple formula. Overwhelm the enemy and do it before anyone else does.

Sometimes it worked: in World War II, or in the Gulf War. Other times it failed: in the Iraq War, or in Vietnam. Military preponderance is a double-edged sword. Big interventions make big targets. They are expensive. If they don't succeed right away, they take longer and cost more, so they rely on great sacrifice and patience on the "home front."

Preponderance governed there too. The stereotype possesses many elements of truth: Americans were the people of plenty. It is the first thing that many foreign visitors notice. The expanse of nearly everything: roads, rooms, meal portions, waistlines, farms, buildings, automobiles, carpets. Even the doors and the doorknobs in America were observed to be thicker, stronger than those elsewhere. The stereotype continues. Rooms are overheated in winter and, following the invention of air-conditioning, chilled like refrigerators in summer. Hairstyles—for women at least, in the late 1940s—and haute couture featured the ample cut. Dean Acheson was one who noticed the sartorial details. The French ambassador once came to visit and Acheson's eye went just below the man's midriff. "Mr. Ambassador, there is now a small oversight accompanying your dress." The man quickly pulled up his fly, so quickly in fact that his tie got caught in it. Acheson could be droll about the oversights of others. When they affected his own appearance, he hated them. He would chastise his tailor for cutting conventional suits. Acheson insisted they be made just right. No wonder some people said he did not look or sound very American.

Having made it through the Depression, Americans liked amplitude and plentitude. The war put them on hold. Dresses and skirts gave way to slacks; trousers lost their cuffs. But these were temporary sacrifices. Behind them a bigger change took place.

The world's fashion capital moved from Paris to New York. The war imposed obvious restrictions on the former—designers and buyers couldn't go there. They would be forced to innovate at home. Paris recovered after the war, and Christian Dior reemerged in a big way in his New Look of 1947 with longer and shapelier skirts, but by now there was competition—from designers and, especially, photographers. Americans resumed their taste for excess. Women's dresses featured rounder cuts with brighter colors; their hats had broader brims; even their aprons were decorated with sequins. Men's shoulders got more padding; ties grew wider and brighter; hats, though fewer men wore them, got bigger; and the soles of shoes got thicker. Menswear also became less formal. Few cutaways or tailcoats were seen; dinner jackets became rare. So did hard collars. A contemporary survey showed that 75 percent of offices permitted men to work in shirtsleeves, 13 percent more said only when it was warm outside; 58 percent allowed men to come in sports shirts. "So steady is the campaign of attrition against the formerly orthodox male costume," proclaimed Frederick Lewis Allen, "that one suspects that its one-hundred-and-twenty-five-year reign may be approaching its end."

Let us recall some more facts and figures. America's gross national product just about doubled during the war. Some fourteen million people had joined the labor force, and more than six times the number of Americans paid income tax in 1946 than had paid in 1940. As we learned in chapter 7, wages and the standard of living also rose. "The American people are in the pleasant predicament of having to learn to live 50 percent better than they have ever lived before" was the verdict of Fred Vinson. More and faster: American war production surpassed the combined production of the entire Axis by 1943, even though they had boosted theirs for nearly a decade. And it kept on growing.

So did the population. It rose from just over 131 million in 1940 to nearly 151 million in 1950, surpassing some predictions by about 10 million. The birth rate, which had been about seventeen per thousand in the 1930s, went up to twenty per thousand by the end of the war and to twenty-five per thousand by 1947. The population of California alone rose by nearly 23 percent.

Americans were more plentiful and younger. They were also larger. Allen has recounted the observations of a teacher talking with her school doctor: "But they're so *big*!" she said. "Big?" said he. "That's the tomato-juice generation you're seeing. Wait till you see the grapefruit-juice generation!" Yet preponderance is also a relative quality. By the standards of the 1950s or 1960s, the people of plenty looked rather meager right after the war. The image of a late-twentieth-century supermarket contrasts obviously with one from 1948 in the *Boston Herald* of a lady retrieving her supply of meat over the counter from three men wearing fedoras. But the lady and the men are smiling. They are plump. There is plenty of meat. It is hard to find a similar image elsewhere. Who in Europe or Asia had such satisfied butchers and customers? Most of these places still felt ruin. America, in spite of inflation and recent shortages, was all right.

John Gunther, now traveling through the Midwest, was impressed by the "ideal geography and almost perfect natural frontiers, by incalculable bulk and wealth and variety and vitality, by a unique and indeed unexampled heritage in democratic ideas and principles— and a country deliberately founded on a good idea." His later list of "Midwest Miscellany" extends for two pages. Some highlights:

> Juke boxes.... Automobiles with wooden bumpers in the winter of 1946–47—as strange a sight as an eagle wearing gloves.... Public worship of vitamins, golf, and Frank Sinatra.... The fact that the most conservative vote is not, contrary to general opinion, that of the farmers but of businessmen in small towns.... Night schools—especially their courses in law.... Motels and tourist camps.... The gap between a basic good will in citizens and a lack of concrete know-how; the gap between sound and generous social ideals and inadequate performance; the gap between what most people believe in as regards political and civic affairs, and what they actually do.

We noted earlier his awe at the size and scope of midwestern institutions such as the *Chicago Tribune*. Here is another:

> Ohio State is a colossus. It has more than seventy buildings, upwards of 14,000 students, a stadium that seats 74,000, its own radio station, a "twilight school" for evening classes, and a vice president—"in charge of education"! ... Among courses offered are: Ice Cream Manufacturing, Elementary Russian, Introduction to Clothing and Textiles, Factors in Successful Marriage, Motor Carrier Organization, The Social Work Approach to Life Adjustments, Pliny and Catullus, Driers, Kilns, and Theory of Firing, Education of Exceptional Children, Epidemic Diseases in

Warfare; Principles of Taxonomy: Monocots and Dicots; Intermediate Japanese; Anatomy of the Horse; Old Provençal; Wood-
lot Management.... Tuition at Ohio State...is of course...
absolutely free to residents of the state. Americans take this phenomenon for granted, but it is another point of unceasing wonder to almost all Europeans.

The final line gives a sign of Gunther's priorities. He noted the
$1,306,514,314 spent on racetracks by Americans in 1945 as con-
trasted with the $100 million bill for cancer research that failed to
pass in the House in 1946. He also reminded us of the growing
income inequality since the war; the fact that some 25 percent of
American troops stationed in Germany had some form of venereal
disease; and that one-third of American marriages now ended in
divorce. Oh, and the Mardi Gras of 1946, "one of the most expensive, crowded, lush and sensational in history, and 750,000 people
saw it."

There was a story told about Herbert Hoover when he was an
old man. "Tell me, child," he asked a young visitor, "what do you
really want in life?" The woman said she was quite happy with what
she had. "I have a nice husband, I have a nice apartment, so the
answer is I want a status quo." His response: "How can you say a
thing like that . . . because I want more. I want to write a better book, I
want to have more friends—I just want more—and I think you should
never sit back and say, 'I want a status quo.'"

Sometimes, though, humility crept back in, only now in the
familiar cynical language of terms like "politics," "power," "empire,"
and "imperial," which had become passé, or dismissive, as in "playing politics" or "it's only politics." This lasted throughout the postwar period and extends even to our own day, despite frequent
attempts to refashion language.

The fact remained that the United States had the most assets, to use Truman's term at Potsdam, and it sought returns. Better that they came compounded in the way to which Americans had grown accustomed. The country grew and grew; maybe it knew that it all someday could be brought down again, maybe even by themselves, but that time was a long way off. Americans were moving up, and they had further to go.

Truman still may have prevaricated. He read the mood of the country, but he did not dismiss the extent of its power. He allowed planning to proceed: for an American general staff of a unified military service; for permanent mobilization of industry, resources, scientific programs for the national defense; for the tighter integration of political, diplomatic, and military functions of government; for a peacetime intelligence service and a peacetime draft. When the new National Security Council came together for the first time in September 1947, Truman ordered it to work in harmony. His new Council on Economic Advisers had already met. Its mission, it now said, was to plan for growth. It also bought into the new Cold War. The mobilization of society and the economy would continue. It would be channeled in particular directions, following the new national security guidance, and for the common good. From the sidelines, Old Baruch was quick to think ahead. In July 1947, for example, he advised purchasing Cuban sugar—in fact, the whole surplus—to keep it out of the hands of the Soviets.

Preponderance, Americans learned, is usually indivisible. The federal government cannot stand apart, for to do so would almost imply an oxymoron. Government budgets usually grew with the economy. The rate of spending by the middle of this war was five times what it had been in the previous one. By the end of 1945 it had risen to around $100 billion, with the national debt in 1946 hitting $269 billion. It would not have been accurate then to posit a choice and contrast between a strong or weak state and society.

The calculus of strength and weakness is one thing; preponderance is another. It relates more to quantity than to quality. It is the appearance of power from plenty as well as the reality. It is, in a word, the power, and the propensity, to overwhelm.

That was the American stereotype at the peak of the nation's power in the world up to that point. The largesse came so easily many people took it for granted. Problems were "solved" by throwing resources at them. Gamal Abdel Nasser, the Egyptian nationalist who knew Americans well, had a nice way of describing it: it was not that Americans sometimes did stupid things, he once said, but that they did stupid things in complicated ways, which made everyone else wonder if they were not missing something. This was a side effect of preponderance. A big country can afford a few mistakes here and there, but doctrinaire stupidity is not one of them.

Sometimes, however, mistakes accumulate hard. It is not easy to say when Americans developed the talent for doing shortsighted things by complication. It goes against the grain of the national stereotype, honed once upon a time by the man who did the most to establish the world's first perception of the new nation, Benjamin Franklin. He hid remarkable complexities behind a veil of captivating simplicity. Perhaps Nasser got it wrong. The ways were not complicated at all; they were just a veil of a different hue, covering up the same reluctance to work through tough decisions. Preponderance was the simplest cover there could be. Nobody could deny it, even if it was much less captivating than a randy old scientist in a fur hat.

Harry Truman, as we have seen, was a less captivating simpleton. Did his everyman exterior cloak remarkable complexities? Probably not. However, it is fair to say that his determination following the war to restore, or at least to preserve, a simpler America—which is hard to say was not genuine—did little to disguise the fact of preponderance. Rather, it reaffirmed it as acceptable, and axiomatic, to the

American people. With preponderance, then, came responsibility, or at least a mantra of responsibility, toward helping to manage the world's problems—hence the Marshall Plan, which was followed by Truman's Point Four Program in 1949.

The United States gave the "mostest" and the fastest, relative to the rest of the world, and to what it had done in its past. Yet all political careers end in failure; all empires decline, eventually. Americans are not used to thinking this way. When it was fashionable, before George W. Bush's intervention in Iraq, to say that the United States would never have another "peer competitor" if the American people and its government were determined to prevent that, many people believed it. The historian does not disabuse them of the idea. For the one historical certainty is that there are no such certainties laid out for us in advance; we take things as they come, then we try to explain how and why they went.

That was the gift Truman imparted to his nation in 1946. He took the preponderance of power; he asked, briefly, how and why; and then did as he was told. Yet the quizzical gesture mattered in the moment, and subsequently. Preponderance could have taken any number of uglier routes; or it could have been resisted, probably with a few terrible consequences. We recall General Marshall's advice to decide problems. Americans had been fighting problems for some time, including the problem of their own size and strength. Now, after a moment of indecision, they aimed to do better.

The solution, provisional but significant, was to build more strength. Strength was not an antidote to fear; it did not destroy it at the source; but it helped. The curious thing about it now was that it did not include an elimination of sentimentality from the national culture. After having tamed that particular strain of the collective psychology, Americans rediscovered it in the 1950s and again in the 1980s, whereas for most people losing or overcoming sentimentality is the first step to amassing strength.

For now Americans overcame the things they did not like by

telling and showing themselves they had more of what they did like. They bought confidence in that way. They armed for arming's sake, physically, materially, mentally.

The war had taught them this. It saw the federal government grow to over three million employees, not including those in military uniform. By 1949 some two million were still in government. It is now a commonplace to say that American productivity and production won the "mechanical" war. The effect went deeper. "The reason you won and we lost," according to Albert Speer, "was that you made total war and we did not." It was total in deed as well as in mind; total in the preponderance of effort, and effect, in a way that could not, however much the American people wanted it, be reversed without great pain and confusion. For preponderance had become so automatic that it could in principle apply to anything: "blood plasma, radar, new drugs, or K rations." In the perceptive words of James Burnham, "They hurled at the enemy overwhelming quantities of supplies, men, shells, food, ships, trucks, tanks, planes, so that the mistakes and crudities of details were buried in the mass." Even books: the war saw the army and the navy print and distribute over six million books in 1943, which quadrupled the following year and was set to double the year after that. The result of all this production, Burnham wrote, was a powerful yet crude imperialism brought about by a superior form of production, but only that. In nearly every other area the United States remained immature and subject to growing pains. We could say this became the essence of the World War II generation, the generation that went on to cheer the line, pay any price, bear any burden, meet any hardship, support any friend, oppose any foe. Total war demanded nothing less. America had to look preponderant, everywhere and forever.

Hence the military-industrial complex. It was a reality long before Ike named it or gave it a slogan. It reached to nearly every part of the defense economy. Research and development, for example, rose to nearly $500 million by 1947. Both the army and the navy spent more in some areas—aeronautics, for example—than they had done during the war. Eisenhower did not invent the problem in 1960. He fretted over it throughout his two terms; so did Truman, who knew a thing or two about waste and inefficiency in the defense industry; but who could stop it? Not he. Not his secretary of defense. Not even the Republican critics of the planned economy. It was not godless Communism or even socialism if you built big to oppose just that. In any event, the complex was now under the management of sound Wall Street men, it was said, like Ferdinand Eberstadt, principal author of the 1947 National Security Act and another one of Baruch's protégés. Their "cold, immensely able . . . spring-steel brain[s]" set the tone and the precedent: they did not question the axiom of preponderance; they paid more attention to the execution, where, as we have seen, savvy and ambitious men made their mark.

Preponderance extended beyond the nation's borders as foreign relations gained in the calculus of national prosperity. The United States contributed nearly 75 percent of the budget of the United Nations Relief and Rehabilitation Administration (UNRRA); some people complained, but largesse had become second nature. So had the thinking that went into postwar assistance to Europe. Today we describe it as a tremendous political, economic, and, above all, diplomatic success. On balance it was.

John Maynard Keynes famously said in reference to the British loan of 1945, "There was no hope of escaping a financial Dunkirk." Keynes had the misfortune to be in command of the British side of it. There was misfortune in more ways than one. First were the accounts: British gold and dollar reserves were by the end of the war less than half their prewar amount, and many times more were owed. Visiting Americans described what would become a stereotype: Leonard Bernstein's visit to London in June 1946 was "a mess. . . . The plane trip was ghastly and a full day overdue. . . . The hotel is dreary beyond description. The food is inedible, what there is of it. The English are very down." Ronald Reagan two years later described much of the same: having to sleep in his coat because he was so cold, hating the fog and coal smoke, and being struck by the "incredible inefficiency" of nearly everything.

Keynes had left this place behind for the "balmy air and bright azalean colour" in Savannah, Georgia, in March 1946. It was the first meeting of the board of governors of the new International Monetary Fund and World Bank, the Bretton Woods institutions Keynes had helped to design. Only they did not come out as he had intended. They did not underwrite an equitable arrangement among the victors of the war and their soon-to-be rehabilitated enemies so much as they bolstered American preponderance and preeminence worldwide.

There were Tories back home who said they had told him so. Now they wondered whether he could pull off the loan their country needed. Keynes was tired and ill and had not long to live. He had seen his ideas take root and prosper, some said, since the dark 1930s, but the Americans now threatened to turn the clock back. He cast himself in the middle somewhere between laissez-faire and the planned economy, whereas he found Americans passionate from both extremes, and at the same time not sure which way to go. At least this was what he told Henry Wallace.

Indecision in this instance was not that simple. Suspicion was in the air. Not all Americans were in a generous mood. Truman had canceled Lend-Lease, the Allied aid program, almost the minute after the last shots were fired. Acheson had been on holiday in Canada and said it never would have happened had he been in town. The culprit was Truman and his inability to read memoranda carefully, but the blame went to Leo Crowley, head of the government agency that administered Lend-Lease. Crowley had made his money in the print industry, then in real estate and in banking, from which he entered politics as a Roosevelt Democrat. FDR found the self-made man useful. He too was known for doing as he was told, often without question and, as it turned out, much good sense. The termination of Lend-Lease not only terrified the British and the French, who depended on it for their survival, but it also annoyed Stalin, who chose naturally to regard the decision as deliberate and entirely political. Other beneficiaries, notably the Chinese, who presently found themselves in the midst of a civil war in which the United States professed an important stake, didn't know what to make of it.

Indecision, and poor decisions, bred more suspicion. Free-traders, now in the American camp, saw the British trying desperately to hang on to their system of imperial preference. A few like Baruch were said even to favor taking sides against the British in economic negotiations because of the threat of "World Wide Cartelization." Others, namely on the British left, accused the United States of misplaced loyalty. The *New Statesman* reported, for example, in November 1946, "It is clear that on the matters that most affect Britain today, the United States is nearly as hostile to the aspirations of Socialist Britain as to the Soviet Union."

This was Keynes's second misfortune. He acted as though the Anglo-American alliance would survive the war unchallenged. He had played the role of architect; now he could be the engineer. But the Americans treated him like a poor and desperate supplicant either way. Fred Vinson, whose origins were in Kentucky, and other Americans spoke to him, Keynes said, in "Cherokee." We've already met his other interlocutor, Will Clayton, a very tall Texan whose cotton brokerage was gargantuan, with some 15 percent of the global market. Roosevelt, who considered Clayton a reactionary, had little time for him, but Clayton had the backing of Baruch and, subsequently, of the group around Acheson, who later relied upon him to mastermind the Marshall Plan. Clayton came up with a deal for Keynes that was less than ideal but not easy to refuse. Instead of the billions of interest-free loans the British had wanted, they got a $3.75 billion loan at 1.62 percent. They also were required to see the Bretton Woods agreements through Parliament and to implement them within a year. Finally, they had to make sterling convertible and to call off import restrictions. It was a tough pill. The British politician Robert Boothby called it an "economic Munich."

From Dunkirk back to Munich with just one loan. Preponderance spoke for itself. But try telling it to the U.S. Senate! It did not like this loan. Why, Vandenberg said, the Russians would complain they weren't getting one, and wouldn't that then mean taking sides? Precisely. Yet hadn't Congress just signed off on more than $13 billion in overall aid and assistance? Now it was asked to sign off on $4 billion more, with the British loan and a $650 million sweetener the negotiators tossed in to be exchanged, upon repayment, for Britain's Lend-Lease obligation. Wallace for one thought Vandenberg and the others had a point. Acheson, for his part, told Wallace "that he never saw such stupendous ignorance in his life as that displayed by the senators."

In spite of these amounts, to which was added a $720 million credit to France in May, most European economies were failing. UNRRA was set to end in 1947. "Food, give us food!" was heard from one end of Europe to another, and beyond. Back in America, the 1945 wheat harvest set a record at 1.123 billion bushels. It was no surprise to hear a western farmer say, "We no longer raise wheat here . . . we manufacture it." The American daily average calorie intake was about thirty-three hundred; in Europe it was between one and two thousand less. European agriculture had suffered a terrible drought in 1946, followed by the worst winter in recent memory. France alone faced an import requirement of between two and three million tons of wheat, for which it could not pay. The wheat crop throughout Europe in 1947 was less than half what it had been before the war; coal production also was much lower.

Hoover had returned from his mission, urging not only food aid but above all the recovery of German industry. There was more at stake than the economic lives of Europeans, he said. There was now the Soviet menace to counter, and it fed on these conditions, as almost everyone knew.

So came the European Reconstruction Program, better known as the Marshall Plan. It was a worthy successor to UNRRA. Ernest Bevin said it was "one of history's greatest acts of statesmanship," living up to Churchill's description of Lend-Lease as America's most unsordid act. It was not sordid, true, but it was not entirely altruistic either. It was accompanied by another policy, the aforementioned Truman Doctrine, which had been announced back in March 1947. The doctrine—an interesting term that had a long history in international affairs, even in the United States (e.g., the Stimson Doctrine, which was the moral embargo on Asian aggressors)—had yet to become a staple of the presidency. Truman's doctrine held that the defense of Greece and Turkey, that is to say, keeping them and the Turkish straits out of Communist hands, required urgent American military and economic assistance. The bureaucratic lead was taken by Acheson, who, when given the cue by the British, jumped into action. Marshall was persuaded, then, with Acheson's help, Truman as well, and finally, with Vandenberg's help, Congress. Truman's speech was followed by a standing ovation; and yet according to Acheson, "This was a tribute to a brave man rather than unanimous acceptance of his policy."

Acheson wrote to sound circumspect, and loyal. He took the floor from Marshall in a fateful meeting with Truman and Vandenberg. He was the one who laid out the consequences, in good lawyerly cadence, of what he charged were the "series of Soviet moves" westward—in Germany, Italy, France. "I can see Senator Vandenberg now," he wrote, "suddenly leaning forward on the sofa in the President's office and saying, 'If you will say that to the whole country, I will support you.'"

But Vandenberg did not, not yet. He added an amendment to boost the authority of the United Nations, just as he would qualify his support for the Marshall Plan by insisting that it be administered independently. "The point I am making," Acheson concluded, "is that Vandenberg exacted as the price of his support a concession to the opposition which contributed to the success of the proposal—whatever it did to its administration." A happy ending, but hardly one that went against the thrust of preponderance.

Nowhere was it felt more than in Germany. Hoover had been right. Germany was the keystone of Europe, and of European recovery. Germany, or what would soon become West Germany, had to feel the brunt of largesse. General Clay was known for an immense will, and an equal amount of persistence. America would go big in Germany. It would finance imports to the tune of billions. It would occupy the most prominent headquarters—the thousand-room former I.G. Farbenindustrie building in Frankfurt, for example, behind which there was a casino that sold thousands of meals, part of it open twenty-two hours per day. Largesse included the black markets. An American member of the occupation could sell a wristwatch—often to fellow Russian occupiers—for up to $1,300. It was not uncommon to see soldiers sporting multiple watches on a single wrist. Lest anyone move to disparage the Russians for their passion for black-market timepieces, American officers felt compelled to remind soldiers to speak respectfully of them to the German people: "[T]he Russians are our allies. They have guts. They kept hordes of jerries off of us and, by God, I never want to fight again. Think it over. You have been warned." An open attitude toward the Russians survived impressions, barely. Clay himself insisted on a tone of hard civility.

His civility would be mostly gone by 1948. The occupation had settled in for the duration. This was decided not by him alone, but by events. It sacrificed efficiency for preponderance, and probably lost some German sympathy. The country was inundated not only with American products and personnel but also with directives, speeches, pep talks, gossip, and ideas. Yet the roads were paved. People were fed. This made an impression too.

The genius of the Marshall Plan was not just its largesse. It was the confidence and good faith it circulated among its beneficiaries by giving them a stake in the production and the distribution. The hand of guidance was not invisible—there were Marshall Planners working throughout Europe—but they made a point of listening and deferring: an intended preponderance, in other words, of goodwill. It succeeded because its beneficiaries had grown convinced that it was right, and came in the right way. This was not true elsewhere, especially in Asia. The recipients of American aid were not sure they liked what lay on the other side of the strings, not to mention the strings themselves; on balance they were looser, but no less effective, in Europe than in Asia.

With the Marshall Plan a total of $13 billion—around $120 billion today—was distributed to Western Europe, which accomplished the goal of seeing these economies recover to launch the glorious boom of the 1950s and early 1960s. Dollar area imports throughout Europe ranged between double and five times what they had been before the war. By 1947 the balance of trade between the United States and Europe was somewhere around seven to one, abetting an annual surplus, by the second quarter of that year, of some $12.5 billion.

Britain had done a similar thing after the defeat of Napoleon. It was a fruitful precedent. It was also a repudiation of the temporary adjustment plans of the interwar period. This one was meant to last. Preponderance, thanks to the Marshall Plan, became a collective venture. It was now the property of the West, driven by consumer societies and welfare states, with global potential, some said. The

ghost of Keynes must have smiled somewhere. The most remarkable thing about the line ascribed in 1971 to Richard Nixon—"We
are all Keynesians now"—was how long it took for somebody,
Republican or Democrat, to say it. The partnership of government
and industry, forged during the war, continued. We have already
called it the national security state. It might also be called a garrison
state, but we would not go that far. It did not sacrifice everything to
military necessity. Rather, it promoted an optimal formula for preponderance whereby the state, the economy, and the nation could
all grow stronger, smarter, and more secure.

Preponderance was not uniform. Redistribution of wealth still lay
on the lips of many survivors of the Great Depression. But even
during the New Deal, redistribution was regarded by many people
as un-American. The politics of economic growth continued into
the war and the postwar period. Among the winners were southern
legislators, who, despite being a minority in Congress, mastered the
division of committee and subcommittee chairmanships, and par-
layed the favors and the autonomy they earned from being loyal
members of Roosevelt's coalition into a prime position in the Cold
War military-industrial complex, a position that some hold to this
day. Dismantling their own complex—that nasty racial one—at
home would be put off just a while longer.

There were other beneficiaries. One statistic cited by Truman
was that 175,000 small firms produced some 70 percent of manu-
factured goods at the start of the war; by the time it ended, the
175,000 small firms produced only 30 percent, while 100 companies got some 70 percent of government contracts. Louis B. Mayer,
head of MGM Pictures, paid himself in 1943 around $1 million.
Charlie Wilson, chairman of General Motors, was the second
highest paid in the country, at $459,041 (in 1943). Walter Reuther,
chief of the United Auto Workers, earned $9,000 the follow-
ing year.

Speaking of General Motors, seven of its officers or directors were directors of DuPont Corporation, for example, and 37 of its executives had 192 seats on the boards of other corporations. DuPont owned around a quarter of GM's stock, worth some $600 million. Even before the war, GM was a behemoth whose net sales (worth around $2.5 billion) accounted for around 7 percent of the country's total manufacturing. It was around twice the size of Ford, producing some 46 percent of the country's automobiles, and involved in some 35 percent of all reconversion, according to John Gunther.

As it happened, 1941 was GM's biggest consumer year. It was able to retool in short order. The story is an instructive one, and unsurprisingly it provided Peter Drucker with a subject for his first and best-known management case study.

Drucker's insight into General Motors was to notice its capacity for decentralization. We shall learn more about this concept in the next chapter. It was related in spirit both to the faith in preponderance and to the semiautonomous principle that lay behind the success of the Marshall Plan. Indeed, it underscored the continuity between wartime production patterns and the postwar national security state and its beneficiaries. Conversion from peace to war and back to peace had to assume an indefinite period of growth. The transitions were messy enough; they would not have survived a fixed business cycle mentality, even if the business cycle was alive and well. The formal separation between policymaking and execution—in Drucker's terms, "central management" and "divisional management"—made possible this flexibility, as well as planning for wartime production in peacetime, and vice versa. This wasn't all seamless; it was, like military planning and warfighting, a succession of ad hoc adaptations, often complicated, by people to circumstances. There were fewer precise rules and precise decisions than a general mind-set, which was harder to reproduce. But it showed that Americans could have it all, or most of it, so long as they kept being preponderant, and so long as they knew themselves to be producers as well as consumers. The free-enterprise system could thrive so long as there was plenty.

Drucker's model corporation was representative of American society, as he put it, and perceived as "an autonomous institution." It showed the country how to produce, how to train, how to prosper, and how to do all that while producing more and faster than the competition. Could we say the same of the American "system"? Friedrich von Hayek's *Road to Serfdom* appeared toward the end of the war, in 1944, but few politicians touted Hayek then as Margaret Thatcher later did by keeping a copy of one or another of his books always in her handbag. A popular presumption was still that some countries would sooner or later become socialist. Let us also remember George Orwell. His *1984* (published in 1949) was a book bred from the war, of rationing, censorship, codification and quantification, and all the other sources of nourishment for the state. What powerful institution relinquishes power after gaining it, whether or not the initial reason for the grab survives? The preponderance of power went deep as well as wide. It infected the consciousness of citizens who now had some experience with the designation "enemy of the state."

Orwell's dystopia sold well in the United States. It confirmed long-standing fears of the new imperial regime. Yet it was written from the left, and the left in America, at least since the demise of the old Bryan Democrats with the New Deal, now backed a strong federal government. Could this have been rejected in 1946? This is another way of asking whether the trend toward the centralization of power—which had been under way well before William Jennings Bryan, the populists, and some progressives tried to wind it back, that is, at least since the end of the Civil War—could be reversed; yet it was done, as Drucker has shown, in particular places and instances.

Were both centralization and its opposite the result of a collective decision? Or was it what historians call "structural," beyond the capacity of groups of human beings to master, resist, or redirect? This was not a question that anyone answered fully at the time. It still confounds us.

Chapter 11

Archipelago

The motor court or motel is a specific solution of the motorist's problem.... There are not enough tourist courts. A good many of them have long since been occupied permanently by veterans and warworkers who have stayed on.

—"The Easy Chair," November 1946

There is a temptation to visualize preponderance as a juggernaut. However, this wasn't the usual way, which is more haphazard and pixelated. This has not stopped Americans from compensating with other, more logical, coherent, and decisive plans. The Joint Chiefs of Staff, for example, published a map of the world in 1946, called an "Outline Command Plan," that divided the world into seven regions or commands: Far East Command, Pacific Command, Alaskan Command, Northeast Command, Atlantic Fleet, Caribbean Command, and European Command. It has since been revised several times, but the basic idea persists as today's unified combatant commands. The impulse behind this was imperial, although the planners who did it may not have so regarded it. Like any good planner, they worked logistics more than strategy. Troops and assets had to be moved and organized as efficiently and as effectively as possible. This meant a partition of the map into regional and subregional zones with "forward deployments," that is, bases and arrangements, eventually alliances, with other armies, each the responsibility of a single commander.

If we look back we can find similar maps. Harold and Margaret Sprout at Princeton, sadly once better known than they are today, produced an important text called *Foundations of National Power* in

1945 for a project sponsored by Jim Forrestal and the navy. It was an anthology of what was called geopolitics. Their division was also regional, with characteristic titles: part 1, "Bases of International Politics"; part 2, "The European Realm of the Great Powers"; part 3, "The Afro-Asian Realm of Rival Imperialisms"; part 4, "The American Realm Between Europe and Asia"; part 5, "Foundations of Peace and a New World Order."

The Sprouts were conservative. They advocated not an entirely new world order but instead an evolution of the existing state system. Other guidebooks advocated similarly, with varying degrees of enthusiasm. There was *U.S. Foreign Policy: Shield of the Republic* (1943) by Walter Lippmann, *Time for Decision* (1944) by Sumner Welles, and of course Willkie's *One World* (1943). All sold well, as well as or even better than their more utopian counterparts during and shortly after the previous war. They were, to use a nice set of comparisons by John Lukacs, like the American people in 1945: generous but not magnanimous, broad-minded but also narrow-minded, idealist but also materialist, communicative but not contemplative, young but also complicated. They knew victory, but they also knew they had to share it and were in a race to possess all they could—not only land but also resources, routes, experts, industries, loyalties. They were also naïve.

It has lately been customary to ask when, how, and why the American archipelago, this collection of islands both physical and virtual, came into being. During the Pacific war, the practice of "island hopping"—hitting the Japanese first on the islands where they were weakest—proved a success. The image stuck; Dos Passos, for example, began his 1945 travelogue, *Tour of Duty*, by going west across the Pacific from one island to another. He heard an army captain say to a Marshall Islander, "You are no more natives than we are.... We're all natives of some place." The American world, like the romantic concept of America, was based on a similar idea. It could rise or fall as do the islands of an archipelago close to sea level by the acceptance or rejection of the American idea, anywhere it liked, a more flexible and perhaps safer form of penetration. For this reason we prefer to amend Henry Luce's American century, to imagine not a simple American world but instead a global archipelago in perpetual motion, afloat, captive to human over physical geography. The historian Stephen Ambrose once called it part of a "rise to globalism" and dated it, as was the custom during the Cold War, to the late interwar years and to World War II. This too was a blurring of boundaries. As we have already noted several times, the mood just after the war was to pull up the drawbridge. But back in Washington, some planners, starting with the occupants of the new Pentagon building, the largest office building in America, kept advancing, following a pattern that had been set at least two generations earlier.

Reconsidering this chronology spatially may help reveal the indecision occurring throughout it. Many people view imperialism, as we have said, as something continuous, like a current. Recall William Bullitt's spreading miasma of Soviet Communism. His former deputy Kennan once equated the same with Americanization, that is, as a disease that feeds upon a weak host. The nineteenth-century maps of the world were colored by imperial rule. This is not exactly how it happens in the real world. Whether sent to establish a trading post or a military "beachhead," imperialists arrive in stages and stay on particular pieces of territory. Americans were not much different. The generation of 1898 extolled the possession of coaling stations (for example, the one at Guantánamo Bay) in order to supply ships, which in turn sailed in order to protect and defend the sea-lanes, the sinews of trade. This was what the British navy had been doing for a couple of centuries. Only when matters got tough in such places, troops were sent in; the beachheads got bigger, and became small, then larger, islands of occupation, and later colonies.

Atomic weaponry accelerated and possibly widened the pattern, but did not fundamentally change it. It was trendy to say that the bomb would eventually lead to a world government, a superstate, or total destruction, but this prediction has proved false, or at least badly premature. Real aims and capabilities counted as much as desires or fears. Thus world government was not synonymous with an all-American world, or with a global utopia. The United States did not, does not, exist everywhere, or nowhere. For all the preponderance described in the previous chapter, its power was as virtual as it was actual.

In practice this meant in 1946 that military victory did not translate automatically into global omnipresence or omnipotence. Americans got much of the credit for that victory, but nobody apart from chauvinists insisted that they get all the credit. So too for the postwar contest. The new world order was not Americans' alone, and Americans to this day insist on a firm distinction between hegemony and empire—and between formal and informal versions of the latter. All would require as much cooperation as sharing a victory, or even more. Referring back to 1898, the historian Ernest May has written that America "had greatness thrust upon it." Maybe so: after the Spanish-American War the United States rated itself a great power, and later, in retrospect, even a nascent superpower. That was a fair diagnosis. However, greatness does not come entirely on its own, or from the whims of politics at home and abroad. It is also, though partly, a choice.

A great power requires a recognition of limits, a habit of rule, and a tradition of empathy in the broad sense, namely, by way of an appreciation of and long experience with the realities of politics, of particularities, and of common opportunities—a sense and instinct, to put it again crudely, of noblesse oblige. Few, if any, great powers exhibit all these traits, but they were not unknown to Americans in the nineteenth century, when, apart from a few infamous moments around 1812, the 1840s, and the 1890s, the country's diplomacy had been rather successful and surprisingly sophisticated. At some point in the early twentieth century the habits receded, but they were not forgotten.

Later Americans could trumpet anomaly, so-called exceptionalism, all they liked, but some people must have known that there was no going back to an imaginary past or to a rewritten present, at least not if they wanted to survive in the world of 1946. Greatness now really was thrust upon them, if they chose it. The American people were called upon to lead. In fact, they may have had little real choice, given what we now know about how dangerous the world then was; but they certainly still had a good number of decisions to make.

This brings us back again to the paradox of Willkie's odd book.

Two years after losing the presidential election to Roosevelt in 1940, Willkie embarked on a journey around the world lasting forty-nine days. On an airplane called the *Gulliver* he traveled to Africa, Europe, Asia, and Latin America. The result was his *One World*, which sold in the millions. What was its appeal? For one thing, its optimism, its sunny message that Americans had no ill will toward other nations and peoples, its admission that the vaunted American way of life had already extended to much of the world, and its implicit redefinition of exceptionalism as an ism of the future. Other nations and peoples in turn, wrote Willkie, looked upon America "with a mixture of respect and hope." Americans liked to read this type of thing. It was the spatial counterpart to Luce's American century but in truth dated back further, to the commercial and imperial exertions of the final decade of the previous one. Willkie was an enthusiast whose favor extended even to the Soviets. Their industry and patriotism impressed him. He could find a way to like anyone so long as they could like him.

The other reason was fear. This was the choice of "one world or none," as the title of a 1946 Federation of American Scientists' paperback, noted in chapter 4, stated it. Fear can make us want to lock things away in boxes, or to divide and conquer, but then we fear the boxes. Willkie provided an alternative. He made one world sound all right, even happy.

Winston Churchill encountered Willkie and described him as a Newfoundland dog, "rushing into the water and coming out again, shaking himself, jumping up on the ladies and putting his paws on their shoulders, wagging his tail and sweeping all the dishes off the table at the same time." Newfoundland dogs could perform a service. Yet Willkie is hard to take seriously in retrospect, for he offered another simplified veil, a half-fiction. Plenty of Americans still liked him. Had he lived to 1948, he might well have defeated Truman.

The book's paradox came from the presumption that the world was all pro-American or pan-American, like the name of the airline, which operated as something close to a monopoly. The image was present in another odd book that has been compared to Willkie's, *The Little Island*, by Margaret Wise Brown, publishing under the pen name Golden MacDonald, which won the Caldecott Medal in children's literature in 1946. It is the story of an island that squares the global circle: "'This little Island is as little as Big is Big.' . . . [A]ll land is one land under the sea. . . . And it was good to be a little Island. A part of the world and a world of its own all surrounded by the bright blue sea."

It is difficult to imagine Americans appreciating such books today to the same degree. The United States has long since stopped pretending to be an island, and the world has long since stopped pretending to look American. Yet these books did not color the entire world red, white, and blue. Their emphasis was less territorial or imperial, in the traditional, nineteenth-century sense, than functional, in the modern, twentieth-century sense. "Americans as a rule have great faith in charters, formulae, and gadgets," the Sprouts wrote. "There seems to be widespread belief that disparities of strength between great and small states can be largely neutralized, that the superior power of the greater states can be effectively shackled, and security for all be thus assured, if only we can contrive the right formula for voting in the world security council, for setting up international police forces, for revising unjust treaties, etc."

Hence the early passion for the United Nations, even among men like the State Department's Jack Hickerson, who would in a couple of years become a hard-boiled Cold Warrior. "I hope and pray," he wrote in March 1946, "that we shall have the privilege of living in a world built on the UNO [United Nation Organisation] conception. I feel so strongly about it that I am willing to go down the line for such a world—and right now." So too among the young founders of the World Federalists—the boosters of world government—such as the one-eyed war hero Cord Meyer, who would in a few years lead the covert political action arm of the CIA.

One world was not inconsistent with many worlds in the midcentury American mind. Its mental map had not spread or shrunk but shifted. The war made popular the polar projection that showed the United States and Europe (and notably the Soviet Union) as virtual next-door neighbors rather than on opposite sides of the world, as the Mercator projection did. A preference during and shortly after the war was for what the geographer Nicholas Spykman touted as the polar azimuthal equidistant projection. He wasn't sure it gave the most accurate representation of American power, for it was centered on the part of the world with the fewest people (the Arctic), but it was an option, even to people who thought about the most populated areas—Africa and Asia—that would soon become the objects, as well as the subjects, of superpower rivalry.

To draw such an archipelago raises an important question. How do you defend the nation's interests in so many places? How, to begin with, do you decide which interests and places matter more than others? The Joint Staff planners in 1946 had the right idea. Archipelagoes are systems of proximity; the islands exist in reference to

one another, as well as to the distant "homeland." A regional division of labor therefore made good sense. Some Americans were
used to thinking regionally. The region they claimed as their
own—the Western Hemisphere or the Americas—is actually several regions whose distances from one end to the other are greater
than those that span the Atlantic. Nevertheless, the region was, and
to some extent still is, considered the United States' "backyard,"
whose nations and cultures have more in common with one
another than with any other group of nations across the sea. The
reasons had something to do with American (as in all the Americas) culture being an amalgam of nearly all others: Eurasian, East
Asian, African, and, not least, Amerindian. But cultural miscege-
nation was not unheard of elsewhere at midcentury. Americans did
not hold a monopoly on it either.

A planner who thought much about all this was not in the armed
services but was a civilian, a diplomat: the aforementioned Sumner
Welles. By 1946 he was well out of office, having been driven there
three years earlier, as we have read, by Bullitt and his fellow con-
spirators.

His earliest experiences in the diplomatic corps were in Latin
America, in Argentina, Cuba, and the Dominican Republic. Whether
this was responsible for his regionalist mind-set cannot be known,
but it's likely. Welles favored the idea that the Americas represented
a special zone of peace. The idea went back several decades and had
elaborated practices of arbitration and norms of international law
that had now made their way to Europe (where lawyers did not hes-
itate to claim authorship) and even to parts of Asia. Most of all,
Welles was enamored with the vision of a world of regions—not a
dystopian one like Orwell's but a synthesis of federated units governed more or less by themselves and in collusion with American-
backed rules and norms.

Welles's regional predilection was shared by others, notably
Monnet and Churchill, although each one of the three drew

distinctions between his formula and the others. Monnet did not consider Welles's plan practical. Churchill preferred a different regional designation, more expansive than Welles's or the one the Joint Chiefs drew, with some of the English-speaking peoples allied in each community. When Henry Wallace asked him if he would include most of the Western Hemisphere, an area regionalists like Welles regarded as part of the American system, Churchill said he thought it was a bad idea to mix "all the colors on the painter's palette" in this way, for what you'd get was "a smudgy grayish brown."

Welles had hoped that the new United Nations would be led by a Security Council made up of regional directorates. This did not happen, although the charter does make room for regional bodies and alliances such as the North Atlantic Treaty. Welles's duties were meanwhile taken over by other, less visionary types. One was a Russian emigré named Leo Pasvolsky, an economist whom Wallace once called "an old dodo." He probably had more say in the end over the makeup of the United Nations than any other person working in the U.S. government. Pasvolsky was no regionalist. The Security Council that came into force was an old-fashioned directorate of the great powers, each with a veto, and presiding over a conglomerate of small powers assembling there for the good of humankind, that is, on a "universalist" basis.

When the Cold War finally ended, sometime in the middle to late 1980s after its short Indian summer (this is meant with irony—there is no phrase to describe such a winter, but the whole thing very nearly did blow up again in 1983), many people began to ask, what next? George Kennan was invited twice to testify in Congress in order to offer an answer. The first time he got a standing ovation; the members of the Senate Committee on Foreign Relations decided they hadn't had enough and invited him back again, even though the octogenarian Kennan had endured several hours of humoring the likes of Joe Biden, Claiborne Pell, and Jesse Helms. Few of them showed up the second time, but no matter. Kennan had made his point before, when, in a delightful exchange with Senator Daniel Patrick Moynihan, he admitted that the great target of his youthful disdain, Woodrow Wilson, had really been ahead of his time and that maybe, finally, the Age of Wilson had arrived. In other words, now that the great Soviet experiment was over we could finally get on with building a new world order of a free, peaceful, democratic community of nations. Why not? Even a man who liked to admit he had no "vision" at all, the then president, George H. W. Bush, didn't mind recycling Wilson's phrase. For his part Moynihan wrote a book called *Pandaemonium* that offered another compelling dystopia of such a world—a tribal free-for-all. It is a nice book, much better written than the two other, more popular expert diagnoses of the moment, Francis Fukuyama's *The End of History and the Last Man* and Samuel P. Huntington's *The Clash of Civilizations and the Remaking of World Order*, neither of which now looks to have been any more accurate than Moynihan's.

Kennan enjoyed his own Indian summer. He had outlived the target of "his" containment doctrine. The senators who rose to applaud him did so not because of what he had to say then but because he had again become fashionable, because he too had survived. Anyway, he had been right, hadn't he? Which now meant that we had been right. Kennan, in spite of having rather little influence on official policy after 1950, and who had spent the past several decades mainly as a bitter gadfly, if and when anybody paid attention to him, was now his nation's great sage, the embodiment of its self-righteousness. Even Moynihan looked to be enjoying the moment too much to press him. For Kennan may have paid some long-belated homage to Wilson but also fell back upon a pre-Wilsonian formula for what ought to come next. The United States, Kennan said, echoing Wallace and Hoover, should try to do all it could to become a normal power, pursuing its interests free from ideology, civilizing missions, crusades, and so on. The U.S. Army had gotten a taste of this in the Philippines, and to a lesser extent in Cuba, right after the 1898 war. It did not like it. Those under occupation liked it even less, and did what many people in their situation do: they fought a brutal insurgency against the occupier. This ended after a few years, but the Philippines got its independence only in 1946. That year, Cuba, now under the rule of Ramón Grau San Martín, welcomed Frank Sinatra for his first performance there. By now American ideology had disabused itself of imperialism, however much the rest of the world abused it for the same. Rather, it pursued what we call informal empire: Sinatra and soda pop, not military governors.

Except in 1946 the United States found itself occupying large pieces of territory, including nearly one-third of Germany and all of Japan. Young officers were put in charge of villages and districts, operating there as satraps. There were also viceroys, General MacArthur in Tokyo and General Clay in Berlin. With them, to the satrapies, came American confections, music, baseball. These were, in other words, islands of America scattered throughout the world. They did not necessarily spread and blur as traditional empires were said to do but rather rose and fell like islands in a rough sea.

Americans learned by trial and error that physical occupation or even coercion isn't necessarily required to decide and influence. You could have an "empire by invitation," at least in name. The epigram was made popular among historians by Norwegian Geir Lundestad, the man who for the past few decades ran the committee that awards the Nobel Peace Prize. Yes, invitations may be accepted or refused. Sometimes the decision to issue them comes from the invitee, not the inviter. Power and influence are "projected," then reflected. So it is important for us to remember—and it is hard to do because American troops remain to this day in both Japan and Germany as well as in any number of other places (and not exactly by invitation)—that the islands are never permanent. They mutate, expand, and contract in relation to the sea. They are temporary nodes of power and influence. That does not mean, however, that they are not at times momentous or, while they last, self-perpetuating both at home and beyond.

Take Konrad Adenauer, for example. The first chancellor of the Federal Republic, Adenauer strove to restore his nation's respect and authority while doing all he could to reassure Europe and the world that West Germany would forever be a responsible world citizen. He knew that he could not do this on his own. This was still "America's Germany." So what happened back in the United States mattered tremendously to someone like Adenauer. It was said that he could always be counted on to stay up for the first primary returns to come in from Dixville Notch, New Hampshire. This is the form of archipelago we mean. Adenauer's radio (or whatever he used to receive the news) was a small island within a larger one called German officialdom within an even larger one called the Federal Republic, all within one called Western Europe. They were components of the American archipelago that was neither strictly formal nor informal but rather some combination of the two that periodically adjusted the terms of membership to meet and overcome crises, and to sustain itself for as long as Americans and others wanted it. The point of this image is not to insist that America at midcentury was indeed exceptional—for every country is, in one way or another—but instead to underscore that the global presence of the United States was so piecemeal precisely because it was more the product of adaptation than of deliberation. In spite of all that postwar planning, the real thinking through came later by way of rationalization and preservation of what Wilson and others contrived as the bitch goddess of national prestige.

How many Americans did want such an archipelago? Not as many in 1946, or even in 1950, as we would like to think. Certainly few said they wanted to keep it by the late 1960s. But just as it takes a person about six months to acquire and reaffirm a new, good habit and a fraction of that time to break it, so too with the imperial habits of nations, just on a calendar of decades rather than months. All things considered, the durability of this particular archipelago is remarkable. How many Americans today are surprised to have visa-free travel around much of the world? Or to be able to use English worldwide? Rather few, probably.

One way or another, an archipelago is not wrapped up so easily. Interests, prejudices, habits persist, and going home is always harder than we think it will be, especially when we have gone abroad on a mission that, however post facto, we have yet to discard.

One old mission that resumed its prominence in the 1940s was the one in China. Throughout the nineteenth and early twentieth centuries, no nation had been a bigger target of American missionaries and merchants. No larger an imagined market of goods, consumers, and souls existed on earth. Roosevelt, who liked to reminisce about his ancestors, China traders who made their fortunes in that market, held such a romantic view. He took special interest in China during the war and was, like many others, charmed by the charismatic Madame Chiang Kai-shek, the wife of the Chinese generalissimo.

The romance was offset by another, less favorable one that came to many Americans who had served with Chinese in the war, and who encountered and resented the venality of Chinese authorities. Like many other aspects of the archipelago, America's views of China were mixed.

"Will China become in actuality the Great Power envisaged by most Americans?" asked the Sprouts in their anthology. "Can the Chinese adapt their ancient culture to the necessities of modern industrialism?" Some are still asking these questions. To many Americans then as now, the fate of China held the fate of the world.

For this reason, quite apart from the arrival of the Cold War, American leaders were vexed by China's civil war. It would divide them more than most people would have predicted. It sounds strange today to imagine that a "Who lost China?" debate would have driven so many people to distraction, and would end a number of brilliant careers. But this was how the archipelago worked. Keeping this particular island in the American sphere turned out to be a drama of the first magnitude.

Most of it took place after our period, that is, after the Communist victory in 1949 and through the Korean War, which lost what little political favor Truman had left. By then he had staked out a firm position in the Cold War, which he applied in equal measure to Soviets and Chinese.

This had not been the case back in 1946. Americans who had been heavily involved in what was known as the China-Burma-India theater during the war were determined to find a compromise between Communists and Nationalists. It was clear to some of these Americans—foreign service officers called China hands, including some who had been born and raised in China as the children of missionaries and who therefore rated highly their powers of empathy—that the Communists were more committed fighters than the Nationlists, who were committed mainly to their own enrichment. This is an unfair oversimplification, but it appeared often in contemporary accounts. Each side, on balance, had keen fighters. The problem was that many were just as keen on fighting each other as on defeating the Japanese, which made the job of the Americans commanding and advising them, notably General Joseph "Vinegar Joe" Stilwell, a sadly maligned figure, extremely difficult. Stilwell was a first-rate field commander but a lousy diplomat. He had so much trouble getting on with Chiang that Roosevelt had to send two additional envoys, Donald Nelson and Patrick Hurley, to make peace between them, among other things.

As often happens in these cases, the envoys chose a side. Nelson and especially Hurley joined the Chiang camp. Stilwell's own partisans included many of the above-mentioned China hands, none of whom was a doctrinaire Communist but who nearly all eventually became tarred with Senator McCarthy's brush for what they said was a pragmatic position in favor of temporary collaboration with Mao's forces. Stilwell's amanuensis became the *Time* reporter Theodore White. This may have been testament to Henry Luce's editorial integrity, for while Luce—himself the son of a missionary to China and a firm partisan of Chiang and the Nationalists—held tight control over the way editors produced his publications, he allowed for some diversity in his writers' reporting. His aim, purportedly, was not to influence politics in the short term but instead to shape perceptions over the long term, China being an exception.

Stilwell had other, more immediate concerns. His enemies had included, on Chiang's side, General Claire Chennault, former commander of the Flying Tigers, the volunteer air support squadrons of Chiang's army, and Chennault's scribe—none other than Joe Alsop, who directed the force of his 250-pound presence against anyone who had a good word to say about Stilwell. Although Alsop slimmed down by nearly one hundred pounds when he returned to Washington after the war, he never altered his views about China, and about the betrayal by the China hands. This was just one reason why much later Alsop, in posing as a liberal contrarian (he was a Roosevelt descendant, after all, though on Eleanor's side) and speaking out against McCarthy, was among the very last passionate defenders of the Vietnam War.

Rather than easing divisions, the Hurley mission worsened them, so Truman sent another missionary to settle differences and restore a neutral, nonpartisan position for the United States. General Marshall dropped into the Chinese snakepit, "[a]rmed with a policy that was twelve months overdue, [and] instructed to create a peace out of the sorrow and bitterness of a raging civil war." Marshall had retired—his health wasn't good—but he did not question the assignment when Truman gave it. Nor did he complain. He merely hung up the phone on the president after saying yes, but this was because he saw Mrs. Marshall approaching in the drive and didn't want her to overhear the conversation. He had promised her, finally, a decent retirement, and feared her reaction.

Marshall spent the better part of 1946 in China before becoming secretary of state, and then, in 1950, secretary of defense. Whereas the last two assignments were successes, this one was a failure. Nobody, not even Marshall, could compel the warring sides together. The only achievement was to have kept them from ganging up on the United States, and in urging, upon his return, the U.S. government to refrain from intervening in this nasty war.

It may have been for the best, but few people said so. The Second World War in the Pacific, in the words of Annalee Jacoby and Teddy White, "cut blindly across . . . the greatest revolution in the history of mankind, the revolution of Asia." What else had the United States done? How could it have "lost" China? "We had temporarily lanced one of the pressure heads and released some of the tension by an enormous letting of blood. But the basic tensions and underlying pressures were still there, accumulating for new crises." Not even Marshall could do anything about that. Chiang and his clique were masters at telling the general what he wanted to hear, and Marshall became adept at saying as little as possible that signaled a certain reaction. His Chinese interlocutors alternated between passive exasperation and active subversion in making it known that they wished he were gone, but when he finally did announce his departure in March—an interim one before the final failure of negotiations, as it happened—the best-informed Americans panicked.

There was indeed little he could do but to act as a buffer and urge caution upon the contenders for power. Anything more was fanciful. Americans didn't have this manner of empire. Their archipelago did not contain this vast island, and probably never could, so they resigned themselves to including a much smaller island, Taiwan. The question was how far outside the archipelago the remainder of

China would lie. Marshall's mission ended with Communists and Nationalists far apart, perhaps further than before. All he could do there was to close the door with a sad bang. It made him few friends in Asia.

Was it a worthy effort? Even the most jaded diplomats—John Melby, for instance, the lover of Lillian Hellman and the keeper of a vivid diary—said so. It was an attempt, probably premature, to find a modus vivendi with people possessing a mission and an ideology that went against what most people said were American values. Yet Asian Communism was complex. It had a different relationship to nationalism, and different terms of reference to what Americans were coming around to contesting in Europe. The remarkable thing is that it took Truman and his successors so long to realize and act upon it. America's influence throughout Asia declined as the United States and its power were equated with repression. "No matter what we do," Melby observed, "we are in the wrong."

A much happier island of the archipelago was Germany. That must sound strange; Germany too was decimated and divided, with an even more dangerous and divided island—Berlin—nestled inside, but its civil war stayed cold, just barely, and the country got more positive attention from Washington. Following a brief moment in the closing hours of the war when it appeared that the Americans would leave the Germans alone, the Truman administration placed Germany at the center of its foreign policy. Other nations in trouble, chiefly China, would take a backseat. This was not so much the result of a clear strategic decision in favor of Germany or Europe— although there certainly were people advocating that—as it was of indecision over what to do, or what could be done, in Asia.

It was only partially a sentimental policy. Americans in Germany in August 1945, including Truman, as we have read, were moved by the destruction they saw, but they knew how close the war had come to being lost, and that it could just as well have been them picking through the rubble of their own cities. Between their meeting at Potsdam and the end of the year, the occupying powers would follow the lead of the occupiers themselves—in America's case, General Clay—and adopt a hostile and independent stance toward their fellow occupiers the Soviets. This led, in turn, to an ever tighter commitment to the survival of West Germany, and West Berlin, as Western outposts. That this also included the granting of rehabilitation, or the willful looking the other way—that is, amnesty—to scores of former enemies is now an established fact. But there were other demands on their attention and resources. The occupations needed collaborators too. The only sin, as General Patton found out when he was dismissed in Bavaria after having disparaged denazification as a political stunt, was to speak too bluntly about it.

Germany's was not the only occupation that was touch and go. In France, for instance, Roosevelt once had in mind importing everything from a new French currency that looked like the U.S. dollar to an occupation authority staffed by American Francophones. This did not happen, mainly because of the fact of General de Gaulle, whom Roosevelt could not bear; the feeling was mutual, but de Gaulle did not confine his hostility to Roosevelt. It was not helped by the delay in recognizing his government.

There was also Japan. In principle it too was to have a joint occupation by the British, Chinese, Soviets, and Americans, but on these islands the United States got its way and became the sole occupier. Here too the occupier looked the other way from capable yet culpable (in their wartime actions) former enemies in the name of security and stability. So too did some of the occupied. Even Hiroshima and its poisoned population got a bright-eyed young American army lieutenant to run their city.

Germany was somewhat different. Germans had to be kept down, went the received wisdom, to prevent them from rearming again. The job that was not done properly after the First World War had to be redone better after the Second, which in effect meant the opposite: helping them rebuild a strong (including, eventually, an armed) and prosperous state. Only the two most powerful nations, the United States and the Soviet Union, could do that. The American occupation adopted this position: Germany also had to be reconverted into a peace-loving society. Only then would it never threaten its neighbors or the wider world. The prospect sounded far-fetched so soon after the war, but what choice did America have? Germany would become the model island with a clear purpose. One American recalled it:

> "The purpose of the Occupation," said Major General Adcock, "is to make certain ..."
> The telephone rang in the General's office in Frankfurt. "Go ahead, Munich," said the General. "Hello, Dorn. Can you hear me? Can you hear me? Fine. I want that report on the sugar beet deal with the Russians as soon as possible. That's right, the sugar beets. Now look, those power plants down there. How much power from Bavaria serves Austria? Yes, Austria? ..."
> "The purpose of the Occupation," he continued to tell me, "is to make certain that Germany can never ..."
> Again the telephone rang. "Hello, Berlin. That you, Boyd? And yourself? Good. Now look, this month's coal production for the Ruhr ..."

We get the point. No matter what the occupiers said they were doing or why, it had above all to work. We are accustomed to tout this attitude as old-fashioned American can-do-ism—here coupled with German willpower and efficiency, and a bit of deviousness on all sides. All were stereotypes and not universally evident, but here and there they drew inspiration. Our observer continues:

> It is chiefly through these [military government] Detachments that the German authorities on the spot receive their orders. This is the point at which the will of Mr. Smith in Duluth is

most keenly felt by Herr Schmidt in Munich, where the desires of Mrs. Shuman in Boston are most sharply felt by Frau Schumann in Stuttgart.... Through this chain of command the American part of Germany is run.... This is America's Germany. In a very real sense, the Germans within this area are our subjects. In a very real sense, they are also our responsibility.

With responsibility came perks. He was blunt:

> The Army of Occupation is also living well. Most men agree that they have never lived so well while in the army. Some have never lived so well before.... The Allied forces are in Germany as conquerors. Conquering has its privileges.... What kind of work do the men of the Occupation do? The majority are "occupied in occupying."

So Americans went to Germany and Germany became more American. Students whose teachers had studied in German universities, or had learned their methods from those who had, went to reconstruct and repopulate those universities. Many of the occupiers had families, and many of their wives and children mingled closely with German families. The occupation established new newspapers modeled on American newspapers, but the editors, language, and style appealed to traditional German readers. Artists came to Germany to perform Wagner operas for the first time since the war. American headquarters and offices proliferated; Germans and Americans collaborated together in designing and making every imaginable product and household good; Germany filled up with Camel cigarettes, hot dogs, American-style country clubs, and, the most ubiquitous of all, Coca-Cola. Coke possessed an entire archipelago of its own: even before the war it was sold in over seventy-five countries. One bottle in 1946 cost as much as a subway fare—a nickel—and the company only twice saw an annual loss, because of sugar shortages.

Some people have always regarded occupations as unpleasant, or even wicked. Surely back then in Germany, Japan, and elsewhere there was some resentment, and sometimes hostility. For this reason we often distinguish between friendly and unfriendly occupations. There aren't many of the former, but Germany was on balance not too unfriendly, at least in the West. More to the point of our archipelago, the occupation, warts and all, was in fashion, at least for the leading occupiers. Many of these people were quite young: in their late twenties or early thirties. Suddenly they were put in charge of whole villages or provinces, or even given ambassadorial rank. To have this in Old Europe at this time must have gone to more than a few heads. They must have felt admired, respected, adored. They were protectors, defenders, promoters of all that they had won in the war and of their own small plot of earth in peace.

This was the case in fact throughout Western Europe, not just Germany. Teddy White, in his roman à clef *The View from the Fortieth Floor*, set in the early 1960s, described the background of his protagonist, Ridge Warren, the director of a large New York publishing house. Warren faced terrible strains on the job, but he then stood, briefly, at the top of the game. Yet this did not compare to what he had done fifteen or so years before, nor was it as easy:

It had seemed in the beginning so natural for the Warrens to go to Europe. The war was over and the Air Force had decided to survey the ruins of Germany. The Strategic Bombing Survey of Germany had held him in Europe in 1945 no more than four months; but then there had been the UNRRA programme in Yugoslavia. Mary had joined him in 1946; and from the first of the aid programmes they had gone to the next, to Greece. And then there had been the Marshall Plan, and the lateral transfer to the Occupation in Germany, as Germany had come alive. And then all the other transfers, each one notch higher than the last until two years before the end, when they had finally

reached Paris. And there, at the heart and centre of the Plan, he
had finally won the rank of Ambassador. The last thing I thor-
oughly believed, reflected Warren, was that it was better to
have won the war than to have lost it.

Speaking of Greece, we can witness another typical scene of
our period: the arrival of several Missouri mules, thanks to the
American aid program, to help the Greeks, who were still in the
middle of a civil war, improve their harvest and to assist somehow
with transporting matériel to the warring parties in the mountains.
One of these mules arrived in the back of a truck to the door of the
American embassy in Athens, accompanied by a confused American sergeant who did not know where to deposit his charge. The
wife of the ambassador, a forceful lady, brushed him aside, mounted
the back of the truck, and sprayed the animal aggressively with her
perfume bottle. "I christen thee Greece!" she exclaimed. She said
the provision of the mules to the Greeks had been her idea.

We call this typical not because Europe was full of diplomats'
wives spraying farm animals with perfume bottles but instead
because it reveals a particular attitude and tone: ostensible in its devotion but carefree, and borderline playful, with its power and presence.
This was before contempt had set in, before George Kennan could
write of his fellow Americans in Germany (in 1954) that "their presence here infuriates me. Everything about them I view with loathing:
their callousness, their softness, their imperviousness to things around
them, their spoiledness, their garrulous conviviality."

There have always been such people whose malodorous presence blemished their country's reputation in the world. For now,
though, briefly, they were outshone by a better sort.

We turn finally to the home island, or, as it was once known, the
great island continent, the United States itself. We have intentionally
not described it in planetary terms, as in a solar system, surrounded

by planets and assorted satellites, for this was a misleading Cold War image. Neither was it a hub with spokes extending in all directions, as Mercator map projections would imply. No, it was an island among islands, soon to comprise multiple world islands—hubs, regions, suburbs, beltways, ghettos, and so on.

Recalling the children's book mentioned at the beginning of this chapter, we note again that the home island and the others were connected, rather than divided, by water, and by decades. Thus it should be no surprise to learn that the United States played an important role in overseeing refugee centers, so-called displaced person centers, throughout Europe after the war. It should be no surprise that the methods used in these centers had much in common with the relief and social work of the Depression years. By mid-1946 the relevant departments of the U.S. government said most should be closed in the American zone in Germany. It should also come as no surprise that Truman put off acting on that recommendation, noting the upcoming midterm elections. Simply put, he said to Secretary Byrnes, "The Poles in this country and the Catholic Church are simply going to have a spa[s]m if we close out these camps."

There were other types of islands at home. We have noted the foresight of the men who built the Pentagon, which was begun a few months before the attack on Pearl Harbor and completed in 1943. It is triple the size of the Empire State Building and contains room for more than twenty-five thousand workers, as well as "eighty-three acres of offices and public spaces, including a shopping center, and seventeen and a half miles of corridors." It is a large island indeed.

The concentration of so much of the country's military command in one site went against the decentralizing grain, as per the dictates of Peter Drucker. Perhaps he had read too much of his own Austro-Hungarian imperial origins into it, yet he had a point. Decentralization, he wrote, may not be "the most efficient" principle. Sometimes it was the opposite; but it could be, in the circumstances of an archipelago of power and influence, the most secure and perhaps the most stable. It is another way of touting the American experiment with federalism, and the American belief in redundancy. "Disperse, disperse, disperse" was the order of the day, following a cursory look at the likely effects of atomic warfare. The Soviets hardened their missile sites many miles underground. Americans did not, or at least not as much. Rather, they made them redundant. For all the preponderance of the Pentagon, the country's military command could in theory survive a direct hit. There were multiple other commands, including at least one in the air twenty-four hours a day, all year round.

The redundancy principle applied to more than military defense. Many of the country's institutions in fact were, in Drucker's words, intellectually cast "as a means to an end which is beyond society." Society and social harmony were not ends in themselves; nor were the power and virtue of the state. Rather, these were all attributes and adornments of something else: the virtue of the individual and its fulfillment in time. Hence Americans' capacity to merge materialism with idealism: "The American who regards social institutions and material goods as ethically valuable *because* they are the means to an ethical goal is neither an idealist nor a naturalist, he is a dualist." Hence the country's obsession with "getting ahead," its passion for competition in nearly all things. Hence its reactive and retrospective need to cover as many bases as possible: if one route failed, try another, and another. Hence, in this respect, its appreciation of opportunities as islands that rise, or fall too. The archipelago was meant to last; the individual islands were not.

Here then was another paradox. One result of decentralization was the comparably low profile of the professional caste of civil servants. They exist in America as in many other places, but they do not occupy the same social role that they do in other countries. Above them exists another, much more visible but transient class of professional appointees. These people, whom Teddy White called the "strange clan of Deciders," enter and leave government in cycles, usually following the party in executive power, and dominate public debates, as well as the most prominent networks of patronage. While broad and apparently permeable, the class, at least back then, was also fickle and not given to offering multiple points and moments of entry. "They recruited their own successors by instinct and fellowship," White noted. "If you did not catch their eye when leaving government, you found yourself in the ten- to fifteen-thousand-dollar basket, pushing brass fittings for an export agency, practising law in a small town, teaching at a small university—or dropping completely from the sight-range of those who made and acted in great decision."

Another result was the Cold War gunbelt—referring to the map of defense expenditure in the United States—which brought the prosperity of the military-industrial complex to the South and the West. These sections—or regions, as they now liked to be called— were still beholden to eastern capital, to eastern ways and eastern priorities. Yet southerners and westerners had grown proud; some among them foresaw the gains that would come with the new Cold War, with suburbanization, with the automobile revolution, with redundancy and dispersal. There would be more islands in their parts of the country, and the islands, beginning with that once sleepy, insular southern small town, Washington, D.C., would keep growing bigger.

Here is the final paradox of the archipelago. The ambivalence about power Americans confronted in 1946 led both to dispersal and, therefore, to more familiarity with the federal government in their lives. It became a less remote island. American culture, like most cultures, would export in singular and import in plural. Willkie's *One World* would do the same, depicting the globe uniformly as America's oyster but described at home—in this case at Jackie Robinson's debut in April 1946 at Roosevelt Stadium in Jersey City—as a "seething mass of humanity, representing all segments of the crazy-quilt we call America. . . . Willkie's 'One World' was right here

on the banks of the Passaic River." Mental maps and real maps con-
verged into an American paradox that remains with us, and confounds our thinking, especially when it comes to decision.

America's self-defined mission after the Cold War was a familiar
one, the old Wilsonian mission, although now it had acquired some
new terminology. In place of new world order (*pace* Bush I) was something called global governance; in place of the world community of
nations was something called globalization. This global consciousness was not new. It is convenient to date it to the moment in 1968
when for the first time a photograph of Earth from space became
widely seen and, arguably for the first time, most people in the world
became aware, literally, that there was a single shared planet. That
realization too had been around for a long time, but it is hard to
prove that most people in the world shared it until the middle or late
twentieth century. Even the nation that became the greatest success
of the New World, the United States, saw its global consciousness
and its global presence emerge in fits and starts, and in sections, from
the trading posts, merchant houses, and capitulations in the nineteenth century to the coaling stations, bases, and multinational corporations in the twentieth, from the Caribbean to the Pacific Rim to
Europe, to the first steps on and photographs from the moon. Americans could argue, as traditional anti-imperialists, that they had neither chosen nor decided to acquire any of these things for their own
sake, but they accepted them as the least dangerous of the alterna-
tives, and did their best to make the most of them. Doing that, in
turn, was a choice, but not one that we could tout as a decision:
empires are man-made; archipelagoes, even global archipelagoes,
are expressions of nature.

In the meantime there was the persistent belief that things
would turn out all right. Jim Forrestal, briefly, guardedly, held on to
it. Here he summarizes a briefing by his old Wall Street colleague
Jack McCloy in November 1945:

The postwar problems are global; that is, the conditions of anarchy, unrest, malnutrition, unemployment, etc., which exist in Europe and the Middle East are duplicated throughout Asia and Southeast Asia—the economic dislocations are profound and far-reaching.... The tremendous position and prestige enjoyed by the United States is the one beacon of hope everywhere, but the dependence upon us to be the salvation for all the ills of the world may not be an unmixed blessing; the disappointment, frustration and bitterness of the end of next winter may be in exact proportion to the confidence expressed in us now.

The year 1946 also would close on a mixed note.

Chapter 12

Midpassage

By the time this issue of Harper's *appears the "constitutional crisis" that Democratic editors—there are some Democratic editors—have been talking about should be precipitated. That crisis, which has occurred a good many times in our history, consists of the loss of the House or both houses by the administration. The current talk about it, however, seems to me pretty belated. We have been in that kind of crisis ever since President Roosevelt died.*

—"The Easy Chair," December 1946

Few people today remember firsthand the twilight era of the crooner. Bing Crosby, Vaughn Monroe, Frank Sinatra, Nat King Cole, Perry Como—all had hits in 1946. Their female counterparts—it is difficult to call them crooners, but the title is loaded anyway—did as well: Doris Day, Jo Stafford, Martha Tilton, Dinah Shore. Today we would call this music soothing, a form of comfort food, but young fans, the "bobby-soxers," swooned for Sinatra especially; they screamed and rioted. Sometimes the police had to be called. This manner of public entertainment predated the rock stars of the 1950s and 1960s; it also predated the adolescence of the baby boomers who later came to dominate the creation and consumption of American popular culture. Nevertheless, the music of the mid-1940s was of a liminal quality, more intimate than the big band sound of the previous decade (although the most popular singers nearly all got their start with big bands), but not yet sultry. There were cross-fertilizations: B. B. King, Bill Haley, and Chet Atkins had launched their careers; Bill Monroe relaunched the Blue Grass Boys. Maybe the war had broken down a few barriers, but the most popular singers stayed well within their genres. The surface, the veneer, held.

One of the most liminal, and certainly one of the most interesting, figures of the era was the lyricist Johnny Mercer. He is known mostly now for his passionate affair with Judy Garland and for his later hits, notably "Moon River." But earlier he had made an important bridge, for a number of reasons. Mercer came at the end of the reign of Tin Pan Alley, which had dominated popular music for a generation. Composers like Irving Berlin and George Gershwin translated popular idiom and taste into song. American music, like American art and American poetry, sought and found this kind of appeal at home and also abroad. Its fans said it spoke to them and sounded just right.

Mercer was a Tin Pan Alley archetype, but he came too late to ride the peak of the trend, and he was different, liminal, in another sense. Many of the Tin Pan Alley men were immigrants or children of immigrants, keen to demonstrate their American bona fides, but their introduction to certain genres—jazz and blues, for example, at the root of so much of American popular music—was second- or third-hand. Not so for Mercer. He came from a good Savannah, Georgia, family, raised by black servants, sung to and enraptured by them. He knew their spirituals, their lullabies, their cadences, their rhythms. Tin Pan Alley men had known all that at a distance; but just when Mercer came onto the scene, the market had shifted. People returned from the war and felt freer to promote the sounds they wanted. "Hillbilly" and "race" music moved up in the charts. These were the sounds Mercer had integrated into his own; he hadn't shied away from that, at least not yet, but now they supplanted Tin Pan Alley, and him.

Mercer and his wife, Ginger, left for Hollywood in 1935. There was a good market there for composers for musicals. He tried his best, but he came up short—professionally, at least. (He would meet Garland there at a party given by Bob and Dolores Hope.) He continued to write nice songs but was overtaken, especially by Oscar

Hammerstein, the king of the lyricists. Mercer returned to Broadway and put his heart into a musical there, *St. Louis Woman,* in 1946. It was a flop. Not all Broadway musicals were. There was a revival of *Show Boat* in 1946, then *Brigadoon* in 1947, *Kiss Me Kate* in 1948, *South Pacific* in 1949. But none was a Mercer production. He "was not a man of the theater.... [He] thought in terms of the song rather than the show."

Maybe so. Tin Pan Alley meanwhile had all but gone. Mercer won his first Academy Award in 1946 and had many more productive years in him, making significant contributions to the American songbook. But for now he had served a purpose. The transition from prewar to postwar music was over.

Hollywood too was in a middle period, although few people there realized or championed it. Many Hollywood actors had roots in vaudeville, and found the transition to film, and then to talkies, uncomfortable. Some just disliked the place: Barbara Stanwyck, a Brooklyn girl born Ruby Stevens, called it "the papier-mâché town." Others adapted. Roles, and role models, changed. Heroes became antiheroes. Easy, fluent actors became hard. Confident men grew unsettled. John Wayne, Bob Hope, and Clark Gable made room for Robert Mitchum, Kirk Douglas, Burt Lancaster, Dana Andrews, Richard Widmark, Sonny Tufts, Alan Ladd, Van Johnson, Robert Ryan, Dan Duryea, Robert Walker, Danny Kaye, Gregory Peck, and finally Montgomery Clift, to name but a few. Jimmy Stewart, one whose career bridged the gap, made his "no war movies" pledge and starred in *It's a Wonderful Life,* released for Christmas 1946. Also on their way out by decade's end were Ingrid Bergman and Betty Grable; in were a resurgent Joan Crawford, Jane Greer, Veronica Lake, Gloria Grahame, a chastened Bette Davis, and "a new screen siren ... a sultry brunette with insolent, smoldering let's-get-to-doing-it eyes by name Lauren Bacall, immediately nicknamed 'The Look.'" She married her costar in *To Have and Have Not* (1944), Humphrey Bogart, in a picture-perfect ceremony the following year.

The changes happened gradually. The highest-earning film in 1946 was Walt Disney's *Song of the South*, followed by *The Best Years of Our Lives*—a paean by Roosevelt's speechwriter Robert Sherwood to the vexed postwar homecoming. It took home eight Academy Awards. Next was *Duel in the Sun*, a gritty, passionate western. The persistence of such stock reminds us that Hollywood is first and foremost an industry, albeit a curious industry that, in John Gunther's charming phrase, even supported its own blackmail. It did comparably well during the war with such hits as *The Outlaw* (1943), another passionate western, featuring a voluptuous Jane Russell. Hollywood provided a stream of predictable, appealing genre films with familiar stars that filled theaters. However, something else had come along.

This was the film noir. Its top earner for 1946, *The Postman Always Rings Twice*, was the third of James M. Cain's dark novels to be made into films. *Double Indemnity* had been released in 1944 and *Mildred Pierce* the following year. *Postman* had already been released with different titles in France and Italy.

What was this genre and why do some people celebrate it? The term was coined in 1946 by a Frenchman, Nino Frank, but the genre in fact dated to just before the war. Well, it wasn't exactly a genre; it was more a style. Ann Douglas has encapsulated it in a couple of wonderfully pregnant sentences:

> [N]oir was a hybrid of glamour and grittiness, exposing the enticingly seamy underside of midcentury America, a world untouched by the national sport of self-justification then reaching Olympic proportions.... [Noir] was peopled not with the gratingly ill-timed figures blotting much of Hollywood's mainstream fare but with wised-up men and worldly women who had none of the right answers but all the smart moves.

In other words, it was also liminal. Like Tin Pan Alley, the Hollywood studio system had begun its decline. The peak year was 1946, with almost $2 billion in box-office receipts and ninety million average weekly attendance. By 1948, Hollywood had become obsessed with the so-called lost audience. Noir films were emblematic of the mood of the industry. It wasn't dead or even sick; it wasn't so cynical as appearances could suggest. Like Alan Ladd in *The Blue Dahlia* (1946), Hollywood had come back from the war to another and more unpleasant world. It still had faith in itself, yet it feared something ahead. What that was it could not say. We are tempted again to attach the cliché "the system" to it, with actors threatened by ambiguous, amorphous, literally obscure antagonists. "I have a feeling something is closing in on me," said Bradford Galt in *The Dark Corner* (1946). "I don't know what it is."

It would be easy to boil these films down to psychological studies in ambiguity for its own sake, coming in more or less two stages, the first displaying the angst of the late Depression and the early war, and the second repackaged for the inner hysteria of the Cold War. But this is too facile. Noir films were not mere symptoms of the times. They could have come at another time. They reflected the melancholic, wary mood of the public and of the 1940s and early 1950s, but they did not hold a monopoly on fear or on fatalism.

They did, however, move between and connect one national frame of mind with another amid the postwar uncertainty. This was a mind that imagined, however fancifully, that it could turn its back upon the rest of the world and be safe, and another that knew just how fanciful that idea was; one that bought into a load of standards, and rules, only to see many of them turned upon their heads. Hollywood had for some time shaped the mood of the nation. Orson Welles later pointed out that the reverse was then the case. More of what had been private, "classified," was then public, and vice versa. Artists, and not only film artists, sought to resist deception and subversion with the same, but out in the open, in the cause, they said, of truth and honesty, and against conformity.

Yet this moment was brief; noir never dominated Hollywood.

At most these films amounted to only about 16 percent of the annual fare. How then to account for the fad and its longevity in the literature? The war had fed fear, naturally, but it may have had to be on the way to being won in order to express this openly. Victory should have made it all right to be scared. It is a tempting proposition, yet unproven. The usual one does not suffice, however. The dark, ominous plots and tone of these films reflect the fear not of the present but of the future: What will come after the war? How long will we survive? Will our world be peaceful and just? Or will we, having just won a great war at the expense of so many millions of lives and with weapons of a destructive power few could have imagined, live in a perpetual gray zone? There were these dangers, the terrors we know of and, more frightening, the ones we do not know, or do not yet even imagine. How likely are they to come? Is there anything at all we can do to prepare for them, or does preparation make things worse by drawing attention to our fear, to our vulnerability? Few people at the time could, or even wanted to, answer those questions. Few trusted themselves to contemplate them all at once. These films pose an even more basic one we have asked in various ways throughout this book: Is it safe to feel free?

Noir films did not necessarily have sad endings—justice may be served—it's just that the leading characters were no longer perfect heroes. Many films dwelt upon a simple question mark, a liminal position, a doubt. Combined with their primitive brand of existentialism—their plots could be almost arbitrary but also could lead to doom—they felt fatalistic. But they were not so much about fate as about chance. Their characters had free will; they could feel and act like condemned people, but they were not in fact doomed. At the same time they were unsure of the world and of themselves, that is, un- or underconfident. The failure to feel confidence expressed itself as a form of haphazard guilt, or an invitation to something worse. If you never knew what was around the next corner, you could, you maybe even should, feel liberated: *nec spe, nec metu*—with no hope, no fear. You did not find comfort in this. You felt the opposite of liberation, even of sanity; the characters in these films almost all feel trapped or hit, although by what they often cannot say. We now know that it was fear—persistent, indelible fear.

Film stars were not immune to the lure of politics. Helen Gahagan Douglas, known as the "darling of the New Dealers," the wife of actor Melvyn Douglas, had come to Washington to counter the appeal of another glamorous wife, Clare Boothe Luce, a playwright, seductress (of, among others, Bernard Baruch), spouse to Henry of Time-Life, and the lady Franklin Roosevelt once called a loose woman. "They watch each other warily," Tris Coffin observed:

> After Mrs. Luce's sparkling lecture to the House on atomic energy, Helen Gahagan Douglas arose with an earnest but not as learned address. Mrs. Luce was witty and intellectual and played on fear. Mrs. Douglas was calling for attention to the healing powers of atomic energy. Clare Boothe Luce glanced across the aisle with a mixture of curiosity and amusement. It was not lost on Mrs. Douglas.... Mrs. Luce is a curious paradox. In some moments, she appeared to be a mysteriously dreamy schoolgirl. At these times, she floated instead of walked.... But when she began to speak on the floor, Mrs. Luce became a clever, shrewd woman fighting with dramatic oratory, cutting satire, feminine charm, and stunning denunciation. She appeared to be cold, intellectual, and an actress.

This was a new generation of reactionary politician. Helen Gahagan Douglas lost the 1950 California Senate race to Richard Nixon. She was called "the Pink Lady" for her alleged Communist sympathies. Nixon would ride that victory to the vice presidency. Clare Boothe Luce would ride hers to ambassadorships to Italy and (briefly) Brazil.

The reactionaries had it in for Harry Truman. They fought his plans for reconversion, such as they were; they denounced him for the strike wave, for wavering over price controls, for the faltering economy. He fought back and succeeded in passing two bills—the Employment Act and the Atomic Energy Act, the second just barely. The trend was running hard against him. He could not have known that he would triumph, again barely, with his reelection in 1948, or that he would leave the presidency in 1953 as one of the least popular political figures in American history. Truman, as we have seen, was used to such booms and busts. It could be said that he almost courted them, just as his Democratic successors—Kennedy and Clinton especially—gained fame as "crisis" presidents, however dire the crises were (in the case of the former) or trivial (in the case of the latter). The midterm elections of 1946 would not disappoint in either regard.

Jimmy Byrnes had begun the year by noting that he had eaten some black-eyed peas, and that this, where he was from, was supposed to bring luck all year. We saw what happened to him. The year, now drawing to a close, proved far from lucky. It attracted some predictable epithets: "The Year of the Bullbat," "A Disastrous Year," "The Year of Frenzy," "The Year of Frustration." Its summer alone, Dean Acheson said, "was a time of almost uninterrupted troubles both in Washington and abroad."

To recapitulate its politics: First, before Wallace, came the tossing overboard of the other most prominent remaining New Dealer, Harold Ickes. The Old Curmudgeon, as he was known, threatened to resign over Truman's backing for a friend, Edwin Pauley, against bribery charges, and found it accepted. He was asked in February 1946:

"Will you leave the Democratic Party?"
The Secretary smiled smugly. "I'll tell you something. I never was a Democrat." He added with the sad wisdom of one who has been through it all, "But this third-party stuff won't work."
A voice called out, "Thank you, Mr. Secretary."
The auditorium echoed with loud applause. It was the final tribute of the Washington correspondents.

Honest Harold stood in the glare of the floodlights set up by a newsreel cameraman. He waved his arm happily and called, "Good-by."

Ickes's departure represented more than the petulance of the New Deal's old guard. The Roosevelt coalition—northern liberals, southern conservatives, and party bosses—had broken down, and now apart. What would replace it wasn't clear. Truman had catered to the last two—with mixed success (and many from both would abandon him in 1948). The first now was disaffected by the Old Curmudgeon's "glorious exodus." Government business meanwhile reverted to the humdrum. "No inspiration," said one departing New Dealer to Coffin. "No one to demand you do the impossible, and giving you confidence you can. No bold adventures."

This may well have been what the country wanted. In California, for example, voters in 1946 turned out the colorful party boss, Robert Kenny, for Earl Warren, a calm, decent, patriotic man who could be called anything but exciting or profound. Few would have expected him to be the vice presidential candidate in 1948, or that he would go on to shepherd some of the most important decisions through the Supreme Court. The country had grown, if not reactionary, at least more conservative. The term "New Dealer" was out of fashion; "liberal" would follow later. No better proof of this is found than in what happened during the 1946 midterm elections. The Republicans' slogan, with credit to the Harry M. Frost Advertising Company, was short and simple: "Had enough?"

Midterm elections are inherently revulsionary. The ruling party in one branch of the government, or part of one branch, if Congress is divided, has been on probation for two years, which is the outer range of the political attention span. By the beginning of the second year, the pride of victory has worn off. The problems you inherited are no longer the fault of your predecessor. They are your problems, it's your war now, as Daniel Patrick Moynihan told Richard

Nixon about Vietnam. When the country turned against Truman, much of it remembered the immediate past when so many of them had given him the benefit of the doubt, or at least said they would try. Now he was skewered on the spit of a hostile Congress. For some reason, he found the result liberating.

In the midterm elections of 1946 the Republicans retook both houses of Congress for the first time since 1928. The New Deal era could be said to have ended there and then. It did not; this took place gradually. In the 1942 midterms, Democrats had lost forty-five seats in the House and eight in the Senate; they also lost the governorships of California, Michigan, and New York. After 1952, Eisenhower and even Congress would uphold the consensus behind the welfare state. Now, though, other Republicans were in season. Their leader was the prim and earnest senator from Ohio, the aforementioned Robert Taft, a presidential son determined, like many sons of famous fathers, to make his mark in contradistinction to what came before, and to what surrounded him.

Taft was a difficult and complicated man. He was also a nostalgic. He was rightly said to be a throwback to the time when America had more choices, when it could afford a Calvin Coolidge in the White House and a detached foreign policy. Taft probably believed in these things. He was not a radical but another reactionary. For he too sought change, just change in reverse to what had happened during his political lifetime at the hands of the Democrats. Only with Eisenhower—who said he ran for office in order to keep the Taft Republicans at bay and, eventually, to defeat them within the party— would there be a genuine conservative in power. For now Truman may have thought he was trying to be just that. His problem was that he provoked in his opposition the determination to show that he was doing just the opposite and threatening the safety of his country.

We have already seen Taft teased by Chet Bowles. Acheson was another who couldn't hold back: Taft, he wrote "had an excellent mind until he made it up." Taft was methodical, tenacious, volatile, and intentionally small-minded. He was also devious. Now and then he betrayed a slight sense of humor and could charm, although he tried not to. He pushed the limits of tolerance for the dirtier mouths of anti-Communism so long as they were favorable to him. He offered himself up as a strong voice in his party, and an heir to its traditional wing; he was no progressive, and had he prevailed in all he sought to do, he probably would have ushered in another Democratic ascendancy. For now, though, Republicans at the Gridiron Club smelled victory:

> Put on your old gray bonnet
> With the Hoover button on it
> And we'll hitch old Dobbin to the shay.
> When the New Deal's over
> We'll be back in clover—
> On Inauguration Day.

Harry Hopkins was known to have said, "To govern the United States, you must move to the right. To win an election, you must move to the left." Truman treated politics this way and, if we believe Clark Clifford, understood his defeat in 1946 to be an invitation to rediscover and restore the liberal tradition of his party. Now, though, the calculus was the other way around. "Don't rock the boat, boys. We're coming into port!" said one GOP mandarin. It certainly looked like it. The Republicans should play it safe. Their party's victory in 1946 would lead, they said, directly to a retaking of the White House two years later.

We now know this did not happen, and it is important to understand why. It was not just that Truman pulled off his remarkable reelection upset. There was a deeper force at work, which was generational. The Solid South—the conservative Democratic wing in

Congress, which had given Truman its strong backing—was getting older, as were others. It became a less reliable quantity. Back in 1944 the average age of the chairmen of at least half a dozen of the most prominent committees in the House and Senate was about seventy-six. Many of them were on their way out, if not already gone. Reforms in committee assignments and membership threw some parts of Congress off balance. The number of committees would be cut by more than half; legislators would get a pay raise; there would be better liaison, more, as we now say, transparency. The reforms "did not advocate the end of Gerontocracy," quipped Stuart Chase, "but you can't get everything at once."

One silver lining to all this, according to the administration, was the enhanced potential for a foreign policy coalition in Congress between conservative Democrats and moderate Republicans. It was boosted by the many diversions of Taft, which left Arthur Vandenberg, the converted internationalist, in a supreme position. Taft had generally deferred to him in foreign policy while protecting domestic prerogatives, but there had always been the possibility of a split. That was unlikely. Vandenberg could hardly have been more cooperative. He was appreciated by Dean Acheson, who paid him the compliment of noting that his mind was not too original but at least it was open.

Vandenberg was from Michigan, which lies in the Midwest. Still today this section of the country is taken to be a barometer. When we ask what is the matter with Kansas, we mean what is the matter with the United States. This is the fixation upon, and sometimes the romance of, the middle position, the heartland, the center, the standard yet special place.

Another well-known but very different midwesterner was George Kennan. He grew up in Wisconsin, and part of him never left it. His enduring parochialism was striking for someone so sensitive, so cosmopolitan and learned. He contrived an analogy where Europe was to the United States as the East Coast of the latter was to the West: "To us in the East, the West looks standardized, bumptious, shallow, crude, and uninteresting, just as all America does to a European." Yet he was glad to dismiss the Far West, having seen it only briefly, as a European would North America, as—in other words—a uniform place devoid of creativity and "inner tension." No wonder a doctrine of containment could emerge from that fearful, contemptuous heart. Keep things in their place, Kennan demanded—even perhaps his own insecure provincialism, against which he devoted a life of experience and education.

Kennan's nostalgia, like that of other isolationists, was also on balance more historical than geographical. Time, not space, cut the worst divisions; nobody could be on both sides of the divide, however much they pretended not to care which side was which or that time built strength; they too would be displaced. On a visit later in life to his alma mater, Princeton, Kennan noticed a light in the window of the rooming house where he once had lived:

Perhaps some other student was now there, much like myself, in many ways, and yet, aside from individual differences, surely with some subtle, undefinable differences in outlook. Those are the differences which mark the distance between generations, and they are the great and important mysteries, for they are an integral part of the total mystery of change. . . . I realized that I am surrounded here by men for whom the people of my generation were partly nuisances and at best regrettable and temporary necessities; that they were skeptical about the difficulties which had stood in our paths and unimpressed with our achievements. . . . Would they soon be rising after us, crowding us, pushing us impatiently toward that ash-heap? Yes. . . . But those of us to whom it had fallen to try to see behind the realities and to unravel the relationships of our civilization—we would not be pushed. There is plenty of space where we stand, space to the point of loneliness and terror.

He nonetheless asked important questions. We could add a few more of our own. Namely, to wonder whether Year Zero, 1945, followed an end after all. Some have said it did not, that 1989 was the real end of the nastiest century of the modern world. Others have sought an appealing comparison. John Lukacs, for example, about as wise a retrospectivist as there is, has written that only 1914 comes close to 1945 in the depth of its rupture and in its effects; but then 1945 in this formulation only finished what 1914 had begun.

We point the finger here at 1946. There it falls on the page, as we have said, as a synecdoche for the century, for the decade, and for the half decade. Gore Vidal pondered it throughout the second half of his life, this golden age—why was it so short? Why, in just a few years between two wars—World War II and Korea—had there been this cultural renaissance that, according to him at least, was unmatched in his lifetime? Why had Auden, Bowles, McCullers, Williams, and his dear Dawn Powell thrived then and not others, at other times, to so high a degree? We would say the answer was bias, Vidal's in particular. Biased especially against war waged in the name of peace, and against the plutocrats who then had captured Harry Truman and had him do their bidding. For some reason then there was this "brief, too little celebrated interregnum," a precious hiatus, that began in late 1945 and lasted through the middle of 1950. In 1946 he began to think about it, decided he liked it, but also that it could not, should not, and was never meant to last.

Vidal did not regard his generation as near dead or lost. He described his creative friends as flowers amid the weeds. The "impetuous and the confident" merely mistook the one for the other in their cultivation of American culture. This is simple snobbery, yes; but

Vidal had a point to make about this moment in history. It marked an end of absolutes, or of seeking absolutes. The war had gone too far. There was too much blood, and the prospect of too much more. For the fortunate who survived all the bloodletting, there was nothing left besides nihilism, or tyranny. Yet even Vidal, one of the most heartless and cynical artists of his generation, had not given up, although he rarely admitted it, here alluding to a famous image of Flaubert's: "[T]here are still cries, still struggles against our condition, against the knowledge that our works and days have value only on the human scale; and those who most clearly remember the secure authority of other times, the ordered universe, the immutable moral hierarchies, are the ones who most protest the black pit."

Vidal left his country and spent the better part of his middle age in Italy. But the United States was no pit. In his own strange, obnoxious way, Vidal too was an American romantic. Part of him craved that brief celebrated interregnum of peace. Part of him must have wished it had never ended. As with many romantics, Vidal's great enemy was Time. He lived to the ripe old age of eighty-six, but in the last third of his life he was bitter, angry, sad, and corpulent. Dawn Powell has written that the greatest enemy of the artist was precisely that. Middle age made a person tired, complacent, and sometimes despondent. Just look at what happened to her friend John Dos Passos. He moved to the political right, as we have said, and had suffered, in Powell's words, a "fatty degeneration." He and his wife were comfortable, idle, satisfied, secure, and therefore suspect. "Dos both trusts and smacks his lips, sops up the gravy and finds reason for this having been the right life for him—a Jesuitism that is dangerous for an active mind. It is thus that priests and philosophers are betrayed, and Dos is part both of these—half ascetic and half sybarite." In September 1947 he and his wife were in a car accident. She was killed. He lost an eye.

Three years before, he had written of the country. He wondered what had happened to its faith in limited government, and its distrust of the opposite. He admitted that the powerful state in wartime had achieved much. He credited the people for protecting and preserving their traditional way of life regardless, even though there was no more territory to conquer at home, apart from Powell's own adopted city. Or as she put it, "New York is not the same city it was, being overrun now with Americans." But, Dos Passos wrote, the American "people are still frontiersmen. Compared to the encrusted centres of habit and ritual and tradition that are being blasted into heaps in the wars across the seas, even our oldest cities are the provincial bivouacs of a raw and fluid civilization that has not yet stiffened into a frame."

He may have been less certain. He met a young bureaucrat in Washington who struck him by his zeal, his devotion, his gravitas. "We are here and we've got to stay here," the man said. "People in this country won't get it through their heads that government is a necessity." A threshold had been crossed. Powell also noticed it. She attributed it to the combination of vice and inventiveness encouraged by the war. It made America closer to an Old World nation.

They were not cynics so much as realists. This is the preferable term, even today. We met them in earlier chapters. They were the survivors, the unsentimental nostalgics, the ironic optimists. They watched and learned from the Depression. They went to war and returned, realists still. They acquired a strange, bifurcated consciousness of historical time, a bit like the new presidential flag Truman had designed that reversed the gaze of the eagle from the claw holding the arrows to the one holding the olive branch. Was this a more realistic appreciation of the present and the future? Or a more pragmatic one?

The gaze was not an immutable fact; it too had been a choice. Yet there were still so many big decisions to make. How much social and economic reform could the country still support? How much should it devote to guns, to butter? These questions did not arise first in the 1960s, when they had become the topic of breakfast-table polemics. They were heard at the outset of this particular American age, and during the war. The country tried to have it all, after briefly facing the prospect of having neither. The eagle did not deceive, but it did not give the whole truth. There was no stark choice to make between peace or war, not then. It makes for a silly contrast. The country would grow accustomed to those, many resembling an experiment in a social science laboratory: Do we intervene or not? Do we bomb or negotiate? Do we oppose this foe or that one? Do we . . .

Americans in 1946 were tired of doing in this way. They must have imagined that the world had not been at peace since 1914 and would continue in this way for the foreseeable future. Their nation, as Baruch observed, always would be preparing for war, fighting it, or recovering from it. History did not guarantee this fate, but it was how things were and maybe still are. Every generation now regards itself as a war or "crisis" generation. There would be no perfect time for readjustment, no long morning to recover from the hangover of war. Every president tries to turn the eagle around, to promise to deliver a simpler, happier, more peaceful life for his fellow citizens. It almost never happens.

On the other hand, the world had changed, mostly for the better, despite appearances. The world of the 1920s was almost an exaggeration of what was nostalgia for the world before 1914. This couldn't happen a second time. That world was gone for good. There were fewer big houses with affordable servants, for example. Construction materials and labor were more expensive, servants no longer served. It was unrealistic and impractical to keep up this way of life in perpetuity. Familiar streets with such houses began to grow unfamiliar. Families split, recombined, and moved on. The only thing you could do after realizing that familiar appearances deceived was to try to forget about it, then improvise.

Worries compounded the fears. Would there be too few jobs, or too much production? Would prosperity also deceive us? How long would it last? "A nation accustomed to the categorical yes and no, to war or peace and prosperity or depression," Eric Goldman wrote, "found itself in the nagging realm of maybe." Maybe it was all true: that prosperity would only bring poverty, that peace would only bring war. Or maybe not. The only certain thing was how fragile the mood and mind of the country were.

For this reason we have blurred the chronology. The year of indecision extended forward and backward. Elections, even nasty midterm elections, don't count the most, even in democracies. They do not decide a country's fate by themselves. Rather, it's the progression of expectations, the cycle and the spiral of events, downward as well as upward, like a multidimensional gyre or another self-promoted microcosm. Students and teachers of history who point to particular years in retrospect also impose a compensatory, decisive gesture—the annohistory—in order to obscure the opposite, that is, chronological indecision. At least that would appear to be the case in 1946, when nearly everything that came to a head—the tension between industry and labor, political disunity, the problems with morale, with housing, with inflation, with the Soviets—had been foreseen in 1944, if not earlier. Bruce Catton went so far as to call the war itself "the high noon of the world's greatest democracy," albeit one that was fluid in time. He has quoted from Baruch's report from February: "The greatest danger that our nation faces, not only in the transition period but also in the long-time future, is the tendency for people to become broken up into blocs and segments, each organized for the narrow interests of the moment."

They were not the only ones to worry about unity and purpose. In a book published in 1946 and dedicated to his grandson and to his grandson's generation's pursuit of the Four Freedoms, Sumner Welles began with the title *Where Are We Heading?* The answer was another set of maybes. Maybe peace, maybe war. Maybe rivalry, maybe cooperation. Maybe confidence, maybe fear. Maybe truth, maybe deception. Maybe commitment and responsibility, maybe, and in spite of their choice, a "haggle with Destiny."

Another was the series of reports prepared for the Twentieth Century Fund by Stuart Chase, which we mentioned back in chapter 1. From 1942 to 1946, they appeared with the following titles: *The Road We Are Traveling, Goals for America, Where's the Money Coming From?, Democracy Under Pressure, Tomorrow's Trade,* and *For This We Fought.* Taken as a whole they give a good impression of the national uncertainty and angst, although the tone is more optimistic than the one found in the forecasts of Welles or Catton. Chase was more interested in expressions than impressions. Also, like Gunther, he was fond of statistics and surveys. He noted, for example, a Roper survey from 1945 that listed the things Americans worried most about in the immediate future and ranked them: "unemployment, Russian relations, the German settlement, the Japanese settlement/ Intermediate problems: labor unions, race frictions, the UNO, veterans/ Minor problems: inflation, relations with England, with France, with China." Another survey, conducted three years before, showed that more than three times as many Americans wanted "medical care for everyone" than did not. Whether they would get this or much of anything else was anyone's guess back in 1942. Chase wrote that with a bit of fraternity, discipline, and organization they well might.

Chase's cautious optimism joined that of a much better-known authority, Arnold Toynbee, whose multivolume *A Study of History* (or rather the abridged edition) was once a staple of American living room bookshelves. He wrote elsewhere that "[c]ivilization, as we know it, is a movement and not a condition, a voyage and not a harbour." There is progress in the world but it comes piecemeal and in the right response to great challenge. That was his main and rather simple idea in all those thousands of pages. Civilization could just drift, but this was unlikely to work any longer, not with the new technologies of war. The challenges had become even bigger; so too, he hoped, would be the responses. Harry Truman must have read some Toynbee. He was a keen recorder and reciter of civilizations:

> The wars between the Hittites and the Egyptians and between Assyria and the Hittites, between Egypt and Babylon are in the same pattern as today.... You don't even have to go that far to learn that real history consists of the life and actions of great men who occupied the stage at the time. Historians' editorializing is in the same class as the modern irresponsible columnist.... Hillaire Belloc tried to smear Gustavus Adolphus because Gustavus was the great Protestant he was! So study men, not historians. Even Gibbon, Green and Guizot were as prejudiced as old man Beard!

Who was old man Beard? We have already come across him in these pages: Charles Beard, like Toynbee, was one of the better-known historians of the time. Back then Beard also was a nostalgic. He equated the psychology of midpassage less with an unruly adolescence than with middle age or even a national menopause: we cannot go back; we do not want to go forward; we conflate the particular with the universal, and existence with utility; and we cannot decide which we dread more, the known or the mysterious. We cannot say exactly why Beard and his wife, Mary, chose *America in Midpassage* for the title of volume 3 of *The Rise of American Civilization*, published in 1939. Did it refer to time or space, a passage through the middle of the country's natural life, or midway between two fates, or maybe divided against itself toward a single fate?

We do know that Charles Beard had had a bad war. He hated it. He blamed Roosevelt for tricking the American people into it. He was one of a small group of historians who viewed this particular intervention not only as a political betrayal—for like Wilson before him, Roosevelt had pledged many times to keep the country out of war—but also as a spiritual departure, almost a perversion, that would only lead in due course to the death of the Republic, either in defeat or in its replacement with an empire. Nearly every account of this and similar moments in history has described it in the spatial terms of volition: a crossroads, a threshold, a crucible. The country and its leaders faced a choice: one direction or the other. Beard did not waste much time there. To him the image was much starker: Roosevelt had pushed the nation off a cliff.

For his part Roosevelt and other chastened onetime Wilsonians described the war, and the imagined postwar, as a rare second chance. They spoke less about American civilization than about Western civilization. They too had read some Toynbee and had heard of Spengler. The era of the world wars rechristened theirs as the world's (or the West's) last moment for salvation.

It was this grand style of thinking, this historicism, that so bothered Beard. He hated the Great Man theory of history; he devoted his life to burying it. If Truman was the archetype of the amateur obsessed with lists of great men, Beard was the anti-Truman. Beard's hero, alternately worshipped and condemned, was his country, America, as he "sat in his study at New Milford, pondering the ways of destiny and the treachery of democratic leaders, and eating his heart out with a vindictive bitterness."

This description of Charles Beard, written by the journalist Max Lerner, may have overstated the case. In truth America at midpassage was less bitter than uncertain about which way it wanted to go: the head said forward, the heart said back. This was the calculus of 1946, and it would last until the mid-1960s, when the historical directions of head and heart were, for complicated generational reasons, reversed. Yet in contrast to the moment after the previous war, there would be no return to normalcy. Postbellum had become postlapsarian. The right appearances, the right mood, had to be kept, however. Americans compensated. They leaned, and still lean, both ways.

Midpassage saw a few more strange couplings. For example, in 1948 Ezra Pound published his *Pisan Cantos*, which did interesting things to the factual record. It was, like Japanese building addresses, an unfamiliar hodgepodge with its own logic, traipsing back and forth around time "purposefully and consistently." This was, some oversimplification notwithstanding, more indecision masquerading as choice. Yet there were many people still alive in the 1940s who remembered, or who knew people who remembered, the previous century, and the Old World. They remembered it not only subjectively but also, they came increasingly to say, objectively. They would have admitted a rupture but, as human nature would dictate, tended to dwell more on the continuities in their lives. For all its revolutionary creed, the United States remained a conservative, or stubbornly evolutionary, society, as well as a highly subjective one. Where its chronologies lapsed, it sought to invent them.

The nation's dilemmas may not have been so metaphysical. The war was in the background. It had not really ended. It remained there. It would take another couple of decades for people to stop marking it in time: "since the war" and so on. To this day, "postwar" is the adjective accepted to mean "contemporary." The Cold War almost certainly would not have been called a war if war had not remained so much a part of everyone's thinking. Still, Americans were not accustomed to talking about war in this way. They were not the extensions or the handmaidens of politics as Clausewitz called them; they were exceptions to the rule, meant to be won by any means necessary, then to be over and done with as quickly as possible. Normal life did not include war. Prewar life could be a source of nostalgia or, in retrospect, a descent into folly; postwar life was meant to be a return to normal peace and prosperity. There would be much of the latter to come during the Cold War, but somehow war itself became normal, later spawning a number of vapid struggles against things some Americans did not like and that appropriated the label: wars on drugs, crime, tobacco, alcohol, prostitution, terrorism, cancer, and so on.

Moving from one position to another, from being disinterested to uninterested in reinventing a distinction between war and peace, took time. It is one reason why many Americans were confused and muddle-headed after the Second World War, and why they took a long time to adjust to the concept of a long Cold War. Yet whereas many of them, like Hoover or Wallace, fought the adjustment on political grounds, the root of it was more cultural than political. This is another reason that a onetime isolationist like Vandenberg could declare himself a founding father of the Cold War and backer of the United Nations, the Marshall Plan, and the North Atlantic Treaty. He had not become an internationalist with the passion of the convert so much as a consistent "insulationist," as we have said. It is not an elegant term but it is a plausible one. To need insulation, protection, security is a defensive, middle position that is bred into a culture, in this instance a culture simultaneously of self-reliance and interdependence. It would be easy to say simply that Americans had finally grown up to realize that security—even the kind they desired—was nearly indivisible, that it required elaborate compromises, alliances, tributaries, and all the rest. They had flirted with this realization at the turn of the century, realized with the First World War that they did not like it much, and then realized again with the Second—which came to pass in part because of the failures to grapple with the aftermath of the First—that collective security for now was the only way forward. Could it be made to work?

Earlier generations knew this even if they did not use the same terminology. The reputations of Franklin, the Adamses, Seward, Hay, Root, and a number of others would hold their own against—or surpass—those of Acheson, Dulles, or Kissinger. They knew war. They knew diplomacy. They also knew power politics. So why did their descendants reinvent a state of diplomatic innocence?

Was that what they needed to justify the sacrifice the wars demanded? Or was this also more reflective than real? Did it come about, in other words, during the postwar years as a way of explaining, or lamenting, why their country no longer made sense to them, why some people chose to flatten the complexities in its history, and why it failed to fulfill the promises made, starting with upholding the Four Freedoms? That would explain the country's persistent divisions during the "consensus" decade of the 1950s as well as the emergence of a popular youth culture that would later annoy, and sometimes terrify, the greatest generation.

After 1946, the country came to notice these contrasts and inconsistencies more consciously than it had in the past. Just as some Americans recently have begun to question the "triumph" of the end of the Cold War, its aftermath, and its legacy in the present day—in a less orderly and still ideologically divided world—interpretations of 1946 will continue to change over time along with the country's self-image. Is America still a power with greatness thrust upon it? If so, what if it chooses to resist rather than acquiesce? That is, what if it instead decides to retreat? This is not another way of asking the perennial question: Is America in decline? Retreat and decline are not synonymous—in rare cases, retreat can be to a nation's expedient advantage—but they are often mutually associated. The usual response, especially among nationalists, is that decline is a choice. If this portrait of 1946 teaches us anything, it is that both rise and decline ought to be more results of a deliberate plan than of a simple choice. In truth, Americans have been unusual and quite fortunate in this regard. The United States has experienced the benefits of the former mainly by indecision, and a pragmatic response to events and opportunities; Americans have been more the consumers than the producers of greatness. It still may be sought and seized, and has been, to many Americans' credit, but it's difficult to will into reality. The same probably doesn't hold, however, for decline.

Speaking of decline, by the end of 1946 Harry Truman and his presidency looked pretty grim. "What had gone wrong?" To Alonzo Hamby, Truman's best sympathetic biographer, it was the noise surrounding Truman's slippages that drowned out recognition of his deeper, evolutionary successes, including a sounder economy, a stronger and more coherent national defense, and a more enduring welfare state, which he failed to connect in a way that the American people could understand. "In a curious reversal of the old maxim that the whole may be less than the sum of its parts, the parts at the time seemed much less than the whole. Even the president's achievements looked like failures." It may not be fair, but it is hard to resist the conclusion that such failure was also the result of so much decisive posturing. To insist over and again that the buck stops here risked that people might actually believe it. Thus Truman got much of the blame, even when his choices were the right ones. So we conclude our tour with a retrospective that appears in his diary, toward the end of 1946. It is as good a summary as any of what his generation of Americans had known of the century so far, and the attitude it held toward what was to come, following his, and our, year of indecision.

Sept. 26, 1918, a few minutes before 4 A.M. a service man of my acquaintance was standing behind a battery of French 75's at a little town called Neuville to the right of the Argonne Forest. A barrage was to be fired by all the guns on the Allied front from Belgium to the Swiss border.

At 4 A.M. that barrage started, at 5 A.M. the infantry in front of my acquaintance's battery went over. At 8 A.M. the artillery including the 75 battery referred to moved forward. That forward movement did not stop until Nov. 11, 1918.

My acquaintance came home, was banqueted and treated as returned soldiers are usually treated by the home people immediately after the tension of war is relieved.

The home people forgot the war. Two years later, turned out the Administration which had successfully conducted our part of the war and turned the clock back.

They began to talk of disarmament. They did disarm themselves, to the point of helplessness. They became fat and rich, special privilege ran the country—ran it to a fall. In 1932 a great leader came forward and rescued the country from chaos and restored the confidence of the people in their government and their institutions.

Then another European war came along. We tried as before to keep out of it. We refused to believe that we could get into it. The great leader warned the country of the possibility. He was vilified, smeared, misrepresented, but kept his courage. As was inevitable we were forced into the war. The country awoke— late, but it awoke and created the greatest war production program in history under the great leader.

The country furnished Russia, Britain, China, Australia and all the allies, guns, tanks, planes, food in unheard of quantities, built, manned and fought the greatest navy in history, created the most powerful and efficient air force ever heard of, and equipped an army of 8 ½ million men and fought them on two fronts 12,000 miles apart and from 3,000 to 7,000 miles from the home base, created the greatest merchant marine in history in order to maintain those two battle fronts.

The collapse of the enemies of liberty came almost simultaneously in May for the eastern front and in August for the western front.

Unfortunately the great leader who had taken the nation through the peace time and war time emergencies passed to his great reward just one month before the German surrender. What a pity for this to happen after twelve long years of the hardest kind of work, three and a half of them in the most terrible of all wars.

My acquaintance who commanded the 75 battery on Sept. 26, 1918, took over.

The same elation filled the home people as filled them after the first world war.

They were happy to have the fighting stop and to quit worrying about their sons and daughters in the armed forces.

Then the reaction set in. Selfishness, greed, jealousy raised their ugly heads. No wartime incentive to keep them down. Labor began to grab all it could get by fair means or foul, farmers began blackmarketing food, industry hoarded inventories and the same old pacifists began to talk disarmament.

But my acquaintance tried to meet every situation and has met them up to now. Can he continue to outface the demagogues, the chiselers, the jealousies?

Time only will tell. The human animal and his emotions change not much from age to age. He must change now or he faces absolute and complete destruction and maybe the insect age or an atmosphereless planet will succeed him.

Acknowledgments

I am indebted to Alex Hoyt, Wendy Wolf, Hugh Van Dusen, and the good team at Viking for all that they do, to Megan Kelley and Joanna Mansbridge for talking with me about the history of Broadway and Hollywood, to Warren Coats and Sahil Mahtani for teaching me about economics, to the librarians at Bilkent University, particularly Semra Kesler and Füsun Yurdakul, for acquiring books, and to Nur Bilge Criss for her peripatetic summer school, where most of this book was written.

Notes

Preface
xiv *"no problem is too intractable"*: Quoted in Dûchene, *Monnet,* 154.

Chapter 1: The Uprooted
1   *made Truman think of "termites"*: Truman, *Off the Record,* 52.
2   *it came "with bland urbanity"*: White and Jacoby, *Thunder,* 266.
3   *the Great Migration*: Figures and other data are from Allen, *Big Change,* Douglas, *Terrible Honesty,* Goodman, ed., *While You Were Gone,* Lingeman, *Noir Forties,* and Ginzberg and Bray, *Uneducated.*
5   *make the most of their "unintended juggernaut"*: Humes, *Over Here,* 2.
7   *"about GIs and how they worry"*: Quoted in Sulzberger, *Long Row of Candles,* 264–65.
8   *"scared of being scared"*: Bradlee, "A Return," n.p. (online).
8   *"In 1946," Ben Bradlee, the journalist*: Ibid.
8   *"Jeff is a combat veteran"*: Quoted in Chase, *For This We Fought,* 3–9.
9   *"When they first get home"*: Ibid., 18–19.
9   *"We want to go home"*: Ibid., 26–27.
10 *"Listen, mister, I don't want"*: Ibid., 5, 12.
10 *"The town cannot lie low"*: Ibid., 13.
11 *were noted for their feistiness*: Weintraub, *Victory Season,* 9.
11 *"'Skinner, what the hell'"*: Bourjaily, *End of My Life,* 111.
12 *It was said they lived*: Aldridge, *After the Lost Generation,* 183, 186, 216.
13 *An "anti-suicide police"*: Jungk, *Tomorrow,* 167.
13 *"Our fight for freedom begins"*: Quoted in Gunther, *Inside U.S.A.,* 687.
14 *"Veteran Beheads Wife"*: Quoted in Graebner, *Age of Doubt,* 22.
14 *Truman appointed a "housing expediter"*: Chase, *For This We Fought,* 74.
16 *"'the victors suffer almost equally'"*: Hoover, *Freedom Betrayed,* xix.
16 *"When these men"*: Hoover, *Crusade Years,* 243–44.
17 *"All these rights," Roosevelt concluded*: Quoted in Goodman, ed., *While You Were Gone,* 129.
17 *a "twenty-year truce"*: Conway, *Sorrows of Belgium,* 4.
22 *an "exuberant confidence"*: Barrett, *Truants,* 32.

Chapter 2 : "Harry Who?"
23 *"I just can't call that man President"*: Quoted in Wallace, *Price of Vision,* 448.
23 *caricaturist's dream of an American everyman*: Kenneth Crawford cited in McCullough, *Truman,* 485.
24 *with a "kick" to them*: Gunther, *Inside U.S.A.,* 341.
24 *"One thing I know about Mr. Truman"*: Ibid.
26 *"to fight for everything you do"*: Quoted in Miller, *Plain Speaking,* 19.
26 *"I wish I was seventeen"*: Truman, *Off the Record,* 225.

27 *"had hoped that someday"*: Truman, *Year of Decisions*, 271.

27 *"the Presiden[t] . . . has more duties and powers"*: Truman, *Off the Record*, 239.

28 *for complexity, for "gray areas"*: Hamby, *Man of the People*, 13.

28 *"erratic, petty, and a cut or two below"*: Ibid., 483.

30 *This was his "mulish streak"*: Coffin, *Missouri Compromise*, 25.

31 *so many "immediate decisions"*: Truman, *Year of Decisions*, 111.

31 *"I am here to make decisions"*: Quoted in Hamby, *Man of the People*, 313.

31 *Truman's method of consultation*: Clifford, *Counsel*, 77.

32 *"I do the very best I know how"*: Quoted in Feis, *From Trust to Terror*, 9.

32 *"a clodhopper who has ambitions"*: Quoted in Dobbs, *Six Months*, 162.

32 *"Well I'm here in the White House"*: Truman, *Off the Record*, 75.

33 *"is an overrated president"*: Alsop, *"I've Seen the Best of It,"* 285.

34 *"Harry," said Bess sternly*: Quoted in Elsey, *Unplanned Life*, 96.

34 *"Every day is Mother's Day"*: Goldman, *Crucial Decade*, 44.

34 *"Now you behave yourself up there"*: Quoted in Miller, *Plain Speaking*, 204.

34 *"piano player in a whorehouse"*: Quoted in Wallace, *Price of Vision*, 478.

35 *because the man couldn't really understand*: Hynd, *Giant Killers*, 190.

35 *"the contrariest cuss in Missouri"*: Quoted in Hamby, *Man of the People*, 152.

35 *"I am obliged to the Big Boss"*: Quoted in Donald, *Citizen Soldier*, 82.

35 *"Mr. Prima Donna"*: Truman, *Off the Record*, 47.

36 *"a most charming and a very clever person"*: Ibid., 51–52.

36 *"first in the council hall"*: Quoted in Gunther, *Inside U.S.A.*, 526.

36 *"the chocolate soldier of Albany"*: Quoted in ibid., 527.

37 *The contrast showed even in the drinks*: Richard Rovere in Finder, ed., *The 40s*, 201.

37 *whom people called "Peanuts"*: Miller, *Plain Speaking*, 66.

37 *"these contrary Kentucky feudists"*: Truman, *Off the Record*, 382.

38 *he distinguished between an "advanced 'Liberal'"*: Ibid., 35.

38 *"switched the ball to the publicized duke"*: Article in the *New York Herald Tribune* described and quoted in Weintraub, *Victory Season*, 99.

40 *"Before I had a chance to answer"*: Truman, *Off the Record*, 15.

40 *"stick peanuts up his nose"*: Quoted in Beisner, *Dean Acheson*, 106.

40 *"Tell Harry to be good"*: Quoted in Yergin, *Shattered Peace*, 185.

Chapter 3: Empire Men

45 *the "[w]hole party was a scream!"*: Quoted in Dobbs, *Six Months*, 97.

46 *"If the oil resources"*: Wallace, *Price of Vision*, 255.

47 *so "unworkable" a "proposition"*: Quoted in Dos Passos, *Tour of Duty*, 312 (there referring to a professor's view of postwar cooperation with the Soviet Union).

47 *"Roosevelt's ardour for social reform"*: Dos Passos, *State of the Nation*, 176.

48 *welcome the "new regimentation"*: Stone, *Truman Era*, xxiv–xxv.

48 *"quiet-spoken" interwar predecessors*: Gillingham, *European Integration*, 28.

52 *"I have no feelings except those"*: Quoted in Acheson, *Sketches from Life*, 154.

52 *"He was," Dean Acheson put it*: Ibid., 148.

53 *"the most honest horse thief"*: Quoted in Wallace, *Price of Vision*, 475.

53 *"Jimmy will handle it"*: Quoted in Elsey, *Unplanned Life*, 135.

53 *"Byrnes' attitude," the columnist Joseph Alsop wrote*: Alsop, *"I've Seen the Best of It,"* 286.

54 *"Do you live here?"*: Quoted in Elsey, *Unplanned Life*, 75.

54 *"Admiral," often adding "five star"*: Truman, *Off the Record*, 11.

54 *"Limeys, Frogs, Wops"*: Elsey, *Unplanned Life*, 25.

55 *"What does State think?"*: Quoted in ibid.

55 *The "Adviser to Presidents"*: Baruch, *Public Years*, 185.

55 *"He had become a great name"*: Catton, *War Lords*, 174.

55 *"Le Grand Bandit Américain"*: Quoted in Baruch, *Public Years*, 112.

56 *"Baruch men," they were called*: Quoted in ibid., 249.

56 *"that old Pooh-bah"*: Quoted in Yergin, *Shattered Peace*, 79.

56 *put him down as a "show-off"*: Quoted in Elsey, *Unplanned Life*, 188.

56 *"[b]y education, training, and profession"*: Kennan, *Kennan Diaries*, 647.

57 *"of the primitives"*: Acheson, *Present at the Creation*, 354ff.

58 *"God-damn Wall Street bastard"*: Drew Pearson quoted in McFarland and Roll, *Louis Johnson*, 146.

58 *"Poor Forrestal," Truman wrote*: Quoted in Hamby, *Man of the People*, 306.

58 *"quiet, animal quality"*: Jonathan Daniels quoted in Yergin, *Shattered Peace*, 206.

58 *"Did you hear the news?"*: Quoted in McFarland and Roll, *Louis Johnson*, 148.

59 *Harriman pursued his passions*: Kennan, *Kennan Diaries*, 393.

60 *"nuttier than a fruitcake"*: Quoted in ibid., 320.

60 *Truman's "battering ram"*: Ibid., 359.

61 *"Lou, you've got to sign"*: Quoted in Elsey, *Unplanned Life*, 196.

61 *"looked like . . . a Truman twin"*: Coffin, *Missouri Compromise*, 18, 30.

61 *"These people have enough"*: Quoted in Clifford, *Counsel*, 78.

62 *"[t]he glittering young man"*: Coffin, *Missouri Compromise*, 41–42.

63 *"took to calling him 'Pauline Davis's counter jumper'"*: Alice Longworth quoted in Alsop, "I've Seen the Best of It," 285.

63 *None was a prototypical "new elite"*: Conway, *Sorrows of Belgium*, 240–41.

63 *"public entrepreneurs" of the middle century*: Eugene Lewis quoted in Graebner, *Age of Doubt*, 66.

Chapter 4: Dynamo

64 *"a little boy on a toboggan"*: Quoted in Dobbs, *Six Months*, 240.

64 *would not be "women and children"*: Truman, *Off the Record*, 55–56.

64 *20 percent of them felt "ashamed"*: Chase, *For This We Fought*, 78.

65 *was now also "boss of the Pacific"*: Walter Trohan quoted in Wallace, *Price of Vision*, 477n.

66 *"A Noiseless Flash"*: Hersey, *Hiroshima*, 3, 4, 32, 82.

67 *could just as easily "happen to us"*: Bourke, *Fear*, 259.

67 *"a blanket of obsolescence"*: Cousins, *Modern Man Is Obsolete*, 8.

68 *"to give society the opportunity"*: Brodie, ed., *Absolute Weapon*, 23.

68 *The onetime "merry, pixy" doctor*: Coffin, *Missouri Compromise*, 207.

68 *"Now I am become Death"*: Quoted in Donald, *Citizen Soldier*, 149.

68 *didn't believe it was real: "Propaganda!"*: Quoted in Laurence, *Dawn over Zero*, 95.

68 *called Oppenheimer a "cry baby"*: Quoted in Donovan, *Conflict and Crisis*, 97.

69 *"missionary for the H-bomb"*: Tris Coffin quoted in McFarland and Roll, *Louis Johnson*, 224.

69 *"a Comic Strip public"*: Powell, *Diaries*, 254.

69 *"like the rapid growth"*: Quoted in Wallace, *Price of Vision*, 583.

69 *"From the skydeck"*: Laurence, *Dawn over Zero*, 231, 237, 239.

71 *"The trouble was that we are playing"*: Quoted in Forrestal, *Forrestal Diaries*, 373.

72 They *"rose in fury"*: Daniel Bell quoted in Katznelson, *Fear Itself*, 430.

72 *full of "fear and awe"*: Byron S. Miller quoted in ibid., 432.

73 *"The answer may determine"*: Quoted in Coffin, *Missouri Compromise*, 225.

73 *"Our secret is an asset"*: Conant, "Atomic Age," 17.

73 *"I agreed with Henry Stimson"*: Wallace, *Price of Vision*, 485–86.

74 *less than its "startling efficiency"*: Frederick Dunn in Brodie, ed., *Absolute Weapon*, 4.

74 *they were said to be "appalled" by it*: Yergin, *Shattered Peace*, 237.

74 *just a "rough sketch"*: Quoted in Baruch, *Public Years*, 361.

74 *too old to be a "messenger boy"*: Ibid.

75 *"What a tall, esteemed"*: Feis, *From Trust to Terror*, 110.

75 *"You know I never do"*: Quoted in Hewlett and Anderson, *New World*, 556.

75 *"on the installment plan"*: John Morton Blum in Wallace, *Price of Vision*, 43.

76 *"silly without being funny"*: Agar, *Unquiet Years*, 57.

76 *"Don't get mad"*: Bob Fitzsimmons quoted in Baruch, *My Own Story*, 65.

76 *"You have no monopoly"*: Quoted in Hewlett and Anderson, *New World*, 605.

76 *"Mr. Baruch has spoken"*: Ibid.

76 *"I don't care what they call me"*: Baruch, *Public Years*, 378.

76 *"Can't you see it's in your interest"*: Ibid.

76 *"Conn must wish"*: Quoted in ibid., 379.

77 *"We are here to make a choice"*: Ibid., 369, 371.

77 *"We should not . . . throw away"*: Quoted in Feis, *From Trust to Terror*, 145.

77 *had been overly "bomb-minded"*: Quoted in Yergin, *Shattered Peace*, 233.

77 *"Let's forget the Baroosh"*: Quoted by Warren Kimball in Woolner, Kimball, and Reynolds, eds., *FDR's World*, 110.

77 *"We believe we are firm"*: Quoted in Yergin, *Shattered Peace*, 239.

78 *Woodrow Wilson called him "Dr. Facts"*: Quoted in Baruch, *My Own Story*, 131.

78 *"like a surgeon"*: Ibid., 248, 253.

79 *"an atomic cocktail"*: Paul Gallico in Goodman, ed., *While You Were Gone*, 62.

79 *a perfume called "GriGri"*: Goldman, *Crucial Decade*, 40–41.

79 *"a new kind of fire"*: Lukacs, *1945*, 8–9.

79 *"like a blast or a storm"*: White, *View from the Fortieth Floor*, 112.

79 *"a bit of near-eternity"*: Jungk, *Tomorrow*, 124.

80 *"Our trouble is not ignorance"*: Carnegie, *How to Stop*, xv.

80 *85 percent of American farms*: Allen, *Big Change*, 191–92.

82 *"During my eighty-seven years"*: Baruch, *My Own Story*, 320.

82 *"[s]haken, beaten, kneaded"*: Jungk, *Tomorrow*, 62–63.

Chapter 5: Four Speeches

85 *"was the product not of a decision"*: Schlesinger, "Origins of the Cold War," 45.

87 *noted that the camaraderie*: Frank Lindsay to the author.

87 *"and there was no stairway"*: Forrestal, *Forrestal Diaries*, 263.

88 *"It is better," John McCloy*: Quoted in Eisenberg, *Drawing the Line*, 101.

89 *"playing their proper role"*: Rowse, *All Souls and Appeasement*, 117.

91 *as ineffable as "the act of love"*: Quoted and described in Alsop, *"I've Seen the Best of It,"* 289–90.

94 *"personally handle Stalin"*: Quoted in Elsey, *Unplanned Life*, 22.

94 *"go to hell"*: Quoted in Harriman and Abel, *Special Envoy*, 452.

94 *he had advised a "firmer" policy*: Forrestal, *Forrestal Diaries*, 172–73.

94 *"certain bigoted Catholics"*: Wallace, *Price of Vision*, 156.

95 *"extraordinarily gifted" people*: Quoted in ibid., 172.

95 *"Stalin at one time"*: Quoted in ibid., 548.

96 *"If bombs fall"*: Quoted in Elsey, *Unplanned Life*, 24.

97 *"encourage the growth of regionalism"*: Quoted in Melby, *Mandate*, 330.

97 *"Build on anyone else"*: Quoted in Kennan, *Kennan Diaries*, 232.

97 *"He shouldn't ask him"*: Elsey, *Unplanned Life*, 134.

97 *"Bullitt is a vivid kind of person"*: Wallace, *Price of Vision*, 61–62, 61n.

98 *"a kind of mystical masochism"*: Utley, *Lost Illusion*, 38.

98 *"[I]n the fifty years"*: Alsop, *"I've Seen the Best of It,"* 294.

99 *Stalin had given a new speech*: This speech (1) and the three described after it (2–4) may be found in (1) J. Stalin, *Speeches Delivered at Meetings of Voters of the Stalin Electoral District* (Moscow: Foreign Languages Publishing House, 1950), 19–44; (2) Robert Rhodes James, ed., *Winston S. Churchill: His Complete Speeches, 1897–1963*, vol. 7: *1943–1949* (New York: Chelsea House, 1974), 7285–93, and on the Web site of the National Churchill Museum, https://www.nationalchurchillmuseum.org/sinews -of-peace-history.html; (3) James F. Byrnes, "Speech of Hope," in U.S. Senate, Committee on Foreign Relations, *Documents on Germany, 1944–1961* (Washington, DC: Government Printing Office, 1961), 55–62; (4) Henry Wallace, "The Way to Peace," in *Vital Speeches of the Day*, vol. 12, no. 24, 738; for the ad-libbed portions, see the appendix to Wallace, *Price of Vision*, 668–69n.

100 *"the Russians need us"*: Quoted in Harriman and Abel, *Special Envoy*, 447.

100 *"liked the little son of a bitch"*: Truman, *Off the Record*, 349.

100 *"I felt that I had heard enough"*: Truman, *Year of Decisions*, 359–60.

101 *"The Success that Failed"*: Byrnes, *Speaking Frankly*, 67.

102 *"only a little further"*: Walter Bedell Smith quoted in Sulzberger, *Long Row of Candles*, 312.

103 *"The sudden spark set off"*: Jones, *Fifteen Weeks*, 8–9.

104 *"bullying, capricious sasquatch"*: Anon. quoted in Kynaston, *Austerity Britain*, 134.

104 *"Molotov and Vyshinsky"*: Nicolson, *Harold Nicolson Diaries*, 378.

105 *He began to act "firm"*: Truman, *Year of Decisions*, 72.

106 *"I'm tired babying the Soviets"*: Truman, *Off the Record*, 80.

106 *"This is one of my greatest pleasures"*: Quoted and described in Coffin, *Missouri Compromise*, 276–77.

107 *"firebrand of war"*: Quoted in Feis, *From Trust to Terror*, 79.

107 *"palette is keyed too high"*: Quoted in Acheson, *Sketches from Life*, 63.

107 *"might wreck the United Nations"*: Quoted in Coffin, *Missouri Compromise*, 275.

107 *"why couldn't we say [them]?"*: Quoted in ibid.

107 *"nothing to do" with the United States*: Quoted in Feis, *From Trust to Terror*, 78.

107 *"it would make a stir"*: Quoted in ibid.

107 *"There is no iron curtain"*: Byrnes, *Speaking Frankly*, 296.

108 *who joked that "Uncle Joe"*: Yergin, *Shattered Peace*, 176.

108 *"Before we were trying"*: Quoted in Elsey, *Unplanned Life*, 138.
108 *"That's not so good"*: Quoted in ibid.
108 *"It ought to come right out"*: Quoted in ibid., 143.
109 *"No one signs a paper"*: Quoted in ibid., 144.
109 the Baron de Charlus of Georgetown: Vidal, *Golden Age*, 321.
109 *"kick the Russians in the balls"*: Quoted in Wallace, *Price of Vision*, 536.
110 *"We all might as well face the facts"*: Clay, *Decision in Germany*, 118.
111 *"The American people want"*: Quoted in ibid., 81.
111 *"Thus the effort to rule Germany"*: Ibid., x.
112 *"went over [it] page by page"*: Wallace, *Price of Vision*, 612–13.
113 *"Question: Mr. President"*: Quoted in Clifford, *Counsel*, 117.
113 *"Can you say whether the Wallace speech"*: Quoted in Coffin, *Missouri Compromise*, 288.
114 *"This will make Jimmy sore"*: Quoted in Feis, *From Trust to Terror*, 162n. (This is unverified, according to Feis.)
114 *"You and I spent fifteen months"*: Quoted in Forrestal, *Forrestal Diaries*, 210.
114 *"Nobody," an editorialist*: Quoted in Goldman, *Crucial Decade*, 40.
114 *divided among themselves*: Lukacs, *1945*, 169.
115 *it was the "general irresolution"*: Ibid., 222.

Chapter 6: Poujades
118 *"I live in an age of fear"*: Quoted in Katznelson, *Fear Itself*, ix.
119 *"And the intensest form of hatred"*: Quoted in Scott, *Domination*, 1.
119 *"The beginning of the Atomic Age"*: Cousins, *Modern Man Is Obsolete*, 7.
119 *"America did the most colossal job"*: Catton, *War Lords*, 305–6.
120 *"The present Western fear"*: Toynbee, *Civilization*, 22–23.
120 *"What pain, then, and how bitter"*: Bourjaily, *End of My Life*, 192.
121 *decried as a dangerous "permissiveness"*: Quoted and described in Bourke, *Fear*, 87–89, 99–102.
122 *"Democracy," Bruce Catton has written*: Catton, *War Lords*, 313.
123 *"pigs are far more intelligent"*: Quoted in Orwell, *A Life*, 281.
124 *martyr and avenger*: Agar, *Unquiet Years*, 90.
125 *"you'll find a hammer"*: Quoted in Andrews, *Washington Witch Hunt*, 111.
125 *a "Mr. Blank"*: Ibid., 22–23.
125 *"About 90% of USA"*: Quoted in Raban, "America's Best Unknown Writer," n.p. (online).
125 *the Hearst Corporation's income*: Lester Markel in Goodman, ed., *While You Were Gone*, 357.
125 *"shiny and tacky" triviality*: Lukacs, *1945*, 198.
125 *the system of "group journalism"*: Drucker, *Adventures of a Bystander*, 225.
126 *"Russia shows by its spy activities"*: Quoted in Gunther, *Inside U.S.A.*, 544–45.

Chapter 7: Coal and Steel
132 *"eloquent of the man"*: Acheson, *Present at the Creation*, photo caption, n.p.
134 *"an attempt to govern"*: Hamby, *Man of the People*, 362.
135 *The war economy had been good*: Figures and other data are from Chase, *For This We Fought*, Catton, *War Lords*, Lingeman, *Noir Forties*, and Goodman, ed., *While You Were Gone*.
137 *"The old boy is still"*: Wallace, *Price of Vision*, 279.

137 *"Who killed OPA?"*: Quoted in Gunther, *Inside U.S.A.*, 333.

138 *"Bowles operated,"* Tris Coffin has written: Coffin, *Missouri Compromise*, 65.

138 *"Senator Taft said dryly"*: Ibid., 152.

139 *"reckless group of selfish men"*: Quoted in Weintraub, *Victory Season*, 324.

139 *"My young infantryman"*: Truman, *Off the Record*, 102.

140 This is what happened: Figures are from Lingeman, *Noir Forties*, and Goldman, *Crucial Decade*.

140 selling *"Welcome Home"* signs: Leo Cherne quoted in Lingeman, *Noir Forties*, 78.

140 find a nickel beer: Figures are from Goldman, *Crucial Decade*, Kunz, *Butter and Guns*, Truman, *Years of Trial and Hope*, and Coffin, *Missouri Compromise*.

141 *"Rosie the Riveter"*: Maurice O'Connell quoted in Goldman, *Crucial Decade*, 13.

141 *"suggestions" for "improvement"*: Drucker, *Concept of the Corporation*, 190.

142 *"another American citizen"*: Catton, *War Lords*, 141.

143 *"There's no holding it"*: Baruch, *Public Years*, 387.

143 *"[w]ith rare exceptions"*: Baruch, *My Own Story*, 252.

144 *"1946 is our year of decision"*: Quoted in McCullough, *Truman*, 480.

144 *"We are having our little troubles now"*: Quoted in Goldman, *Crucial Decade*, 20–21.

145 *"it would seem, only one thing"*: Gunther, *Inside U.S.A.*, 622.

145 *"He is a Hitler at heart"*: Truman, *Off the Record*, 103.

145 *"Big John" impressed Truman*: Coffin, *Missouri Compromise*, 192.

146 *"There was only one thing . . . to do"*: Truman, *Off the Record*, 104.

146 *"The White House is open to anybody"*: Quoted in Clifford, *Counsel*, 95.

146 *"I brought you gentlemen here"*: Quoted in Coffin, *Missouri Compromise*, 194–95.

146 *"Well then," Truman said*: Quoted in Goldman, *Crucial Decade*, 23.

146 *"The idea of drafting men"*: Quoted in Coffin, *Missouri Compromise*, 202.

147 *"Do you agree with Whitney"*: Quoted and described in ibid.

147 *"flouted, vilified, and misrepresented"*: Quoted in Clifford, *Counsel*, 89.

148 *"We have an agreement!"*: Quoted and described in ibid., 90–91.

148 *"The House chamber erupted"*: Ibid.

149 *"a promontory of American self-satisfaction"*: Dawidoff, "Commager's *The American Mind*," 449.

151 liberate the backbone, and the ego: Madariaga, *On Hamlet*, 11–13.

Chapter 8: New York City

152 *"reputations, many of them fraudulent"*: Gunther, *Inside U.S.A.*, 550.

152 *"a Constantinople, a great Bazaar"*: Frank O'Hara quoted in Perl, *New Art City*, 4.

153 *"a European city"*: Quoted in Gunther, *Inside U.S.A.*, 552.

154 *"anything from Malabar spices"*: Ibid., 553, 556, 576–77.

155 *"Wait until after the war"*: Bourjaily, *End of My Life*, 38–39.

156 *"1919! 1919!" exclaimed Delmore Schwartz*: Quoted in Barrett, *Truants*, 31.

157 They were at once *"terribly aware"*: John Aldridge, introduction to Bourjaily, *End of My Life*, xiii.

158 *"would not be writing books"*: Aldridge, *After the Lost Generation*, 59–60.

159 back to the great moderns: Barrett, *Truants*, 72.

159 *"The influence of* The New Yorker*"*: Aldridge, *After the Lost Generation*, 146.

160 *"We'd heard rumors"*: Lillian Ross in Finder, ed., *The 40s*, 329–31.

161 *"was as delightful a place"*: Vidal, *United States*, 306.

161 *"our best comic novelist"*: Ibid., 306–7.

162 *"Luciferian-looking young man"*: Powell, *Diaries*, 337–38.

162 *"somberly riding geniuses"*: Ibid., 266.

162 *"a Bolingbroke, a born usurper"*: Vidal, *United States*, 39.

162 *"In many ways, Mr. O'Hara's writing"*: Ibid., 336, 339.

163 *"Alfred insists so much"*: Quoted in Barrett, *Truants*, 46.

163 *"felt this chill and withdrew"*: Ibid., 47.

164 *"hour of the women"*: Atina Grossmann in Bessel and Schumann, eds., *Life After Death*, 94.

164 *"The language of our current American drama"*: Quoted in Barrett, *Truants*, 66.

164 *"mechanical and doughy"*: Quoted in Goodman, ed., *While You Were Gone*, 466.

165 *"It was all wonderful"*: Gibbs in ibid., 482.

165 *"gift of suggesting a wide range"*: Gibbs quoted in Finder, ed., *The 40s*, 508.

166 *"Everyone knew that the theater"*: Vidal, *Golden Age*, 317.

166 *"like publishers, regarding the author"*: Powell, *Diaries*, 50, 142.

166 *"was the talk of the season"*: Ibid., 240.

166 a *"real Wagnerian conductor"*: Bernstein, *Leonard Bernstein Letters*, 202.

167 *"painting out of the unconscious"*: Quoted in Leja, *Reframing Abstract Expressionism*, 127.

167 *"New York was a magnificent symbol"*: Perl, *New Art City*, 10–11, 25, 66.

170 *"[W]hat did I have to hold on to?"*: Barrett, *Truants*, 11.

171 *"[a] tall, distinguished looking white-haired lady"*: Powell, *Diaries*, 339.

171 *"Look at the jewels"*: Quoted in Vidal, *United States*, 326. The quotation comes from Powell's *A Time to Be Born* (1942).

Chapter 9: Gaze Homeward

172 *"You know, this whole matter"*: Quoted in Wallace, *Price of Vision*, 373.

172 Truman *"is a small man"*: Ibid., 374.

173 with *"a big grin"*: Hamby, *Man of the People*, 278.

173 *"Wallace's global stare"*: Quoted in Clifford, *Counsel*, 113.

174 who concurred with the epithet: Wallace, *Price of Vision*, 478.

174 The mystical bent of *"Farmer Wallace"*: Quoted by John Morton Blum in ibid., 10.

175 *"Progressives," he pointed out*: Ibid., 17.

176 *"facts rather make it appear"*: Ibid., 591–92.

177 *"a rather mousy little man"*: Ibid., 512.

177 *"very likeable people"*: Ibid., 513.

177 *"Wallace is nothing but a cat bastard"*: Quoted in Yergin, *Shattered Peace*, 246.

178 an *"umpire"* between interest groups: Quoted in Hamby, *Man of the People*, 217.

178 How else to explain popular book sales?: Louis Gannett in Goodman, ed., *While You Were Gone*, 447–53.

179 *"hold the outside world too unimportant"*: Kennan, *Kennan Diaries*, 360.

179 turned to the former, to *"refined nostalgia"*: Burnham, *Struggle*, 235.

179 the devils and *"giddy minds"*: The quote is from the title of a book (*Giddy Minds and Foreign Quarrels*) published by Beard in 1939, from Shakespeare's *Henry IV, Part II*.

180 *"Oh, won't it be wonderful"*: A. P. Herbert quoted in Conradi, *Very English Hero*, 269n.

180 Your will came from the heart: Lukacs, *1945*, 211.

181 "*[M]ore than a mere newspaper*": Gunther, *Inside U.S.A.*, 359.
185 "*[b]eyond and beneath the inflation*": Lukacs, *1945*, 242.
186 "*Mr. President, this is Harry Truman*": Quoted in Miller, *Plain Speaking*, 237–38.
187 "*I saw that great big tears*": Ibid., 238.
188 "*There ensued a period*": Hoover, *Freedom Betrayed*, 569.

Chapter 10: Preponderance
191 "*Mr. Ambassador, there is now a small oversight*": David Acheson to the author.
191 "*So steady is the campaign*": Allen, *Big Change*, 231.
192 *Let us recall some more facts*: Figures are from Murray and Millett, *War to Be Won*, Allen, *Big Change*, Gunther, *Inside U.S.A.*, Goodman, ed., *While You Were Gone*, Yergin, *Shattered Peace*, Woolner, Kimball, and Reynolds, eds., *FDR's World*, Hewlett and Anderson, *New World*, Kunz, *Butter and Guns*, Jones, *Fifteen Weeks*, Mezerik, *Revolt*, and Lowe, *Savage Continent*.
192 "*The American people are in the pleasant predicament*": Quoted in Goldman, *Crucial Decade*, 14.
192 "*But they're so big!*": Quoted in Allen, *Big Change*, 204.
193 *was impressed by the "ideal geography"*: Gunther, *Inside U.S.A.*, ix.
193 "*Juke boxes. . . . Automobiles*": Ibid., 280–82.
193 "*Ohio State is a colossus*": Ibid., 454–55.
194 "*one of the most expensive*": Ibid., 813.
194 "*Tell me, child*": Hoover, *Crusade Years*, xxxviii.
194 "*it's only politics*": Carl Becker in Sprout and Sprout, eds., *Foundations*, 19.
198 *won the "mechanical" war*: A sergeant quoted in Dos Passos, *Tour of Duty*, 14.
198 "*The reason you won*": Quoted in Fairlie, *Kennedy Promise*, 113.
198 "*blood plasma, radar, new drugs*": Burnham, *Struggle*, 5.
199 "*cold, immensely able*": Catton, *War Lords*, 204–5.
199 "*There was no hope of escaping*": Quoted in Yergin, *Shattered Peace*, 177.
199 *London in June 1946 was "a mess"*: Bernstein, *Leonard Bernstein Letters*, 198.
200 *struck by the "incredible inefficiency"*: Quoted in Kynaston, *Austerity Britain*, 315.
200 "*balmy air and bright azalean colour*": Quoted in Martin, "Were We Bullied?" 16.
201 "*World Wide Cartelization*": Wallace, *Price of Vision*, 468.
201 "*It is clear that on the matters*": Quoted in Kynaston, *Austerity Britain*, 134.
202 *an "economic Munich"*: Quoted in Kunz, *Butter and Guns*, 21.
202 "*that he never saw such stupendous ignorance*": Paraphrased in Wallace, *Price of Vision*, 526–27.
202 "*Food, give us food!*" Quoted in Jones, *Fifteen Weeks*, 83.
202 "*We no longer raise wheat*": Quoted in Gunther, *Inside U.S.A.*, 137.
203 "*one of history's greatest acts*": Quoted in Acheson, *Sketches from Life*, 2.
203 "*This was a tribute*": Acheson, *Present at the Creation*, 223.
203 "*series of Soviet moves*": Acheson, *Sketches from Life*, 128.
203 "*I can see Senator Vandenberg now*": Ibid.
204 "*The point I am making*": Ibid., 129.
204 *An American member of the occupation*: Bach, *America's Germany*, 64.
204 "*[T]he Russians are our allies*": Order of Frank W. Ebey, quoted in Sulzberger, *Long Row of Candles*, 308.

206 *"We are all Keynesians now"*: Likely coined by Milton Friedman (and not meant as a compliment).

208 *"an autonomous institution"*: Drucker, *Concept of the Corporation*, 13.

Chapter 11: Archipelago

210 *"Outline Command Plan"*: Catoire, "A CINC," n.p. (online).

211 *"Bases of International Politics"*: Sprout and Sprout, eds., *Foundations*, v.

211 *"You are no more natives"*: Quoted in Dos Passos, *Tour of Duty*, 17.

212 *"rise to globalism"*: The title of a book by Stephen E. Ambrose.

213 *"had greatness thrust upon it"*: May, *Imperial Democracy*, 270.

214 *"with a mixture of respect and hope"*: Quoted in Thompson, *There Is a Spirit*, 167. (Thompson disagreed.)

214 *"one world or none"*: Quoted in Katznelson, *Fear Itself*, 414.

215 *"rushing into the water"*: Paraphrased in Wallace, *Price of Vision*, 207.

215 *"This little Island"*: Brown, *Little Island*, n.p., described in Graebner, *Age of Doubt*, 71.

215 *"Americans as a rule"*: Sprout and Sprout, eds., *Foundations*, 732.

216 *"I hope and pray"*: Quoted in Yergin, *Shattered Peace*, 187.

218 *"all the colors on the painter's palette"*: Paraphrased in Wallace, *Price of Vision*, 208.

218 *"an old dodo"*: Ibid., 263.

221 This was still *"America's Germany"*: Title of books by Julian Sebastian Bach and Thomas Alan Schwartz.

222 *"Will China become in actuality"*: Sprout and Sprout, eds., *Foundations*, 548.

224 His aim, purportedly: Drucker, *Adventures of a Bystander*, 240–42.

224 *"[a]rmed with a policy"*: White and Jacoby, *Thunder*, 292.

225 *"cut blindly across"*: Ibid., xiii.

225 *"We had temporarily lanced"*: Ibid.

226 *"No matter what we do"*: Melby, *Mandate*, 38.

228 *"'The purpose of the Occupation'"*: Quoted in Bach, *America's Germany*, 3–4.

228 *"It is chiefly through these"*: Ibid., 10–11.

229 *"The Army of Occupation"*: Ibid., 31, 38.

229 *Camel cigarettes, hot dogs*: Alsop, "I've Seen the Best of It," 314.

229 *cost as much as a subway fare*: Gunther, *Inside U.S.A.*, 785–86.

230 *"It had seemed in the beginning"*: White, *View from the Fortieth Floor*, 120.

231 *"I christen thee Greece!"*: Quoted in Alsop, "I've Seen the Best of It," 403.

231 *"their presence here infuriates me"*: Kennan, *Kennan Diaries*, 343.

232 *"The Poles in this country"*: Quoted in Cohen, *In War's Wake*, 36.

232 *"eighty-three acres of offices"*: McFarland and Roll, *Louis Johnson*, 155.

232 *"the most efficient principle"*: Drucker, *Concept of the Corporation*, 119.

233 *"Disperse, disperse, disperse"*: Dr. Ogburn quoted in Mezerik, *Revolt*, 283.

233 *"as a means to an end"*: Drucker, *Concept of the Corporation*, 130.

233 *"The American who regards social institutions"*: Ibid., 132, 151–52.

233 *"strange clan of Deciders"*: White, *View from the Fortieth Floor*, 122.

234 *"They recruited their own successors"*: Ibid.

234 *"seething mass of humanity"*: Wendell Smith quoted in Weintraub, *Victory Season*, 106.

236 *"The postwar problems are global"*: Forrestal, *Forrestal Diaries*, 105–6.

Chapter 12: Midpassage

237 the "bobby-soxers": Paul Gallico in Goodman, ed., *While You Were Gone*, 45.
239 "was not a man of the theater": Martin Gottfried quoted in Furia, *Poets*, 275.
239 "the papier-mâché town": Quoted in Wilson, *A Life*, 181.
239 "no war movies" pledge: Alex Hoyt to the author.
239 "a new screen siren": Gallico in Goodman, ed., *While You Were Gone*, 53.
240 "[N]oir was a hybrid": Douglas, "Day into *Noir*," n.p.
240 The peak year was 1946: Figures are from Lingeman, *Noir Forties*.
243 "darling of the New Dealers": Coffin, *Missouri Compromise*, 97.
243 "They watch each other warily": Ibid., 97–99.
244 "The Year of the Bullbat": Goldman, *Crucial Decade*, 41.
244 "A Disastrous Year": Donovan, *Conflict and Crisis*, 163.
244 "The Year of Frenzy": Goldman, *Crucial Decade*, 41.
244 "The Year of Frustration": Ibid.
244 "was a time of almost uninterrupted troubles": Acheson, *Present at the Creation*, 183.
244 "'Will you leave the Democratic Party?'": Quoted and described in Coffin, *Missouri Compromise*, 60.
245 the Old Curmudgeon's "glorious exodus": Ibid., 62.
245 "No inspiration," said one departing New Dealer: Quoted in ibid., 64.
246 "had an excellent mind": Acheson, *Sketches from Life*, 133.
247 "Put on your old gray bonnet": Quoted in Gunther, *Inside U.S.A.*, 430.
247 "To govern the United States": Quoted in Vidal, *Golden Age*, 334.
247 "Don't rock the boat, boys": Henry P. Fletcher quoted in Coffin, *Missouri Compromise*, 82.
248 "did not advocate the end of Gerontocracy": Chase, *For This We Fought*, 110.
249 "To us in the East": Kennan, *Kennan Diaries*, 350.
249 "Perhaps some other student": Ibid., 235.
250 "brief, too little celebrated interregnum": Vidal, *United States*, 857.
250 "impetuous and the confident": Ibid., 12.
251 "[T]here are still cries": Ibid., 17.
251 a "fatty degeneration": Powell, *Diaries*, 181.
252 "New York is not the same city": Quoted (from 1947) in John Guare, introduction to Powell, *Locusts*, ix.
252 "people are still frontiersmen": Dos Passos, *State of the Nation*, 5–6.
252 "We are here and we've got to stay here": Quoted in ibid., 146.
254 "A nation accustomed to the categorical": Goldman, *Crucial Decade*, 14.
254 "the high noon of the world's greatest democracy": Catton, *War Lords*, 226.
254 "The greatest danger that our nation faces": Quoted in ibid., 227.
255 "haggle with Destiny": Welles, *Where Are We Heading?*, 338.
255 "unemployment, Russian relations": Chase, *For This We Fought*, 32–33.
255 "[c]ivilization, as we know it": Toynbee, *Civilization*, 55.
256 "The wars between the Hittites and the Egyptians": Truman, *Off the Record*, 186–87.
257 "sat in his study at New Milford": Lerner, "Charles Beard," 23.
258 "purposefully and consistently": Graebner, *Age of Doubt*, 56.
261 "What had gone wrong?": Hamby, *Man of the People*, 384.
261 "In a curious reversal": Ibid.
261 "Sept. 26, 1918": Truman, *Off the Record*, 98–99.

Bibliography

Acheson, Dean. *Present at the Creation: My Years in the State Department.* New York: W. W. Norton, 1987. Originally published 1969.

———. *Sketches from Life of Men I Have Known.* New York: Harper & Brothers, 1961.

Adams, Henry. *The Education of Henry Adams: A Centennial Version.* Edited by Edward Chalfant and Conrad Edick Wright. Boston: Massachusetts Historical Society, 2007.

Agar, Herbert. *The Unquiet Years: U.S.A., 1945–1955.* London: Rupert Hart-Davis, 1957.

Aldridge, John W. *After the Lost Generation: A Critical Study of the Writers of Two Wars.* New York: Noonday Press, 1958. Originally published 1951.

Allen, Frederick Lewis. *The Big Change: America Transforms Itself, 1900–1950.* New York: Harper & Brothers, 1952.

Alsop, Joseph W., with Adam Platt. *"I've Seen the Best of It": Memoirs.* Rev. ed. Mount Jackson, VA: Axios, 2009.

Ambrose, Stephen. *Rise to Globalism: American Foreign Policy Since 1938.* 4th ed. New York: Penguin, 1985.

Andrews, Bert. *Washington Witch Hunt.* New York: Random House, 1948.

Bach, Julian Sebastian. *America's Germany: An Account of the Occupation.* New York: Random House, 1946.

Barrett, William. *The Truants: Adventures Among the Intellectuals.* Garden City, NY: Anchor, 1982.

Baruch, Bernard M. *Baruch: My Own Story.* New York: Henry Holt, 1957.

———. *Baruch: The Public Years.* New York: Holt, Rinehart & Winston, 1960.

Beard, Charles A. *Giddy Minds and Foreign Quarrels.* New York: Macmillan, 1939.

Beisner, Robert L. *Dean Acheson: A Life in the Cold War.* Oxford: Oxford University Press, 2006.

Bell, Clive. *Civilization: An Essay.* West Drayton, UK: Penguin, 1947. Originally published 1928.

Bernstein, Leonard. *The Leonard Bernstein Letters.* Edited by Nigel Simeone. New Haven, CT: Yale University Press, 2013.

Bessel, Richard, and Dirk Schumann, eds. *Life After Death: Approaches to a Cultural and Social History of Europe During the 1940s and 1950s.* Cambridge: Cambridge University Press, 2003.

Bohlen, Charles E. *Witness to History, 1929–1969.* New York: W. W. Norton, 1973.

Bourjaily, Vance. *The End of My Life.* New York: Arbor House, 1984.

Bourke, Joanna. *Fear: A Cultural History.* 2nd ed. Emeryville, CA: Shoemaker & Hoard, 2006.

Bradlee, Benjamin. "A Return: When We Were Young, and at War." *New Yorker,* October 2, 2006.

Brodie, Bernard, ed. *The Absolute Weapon: Atomic Power and World Order.* New York: Harcourt, Brace, 1946.

Brody, Richard. "'Film Noir': The Elusive Genre." *New Yorker,* July 23, 2014.

Brown, Margaret Wise. [Golden Mac Donald, pseud.] *The Little Island.* Garden City, NY: Doubleday, 1946.

Burnham, James. *The Managerial Revolution.* New York: John Day, 1941.

————. *The Struggle for the World*. New York: John Day, 1947.

Burns, James MacGregor. *Leadership*. New York: Harper & Row, 1978.

Buruma, Ian. *Year Zero: A History of 1945*. New York: Penguin Press, 2013.

Byrnes, James F. *Speaking Frankly*. New York and London: Harper & Brothers, 1947.

Carnegie, Dale. *How to Stop Worrying and Start Living*. New York: Simon & Schuster, 1948.

Catoire, Richard G. "A CINC for Sub-Saharan Africa? Rethinking the Unified Command Plan." *Parameters* 30 (2000): 102–17.

Catton, Bruce. *The War Lords of Washington*. Rev. ed. Westport, CT: Greenwood Press, 1969. Originally published 1948.

Chase, Stuart. *For This We Fought*. New York: Twentieth Century Fund, 1946.

Clay, Lucius D. *Decision in Germany*. London: William Heinemann, 1950.

Clifford, Clark, with Richard Holbrooke. *Counsel to the President: A Memoir*. New York: Random House, 1991.

Coffin, Tris. *Missouri Compromise*. Boston: Little, Brown, 1947.

Cohen, Gerard Daniel. *In War's Wake: Europe's Displaced Persons in the Postwar Order*. Oxford: Oxford University Press, 2012.

Conant, James B. "The Atomic Age." Washington, DC: National War College, September 16, 1946.

Conradi, Peter J. *A Very English Hero: The Making of Frank Thompson*. London: Bloomsbury, 2012.

Conway, Martin. *The Sorrows of Belgium: Liberation and Political Reconstruction, 1944–1947*. Oxford: Oxford University Press, 2012.

Cooper, Duff. *The Duff Cooper Diaries, 1915–1951*. Edited by John Julius Norwich. London: Phoenix, 2006.

Cousins, Norman. *Modern Man Is Obsolete*. New York: Viking, 1945.

Cozzens, James Gould. *Guard of Honor*. New York: Harcourt Brace Jovanovich, 1976. Originally published 1948.

Cripps, Thomas. *Making Movies Black: The Hollywood Message Movie from World War II to the Civil Rights Era*. Oxford: Oxford University Press, 1993.

Dawidoff, Robert. "Commager's *The American Mind*: A Reconsideration." *Reviews in American History* 12 (1984): 449–62.

Deery, Phillip. *Red Apple: Communism and McCarthyism in Cold War New York*. Bronx, NY: Fordham University Press, 2014.

DeVoto, Bernard. *The Year of Decision: 1846*. New York: Houghton Mifflin, 1984. Originally published 1943.

Dewey, John. *Problems of Men*. New York: Philosophical Library, 1946.

Dobbs, Michael. *Six Months in 1945: FDR, Stalin, Churchill, and Truman—From World War to Cold War*. New York: Alfred A. Knopf, 2012.

Donald, Aida D. *Citizen Soldier: A Life of Harry S. Truman*. New York: Basic Books, 2012.

Donovan, Robert J. *Conflict and Crisis: The Presidency of Harry S. Truman, 1945–1948*. Columbia: University of Missouri Press, 1996. Originally published 1977.

————. *Tumultuous Years: The Presidency of Harry S. Truman, 1949–1953*. New York: W. W. Norton, 1982.

Dos Passos, John. *Midcentury*. Boston: Houghton Mifflin, 1961.

———. *State of the Nation.* London: George Routledge & Sons, 1945.

———. *Tour of Duty.* Boston: Houghton Mifflin, 1946.

Douglas, Ann. "Day into Noir." *Vanity Fair,* March 2007.

———. *Terrible Honesty: Mongrel Manhattan in the 1920s.* New York: Farrar, Straus & Giroux, 1995.

Douglas, Norman. *Late Harvest.* London: Lindsay Drummond, 1946.

Drucker, Peter F. *Adventures of a Bystander.* New York: Harper & Row, 1978.

———. *Concept of the Corporation.* Boston: Beacon, 1960. Originally published 1946.

Dûchene, François. *Jean Monnet: The First Statesman of Interdependence.* New York: W. W. Norton, 1980.

Eckes, Alfred E., Jr., and Thomas W. Zeiler. *Globalization and the American Century.* Cambridge: Cambridge University Press, 2003.

Eisenberg, Carolyn. *Drawing the Line: The American Decision to Divide Germany, 1944–1949.* Cambridge: Cambridge University Press, 1996.

Eisenhower, Dwight D. *The Eisenhower Diaries.* Edited by Robert H. Ferrell. New York: W. W. Norton, 1981.

Elsey, George M. *An Unplanned Life: A Memoir.* Columbia: University of Missouri Press, 2005.

Fairlie, Henry. *The Kennedy Promise: The Politics of Expectation.* London: Eyre Methuen, 1973.

Feis, Herbert. *From Trust to Terror: The Onset of the Cold War, 1945–1950.* New York: W. W. Norton, 1970.

Finder, Henry, ed. *The 40s: The Story of a Decade.* New York: Random House, 2014.

Forrestal, James. *The Forrestal Diaries.* Edited by Walter Millis. New York: Viking, 1951.

Frederickson, Karl A. *Cold War Dixie: Militarization and Modernization in the American South.* Athens: University of Georgia Press, 2013.

Friedberg, Aaron L. *In the Shadow of the Garrison State.* Princeton, NJ: Princeton University Press, 2000.

Furia, Philip. *The Poets of Tin Pan Alley: A History of America's Greatest Lyricists.* New York: Oxford University Press, 1990.

———. *Skylark: The Life and Times of Johnny Mercer.* New York: St. Martin's, 2003.

Gaddis, John Lewis. *The United States and the Origins of the Cold War, 1941–1947.* New York: Columbia University Press, 1972.

Gillingham, John. *European Integration, 1950–2003: Superstate or New Market Economy?* New York: Cambridge University Press, 2003.

Ginzberg, Eli, and Douglas W. Bray. *The Uneducated.* New York: Columbia University Press, 1953.

Goldman, Eric F. *The Crucial Decade—And After: America, 1945–1960.* New York: Alfred A. Knopf, 1966.

Goodman, Jack, ed. *While You Were Gone: A Report on Wartime Life in the United States.* 2nd ed. New York: Da Capo, 1974.

Graebner, William. *The Age of Doubt: American Thought and Culture in the 1940s.* Boston: Twayne, 1991.

Greif, Mark. *The Age of the Crisis of Man: Thought and Fiction in America, 1933–1973.* Princeton, NJ: Princeton University Press, 2015.

Gunther, John. *Inside U.S.A.* New York: Harper & Brothers, 1947.

Hamby, Alonzo L. *Man of the People: A Life of Harry S. Truman.* Oxford: Oxford University Press, 1998. Originally published 1995.

Handlin, Oscar. *One World: The Origins of an American Concept.* Oxford: Oxford University Press, 1974.

———. *The Uprooted: The Epic Story of the Great Migrations That Made the American People.* 2nd ed. Boston: Little, Brown, 1979.

Harbutt, Fraser J. *The Cold War Era.* Oxford: Blackwell, 2002.

———. *The Iron Curtain: Churchill, America and the Origins of the Cold War.* Oxford: Oxford University Press, 1986.

Harriman, W. Averell, and Elie Abel. *Special Envoy to Churchill and Stalin, 1941–1946.* New York: Random House, 1975.

Hersey, John. *Hiroshima.* New York: Alfred A. Knopf, 1946.

Hewlett, Richard G., and Oscar E. Anderson Jr. *The New World, 1939/1946.* University Park: Pennsylvania State University Press, 1962.

Hofstadter, Richard. *America at 1750: A Social Portrait.* New York: Vintage, 1973. Originally published 1971.

Hoover, Herbert. *The Crusade Years, 1933–1955: Herbert Hoover's Lost Memoir of the New Deal Era and Its Aftermath.* Edited by George H. Nash. Stanford, CA: Hoover Institution Press, 2013.

———. *Freedom Betrayed: Herbert Hoover's Secret History of the Second World War and Its Aftermath.* Edited by George H. Nash. Stanford, CA: Hoover Institution Press, 2011.

Humes, Edward. *Over Here: How the G.I. Bill Transformed the American Dream.* Orlando, FL: Harcourt, 2006.

Hynd, Alan. *The Giant Killers.* New York: Robert H. McBride & Company, 1945.

Jones, Joseph M. *The Fifteen Weeks.* New York: Viking, 1955.

Jones, Thomas. *A Diary with Letters, 1931–1950.* London: Oxford University Press, 1954.

Judt, Tony. *Postwar: A History of Europe Since 1945.* New York: Penguin, 2005.

Jungk, Robert. *Tomorrow Is Already Here: Scenes from a Man-Made World.* London: Rupert Hart-Davis, 1954.

Katznelson, Ira. *Fear Itself: The New Deal and the Origins of Our Time.* New York: Liveright, 2013.

Kennan, George F. *The Kennan Diaries.* Edited by Frank Costigliola. New York: W. W. Norton, 2014.

———. ["X," pseud.] "The Sources of Soviet Conduct." *Foreign Affairs* 25, no. 4 (July 1947): 566–82.

Kravchenko, Victor. *I Chose Freedom.* London: Robert Hale, 1947.

Kunz, Diane B. *Butter and Guns: America's Cold War Economic Diplomacy.* New York: Free Press, 1997.

Kynaston, David. *Austerity Britain, 1945–1951.* London: Bloomsbury, 2007.

Laurence, William L. *Dawn over Zero: The Story of the Atomic Bomb.* London: Museum Press, 1947.

Leahy, William D. *I Was There.* New York: Whittlesey House, 1950.

Leffler, Melvyn. *A Preponderance of Power: National Security, the Truman Administration, and the Cold War.* Stanford, CA: Stanford University Press, 1992.

Leja, Michael. *Reframing Abstract Expressionism: Subjectivity and Painting in the 1940s.* New Haven, CT: Yale University Press, 1993.

Lerner, Max. "Charles Beard: Civilization and the Devils." *New Republic* 119, no. 18 (November 1, 1948), 21–24.

Leuchtenburg, William. *The Perils of Prosperity: 1914–1932*. Chicago: University of Chicago Press, 1958.

Lingeman, Richard. *The Noir Forties: The American People from Victory to Cold War*. New York: Nation Books, 2012.

Lowe, Keith. *Savage Continent: Europe in the Aftermath of World War II*. New York: St. Martin's, 2012.

Lukacs, John. *June 1941: Hitler and Stalin*. New Haven, CT: Yale University Press, 2006.

———. *1945: Year Zero*. Garden City, NY: Doubleday, 1978.

Lundestad, Geir. *The United States and Western Europe Since 1945: From "Empire" by Invitation to Transatlantic Drift*. Oxford: Oxford University Press, 2003.

Madariaga, Salvador de. *On Hamlet*. 2nd ed. London: Frank Cass, 1964.

Maharidge, Dale. *Bringing Mulligan Home: The Other Side of the Good War*. New York: Public Affairs, 2013.

Mailer, Norman. *The Naked and the Dead*. 50th anniversary ed. New York: Henry Holt, 1998.

Markusen, Ann, Peter Hall, Scott Campbell, and Sabina Deitrick. *The Rise of the Gunbelt: The Military Remapping of Industrial America*. Oxford: Oxford University Press, 1991.

Martin, Jamie. "Were We Bullied?" *London Review of Books*, November 21, 2013.

May, Ernest R., ed. *American Cold War Strategy: Interpreting NSC 68*. Boston: Bedford/St. Martin's, 1993.

———. *Imperial Democracy: The Emergence of America as a Great Power*. Chicago: Imprint Publications, 1991. Originally published 1961.

May, Lary. *The Big Tomorrow: Hollywood and the Politics of the American Way*. Chicago: University of Chicago Press, 2000.

McCullough, David. *Truman*. New York: Simon & Schuster, 1992.

McFarland, Keith D., and David L. Roll. *Louis Johnson and the Arming of America*. Bloomington: Indiana University Press, 2005.

Melby, John F. *The Mandate of Heaven: Record of a Civil War in China, 1945–49*. Toronto: Anchor, 1968.

Mezerik, A. G. *The Revolt of the South and the West*. New York: Duell, Sloan & Pearce, 1946.

Miller, Merle. *Plain Speaking: An Oral Biography of Harry S. Truman*. 3rd ed. New York: Berkley, 1984.

Mitchell, Joseph. *Up in the Old Hotel and Other Stories*. New York: Pantheon, 1992.

Moskin, J. Robert. *Mr. Truman's War: The Final Victories of World War II and the Birth of the Postwar World*. New York: Random House, 1996.

Moynihan, Daniel Patrick. *Pandaemonium: Ethnicity in International Politics*. Oxford: Oxford University Press, 1993.

Murray, Williamson, and Allan R. Millett. *A War to Be Won: Fighting the Second World War*. Cambridge, MA: Belknap Press of Harvard University Press, 2000.

Neustadt, Richard E. *Presidential Power: The Politics of Leadership*. New York: John Wiley & Sons, 1960.

Nevins, Allan. *Ordeal of the Union*. New York: Charles Scribner's Sons, 1947.

Nichols, Christopher McKnight. *Promise and Peril: America at the Dawn of a Global Age*. Cambridge, MA: Harvard University Press, 2011.

Nicolson, Harold. *The Harold Nicolson Diaries, 1907–1964.* Edited by Nigel Nicolson. London: Phoenix, 2005.

Ninkovich, Frank. *Modernity and Power: A History of the Domino Theory in the Twentieth Century.* Chicago: University of Chicago Press, 1994.

O'Hara, John. *Hellbox.* 3rd ed. New York: Popular Library, 1947.

———. *Pipe Night.* 3rd ed. New York: Bantam, 1966.

Orwell, George. *A Life in Letters.* Selected and annotated by Peter Davison. New York: Liveright, 2010.

———. "Second Thoughts on James Burnham." *Polemic,* Summer 1946.

———. *Why I Write.* London: Penguin, 1984.

Packer, George. *The Unwinding: An Inner History of the New America.* New York: Farrar, Straus & Giroux, 2013.

Pells, Richard. *Not Like Us: How Europeans Have Loved, Hated, and Transformed American Culture Since World War II.* New York: Basic Books, 1997.

Perl, Jed. *New Art City: Manhattan at Mid-Century.* New York: Alfred A. Knopf, 2005.

Powell, Dawn. *The Diaries of Dawn Powell, 1931–1965.* Edited by Tim Page. South Royalton, VT: Steerforth Press, 1995.

———. *The Locusts Have No King.* New York: Yarrow Press, 1990. Originally published 1948.

Powers, J. F. *Suitable Accommodations: An Autobiographical Story of Family Life; The Letters of J. F. Powers, 1942–1963.* Edited by Katherine A. Powers. New York: Farrar, Straus & Giroux, 2013.

Raban, Jonathan. "America's Best Unknown Writer [William Gaddis]." *New York Review of Books,* October 10, 2013.

Reid-Henry, Simon. "When Years Are Celebs." *Intelligent Life,* March/April 2014.

Reves, Emery. *The Anatomy of Peace.* 10th ed. New York: Harper & Brothers, 1946.

Rowse, A. L. *All Souls and Appeasement: A Contribution to Contemporary History.* London: Macmillan, 1961.

Runciman, David. "Counter-Counter Revolution." *London Review of Books,* September 26, 2013.

Salter, James. "Postscript: Peter Matthiessen (1927–2014)." *New Yorker,* April 14, 2014.

Schlesinger, Arthur, Jr. *The Letters of Arthur Schlesinger, Jr.* Edited by Andrew Schlesinger and Stephen Schlesinger. New York: Random House, 2013.

———. "Origins of the Cold War." *Foreign Affairs* 46, no. 1 (1967): 22–52.

Schrecker, Ellen. *The Age of McCarthyism.* Boston: Bedford, 1994.

Schulten, Susan. "World War II Led to a Revolution in Cartography." *New Republic,* May 20, 2014.

Schwartz, Thomas Alan. *America's Germany: John J. McCloy and the Federal Republic of Germany.* Cambridge, MA: Harvard University Press, 1991.

Scott, James C. *Domination and the Arts of Resistance: Hidden Transcripts.* New Haven, CT: Yale University Press, 1990.

Short, Philip. *Mitterrand: A Study in Ambiguity.* London: Bodley Head, 2013.

Sitwell, Osbert. *The Scarlet Tree.* London: Macmillan, 1949.

Sluga, Glenda. *Internationalism in the Age of Nationalism.* Philadelphia: University of Pennsylvania Press, 2013.

Sollors, Werner. *The Temptation of Despair: Tales of the 1940s.* Cambridge, MA: Belknap Press of Harvard University Press, 2014.

Sprout, Harold, and Margaret Sprout, eds. *Foundations of National Power: Readings on World Politics and American Security.* Princeton, NJ: Princeton University Press, 1945.

Spykman, Nicholas J. *The Geography of the Peace.* New York: Harcourt, Brace, 1944.

Stone, I. F. *The Truman Era, 1945–1952.* 2nd ed. Boston: Little, Brown, 1972.

Stromberg, Roland N. *Collective Security and American Foreign Policy: From the League of Nations to NATO.* New York: Frederick A. Praeger, 1963.

Sulzberger, C. L. *A Long Row of Candles: Memoirs and Diaries, 1934–1954.* Toronto: Macmillan, 1969.

Terkel, Studs. *"The Good War": An Oral History of World War II.* New York: Pantheon, 1984.

Thompson, Frank. *There Is a Spirit in Europe.* London: Victor Gollancz, 1948.

Toye, Richard. "From 'Consensus' to 'Common Ground': The Rhetoric of the Postwar Settlement and Its Collapse." *Journal of Contemporary History* 48, no. 1 (2012): 3–23.

Toynbee, Arnold J. *Civilization on Trial.* New York: Oxford University Press, 1948.

Trachtenberg, Marc. *A Constructed Peace: The Making of the European Settlement, 1945–1963.* Princeton, NJ: Princeton University Press, 1999.

Trilling, Lionel. *The Middle of the Journey.* New York: Viking, 1947.

Truman S. Harry. *Off the Record: The Private Papers of Harry S. Truman.* Edited by Robert H. Ferrell. Columbia: University of Missouri Press, 1997. Originally published 1980.

———. *Year of Decisions.* Garden City, NY: Doubleday, 1955.

———. *Years of Trial and Hope, 1946–1953.* London: Hodder & Stoughton, 1956.

Utley, Freda. *Lost Illusion.* London: George Allen & Unwin, 1949.

Vidal, Gore. *The Golden Age.* New York: Doubleday, 2000.

———. *Screening History.* Cambridge, MA: Harvard University Press, 1992.

———. *United States: Essays 1952–1992.* New York: Random House, 1993.

Wallace, Henry A. *The Century of the Common Man.* Edited by Russell Lord. New York: Reynal & Hitchcock, 1943.

———. *Must We Have a Century of Fear?* New York: Progressive Citizens of America, 1949.

———. *The Price of Vision: The Diary of Henry A. Wallace, 1942–1946.* Edited by John Morton Blum. Boston: Houghton Mifflin, 1973.

———. *Sixty Million Jobs.* New York: Simon & Schuster, 1945.

Weintraub, Robert. *The Victory Season: The End of World War II and the Birth of Baseball's Golden Age.* New York: Little, Brown, 2013.

Welles, Orson. Interview with Michael Parkinson, *Parkinson,* BBC, 1974.

Welles, Sumner. *The Time for Decision.* New York: Harper & Brothers, 1944.

———. *Where Are We Heading?* New York: Harper & Brothers, 1946.

White, Theodore H. *The View from the Fortieth Floor.* 2nd ed. London: Pan, 1963.

White, Theodore H., and Annalee Jacoby. *Thunder Out of China.* New York: William Sloane Associates, 1946.

Willkie, Wendell. *One World.* New York: Pocket Books, 1943.

Wilson, Victoria. *A Life of Barbara Stanwyck: Steel True, 1907–1940.* New York: Simon & Schuster, 2013.

Woolner, David B., Warren F. Kimball, and David Reynolds, eds. *FDR's World: War, Peace, and Legacies.* New York: Palgrave Macmillan, 2008.

Yergin, Daniel. *Shattered Peace: The Origins of the Cold War and the National Security State.* 2nd ed. Boston: Houghton Mifflin, 1978.

Index